What has straw in common with wheat? declares the Lord.
Is not my word like fire, declares the Lord,
and like a hammer that breaks the rock in pieces?

Jeremiah 23:29

We speak, not in the words which man's wisdom teaches,
but which the Spirit teaches,
combining spiritual ideas with spiritual words.

1 Corinthians 2:13

Our gospel came to you not only in word,
but also in power and in the Holy Spirit and with full conviction.

1 Thessalonians 1:5

Preaching by Comparison:

Supernatural Power in Bible Application

Daniel W. Sheard

ISBN: 979-8-9875309-2-4
Place of publication: Elizabethtown, PA

Chapter 12 was published earlier under the title, "Preaching in the *Hear* and Now: The Circumstantial Quality of the Preaching Engagement," in the *Journal of the Evangelical Homiletics Society* 4:2 (2004):10-22 © and is reproduced here with modifications and gracious permission.

Original Cover Design by Benjamin Sheard

Acknowledgements

To Mary Sue, the mirror of Christlikeness and a walking parable,
To Andrew, the student who has surpassed the teacher,
To Lauren, Bekah, and Benny, specialists in detail-capture and its accompanying laughter,
To Stephen Wright of Spurgeon's College, encourager and mentor,
To my friends at Summit International School of Ministry, colleagues in supernatural application,
To Walter Sheard, master of the metaphoric homily, "feed the sheep," John 21:16,
To Shirley Sheard, who understood the main thing (John 12:32),
To the thousands of simple, unschooled readers who desire to learn the ways of Jesus,
This book is for you, to help you delight in finding spiritual words for biblical ideas.

Contents

Foreword

Why are vivid illustrations and relevant applications so difficult to find? We can perhaps remember (or vaguely remember) a time when we witnessed a preacher make use of his entire seminary repertoire, calling on the powers of learned scholars, revealing the secret insights of extra-biblical texts, and spitting mouthfuls of Greek and Hebrew, only to walk out of the service still feeling the angst for tomorrow's dreaded meeting.

If we are in the business of speaking, we can perhaps (or certainly) remember a time when we spent hours meditating on, studying, praying over, and deducing the main point of a sermon text, only to be left unsure how to proclaim it to the member who is dreading her meeting the next morning.

I think illustration and application are hard to produce because somewhere along the way we were taught, either explicitly or implicitly, that the skills and tools necessary for understanding the Bible are the only tools necessary for engaging illustration and application. This is what happened to me. I attended a school that valued Scripture as the authoritative Word of God and consequently valued the careful, hard work of breaking down its grammar, syntax, and discourse. This meant that the lion's share of my seminary years focused on acquiring the tools of exegetical mining, descending into the depths of Scripture to unearth the treasures of wisdom and knowledge hidden in Christ, revealed in his Word. This was important. This was good.

However, after leaving the confines of a highly educated community bound together with similar values and specialized vocabulary, I am still learning that my mining tools are only some of the necessary instruments for ministry "in the real world." There is the text, always giving light, but then there are the people, always needing light.

My inherited assumption was that unearthing light through exegesis and prayer *was* the business of giving it away. Yet, it is becoming clear (through experience and my dad's long-suffering reminders) that there are degrees of separation between the mine shafts and the jewelry store. Our exegetical insights, however devotional to us, are often crude abstractions, needing to be cut and polished with the tools of Spirit-dependent communication before others can truly understand the text and clearly see its export for daily life.

This means that training for speaking ministry is a lot like training our bodies. If I want to get good at an activity, say rock climbing, the *best thing* I can do is go out and rock climb. I might think that a solid pull-up regimen would also do the trick, since the two activities look similar and even use a lot of the same muscles. While strengthening my upper body through pull-ups may help, it is not the best thing I can do to reach my goal of becoming a better rock climber. This is because our bodies respond in a unique way to each activity—the precise set of muscles activated, the magnitude and frequency of muscle firing, the use of hand-eye coordination, etc. In the field of exercise science, this is a fundamental idea called the *specificity principle*. If I want to acquire or improve my rock-climbing abilities, the specificity principle tells me that the best training I can do is go rock climbing.

Similarly, it is perhaps flawed to assume (or argue) that training in exegesis will also function to train students in communication. That is, becoming a trained text-breaker-downer does *not* automatically strengthen our text-communicating muscles. We need to adopt a preaching specificity principle, that recognizes and accepts there are two related-but-different activities happening: exegeting a text (activity A) and explaining a text (activity B). The former aims to uncover what God revealed centuries ago, and the latter aims to lead myself and others into what it means for us today. To be sure, the spiritual work of exegesis is intertwined to the spiritual work of explanation (just like pull ups are related to rock climbing), but in the end, recognizing these as distinct tasks helps us understand the unique challenges and training regimens needed for communicating a text.

Once we complete this move, to distinguish exegesis from explanation, we can recognize and accept that faithful interpretation depends on *both* activities (exegeting *and* explaining). To claim that faithful interpretation depends on our exegesis is only to affirm a truism among theological conservatives. However, to claim that faithful interpretation depends upon how we explain a text is one of the primary insights and contributions of this book, the full rationale and implications of which are fleshed out in the pages that follow.

In short, my dad helps us see that the process of interpreting a text does not end with our ability to extract and understand an abstraction. In other words, identifying the main point of a passage should not always be equated with interpreting a text. Instead, we should remember that the infinite God of glory revealed Himself to us in human words and even human flesh *so that we would trust, feel, and act in accord with righteousness in time and space, walking in the good works that He prepared for us*. God commands us to renew our minds, but in the same breath He also tells us to present our bodies as living sacrifices (Rom 12:1-2). This means that the process of faithful interpretation ends *after* we have helped hearers grasp the reality of the text and embrace a vision for living it out in their context.

So, the book you hold aims to inspire and tutor us in the power of explanation, but this does not mean it is about tips and tricks for illustrating and applying. The following content aims to refine our models of spiritual communication-- illustration, application, and preaching itself–and conform them to what Scripture teaches, acquiring tools fit for the task along the way. Adjusting a working model is never easy and, like growing pains, real learning is often accompanied by some measure of discomfort. As you read, you should expect to be challenged in at least two ways.

First, some of the ideas in this book will challenge popular terms whose definitions you have accepted and will challenge paradigms that you have found useful. I can still hear my dad's voice over the phone rise in pitch and excitement to remind me again, "but Andrew, illustrating *is* explaining the text." Whether you agree with everything in this book or not, may the Lord give you humility and teachability as you aim to grow in your understanding of communicating God's Word on God's terms.

Second, these redefinitions and model adjustments will challenge your understanding of what faithful preaching means. Many people define faithful preaching as careful expositing (i.e., explaining) God's word. But, as mentioned above, if illustration and application are central to the task of properly explaining a text, then it follows that illustration and application along the grain of analogy and correspondence are central to the task of faithful preaching.

This puts most of us in an awkward position. We have probably received little to no formal training in the art of communication. Compared to the dozens or even hundreds of theological books that we have consumed, this may be the first that you have ever picked up focusing on illustration and application. If this understanding of faithful preaching is correct, it increases the urgency of a book like this to be read and implemented in and for local congregations. May the Lord's love for you and your hearers fill you with hope as you aim to run hard after faithful preaching.

So, when it comes to illustrating and applying spiritual truths, most of us cut our teeth on desperate prayer, Google searches, and inspiration. By writing this book my dad hopes to equip people like you and me with conviction and tools to pursue thoughtful, faithful communication in preaching, teaching, and in life. He has taken his insights from years of training in both the activities of exegeting texts and communicating texts to coach those of us who have always conflated the two. Most of all, I know he wants us to grow in wonder at the light of Christ revealed in Scripture, and in so doing, grow in joy and skill at sharing that light with others.

Andrew Sheard, M.Div.
Weare, NH

An Introduction to Being Possessed by the Majesty

When I read the Bible, my mind is flooded with wonder, fear, holiness, and countless other emotions and connections. The nature and texture of the Word of God is overflowing with majesty, and I am possessed by it.

These pages represent a lifelong journey of wonderment and a glimpse into the glory of God. I have learned to love my mornings in His word, and I increasingly linger in that Presence. This simple practice has become the observational basis for my preaching.

I have struggled over the years with how to communicate the stream of the Spirit's voice in a way that others can understand. I have attempted here to chronicle that process.

The ensuing chapters provide a mindset of observation and the consequential pouring out of that ever-flowing stream of communication. To use another metaphor, there is an ever-widening tapestry of God's master quilt, one that is accessible and fantastic. People that listen deserve an optimistic panorama in all its full-orbed beauty.

God is constantly communicating, connecting our current circumstances to His living word, the Bible. People should be shown that with power and clarity. They deserve our very best communication effort and need to see our enjoyment in that task.

Magnitude

Most preachers fail to capture the magnitude of God's spoken volume. Not only is He talking quietly, but He is also shouting.

The problem, in part, is that we do not guard against the accumulating voices of men, phones, devices, hobbies, and friends that risk locking out that Spirit-shouting love of God. Our lives can be cluttered by a thousand competing distractions that serve as disturbances that interfere with the most important thing, the majesty of God's voice.

Beyond the competing chatter, when we look at our task from a human point of view, sometimes the Bible is hard to understand. We can get discouraged or demotivated to read and prepare. Even the Apostle Peter told his readers in 2 Peter 3:16 that he struggled to understand Paul's letters. Yet, he warns us not to twist what we read.

Exposition of the Bible is not about human processes; it is not just textual mechanics. It is being possessed by God and His clear vocalizations, both in the precise words of scripture and in the created world.

In a way, the Bible is an explosion of excitement. When our hearts are right, the Spirit Himself reveals the scope and magnitude of God's activity, and just as Jesus told the woman at the well in John 4, His word is like a spring of living water bursting into our lives, full to overflowing.

The scriptures are God's voice to us, capped with Jesus Himself, the living Word. Today, the Holy Spirit of God is excited to communicate, and He wants us to live that Trinitarian connection in all its cognitive and emotional meaning.

When we are full of God Himself, we are then best prepared to spill over into the lives of others. It stands to reason that before we can capture others with that fantastic, relational dynamic which we have come to experience, we ourselves need to be possessed by Him.

This book is about being captured, and in turn, capturing others. The process is supernatural. We should divinely inspire people to journey with us through the pages of scripture, making countless connections to the world in which we live. The engagement, wonder, fear, or whatever you want to call what happens upon close encounter with the Spirit of God, are the waters upon which we are about to voyage.

Jesus Preached by Comparison

Jesus preached in parables. The term parable means 'to throw alongside.' In other words, Jesus preached by comparison. He modeled the importance of illustration in communicating key ideas. It is the focus of this book.

How can we find common ground between text and audience so that quality communication can take place? It is about being honest enough to admit that good information and accurate exposition are only two pieces of the preaching puzzle.

Preaching is about overcoming culture gaps when speaking expositionally so that a listener can encounter a living God. It is about understanding communication barriers, identifying them, and moving from textual comprehension issues into the realm of meeting the God of gods in the common places of life. Preaching must connect these two components.

Naturally, any preaching audience is part of a genus, that is sinful humanity. They possess a condition that plagues all of us who live in the flesh and get up in the morning, only to put our pants on one leg at a time.

Our communication task begins with taking a close look at the incarnated Savior who overcame the limitations of our depraved condition by teaching with spiritual connection and by using the concrete world. These are the very reasons for writing a book on illustration and application. We must learn how Jesus managed to engage common people.

What is Bible Application and How is It Different from Illustration?

Bible application is not telling people how to do things. It is an engagement between the speaker, the listener, and God, where the message of the text brings correlation to a shared common experience. Preaching is also not about telling people how they need to feel. Most of us resent being told we should not feel a certain way, when in fact, it is hard to escape our human dilemmas.

The preacher should be all about participation with the practical outworkings of the scriptures. We invite the audience to connect with God in a supernatural way through storied delivery, concrete scenarios, and open-ended questions that are hopeful or confrontational in nature.

Bible application is a journey that challenges assumptions and dismantles false thinking, always with the view to present a new world of Christ-centered possibilities. Change does not just happen through logical discourse but also through accurate comparisons. We intentionally challenge hurtful assumptions and entrenched ideas by drawing pictures to which common people can relate.

By way of formal definition, I need to say at the outset that I find very little difference between illustration and application. The former is typically a specific instance of the latter, and illustration seems to be a precise imaging process, often with narrative, but not necessarily.

Illustration is typically seen or understood as the localization or picturing of application. However, these differentiations break down in real life because someone can easily give a pictured application of a passage that has both particular and universal applications. In any event, I often use the terms interchangeably throughout this work.

Within the ongoing discussion about common language for spiritual engagement that is constantly present in the contemporary Evangelical world, there still exists very little by way of teaching the nuts and bolts of sermon illustration in the English language. Moving forward in this area requires dealing with the integrity process of text-to-figure mechanics.

Hopefully, the reader will find the ensuing chapters valuable in learning both simple and complex Bible application, being faithful to both the scriptures and the audience. Whether you are just curious about the subject or are a seasoned preacher, you will find in these pages valuable ways to illustrate textual nuances that, through the Holy Spirit's influence, will change the lives of listeners.

Questions for Engagement

1. How does the 'magnitude' of God's spoken volume change the quality of illustration?
2. How is Jesus' method different from many modern-day approaches to preaching?
3. How are Bible application and illustration different?

Part One: From the Majesty of God to the Material of Man

1   Preaching by Comparison

Jesus taught by comparison. He did not give technical lectures, mesmerizing descriptions of how He created the universe, or even long suspenseful stories. He just often rolled out shocking snippets that jolted people by showing connections between the spiritual and concrete worlds.

This is our task too. Preaching by comparison involves drawing connections between the text and the common experience of speaker and listener.

Why did the God of the universe make His speech so common, so provocative? The answer is clear: He wanted us to share His glory and demonstrate that the world and its contents are teeming with Christ-infused meaning, every last molecule.

Preaching is showing people how their lives already resonate with the eternal, life-giving message of the Bible. For some, their perceptions of the universe do not resonate with God's enduring purposes.

Parables, Jesus' principle means of teaching, are comparisons at the root. They are constructions that give delight to the listener because the audience already knows the truth but has likely never seen it.

Jesus' way should be our way when we talk to people. We in essence say by our manner, "Let me show you how God is already at work in your life. Let me show you the eternal truths that you already know."

For sure, there are technical categories for parables, differing rhetorical means of comparison. Some are explicit, like the 8 times in the book of Matthew where Jesus says, "The kingdom of Heaven is like…." However, some are implicit, for example when Jesus just drops a parable like this one: "Can a blind man lead a blind man? Will they not both fall into a pit?" (Luke 6:39).

Similarly, when Jesus begins His great parabolic discourse in Matthew 13, He just begins with, "A sower went out to sow…." There is no introduction, where Jesus says, "I am about to tell you a series of parables that are comparisons. They will teach you spiritual principles using knowledge you already have and could change your lives."

Jesus' strategy was to simply show people the truth they already knew and experienced but had intentionally ignored, suppressed, or were just too busy to notice. Certainly, they were blinded by sin.

Jesus was all about experiential resonance. For example, after Peter's threefold denial and failure in Jerusalem during the trials of Jesus, Peter and six companions go fishing back on Galilee Lake. Unknown to them, the anonymous Jesus tells them to throw the net on the other side of the boat. They complain and self-admit, like good fishermen, they were skunked. After doing what Jesus told them to do, they have a massive haul.

When the disciples reflect on what was happening in the moment, they recognize their Master and bring the breaking nets to shore. Jesus had prepared a fire with some barbecued fish and baked bread. He tells them, "Bring some of the fish that you have just caught" (John 21:10).

Why did Jesus do this? He already had breakfast cooked. The answer seems clear. He wants us to partner with Him. He wants to delight in us, in our part.

"I have some fish here. You bring some of yours too."

He wants us to see how our human experience is superintended by a loving God and how our own circumstances teach us about eternal verities. Our material world has connection to Divine purpose and instruction.

This is very similar to how Jesus ends His parabolic discourse in Matthew 13:52, when He says that if we are fully instructed in the kingdom of heaven, we bring out of our treasure new things and old things. We are in a constant habit of past reflection and present renewal. Parables show us that God was there all the time, that He is sovereign over every molecule in the universe.

> For by him all things were created, in heaven and on earth, visible and invisible, whether thrones or dominions or rulers or authorities—all things were created through him and for him. And he is before all things, and in him all things hold together. (Col. 1:16-17).

The truth we **catch** is part of God's plan. It is prepared for us in advance to do (Eph. 2:10). He leads us on the path of recognition. As I discover what He is teaching me in the word of God, I realize that it is exactly what He has been telling me by His Spirit for years.

Life is about discovery, discovery of the magnitude of God; it is about marveling. We begin to see God's work in everything.

This idea radically changes how we preach the Bible. The integration of specific revelation and general revelation becomes clear.

Jesus' use of common things—nature, people, animals, the sea, agriculture, and a host of other tangibles—is a lesson in simplicity. It is a lesson in integration of life, how the natural world points to the Bible and the Bible back to the Author of the natural world.

How This Idea Changes Preaching Strategy

When someone enters the pulpit or "goes up front," or stands to share from the scriptures, what is in the mind of that expository preacher? Hopefully, that person understands his/her role as more than simply, "explaining the text."

The idea of "explaining the text" has no reference to the audience. The preacher must say, "I am here to explain the text *to the audience*." More than this, the preacher must say, "I am here to explain the text from within a framework that the audience can get caught up in *what they already know to be true*, the certainties revealed to them in scripture."

If I could go a couple steps further, the preacher must understand that those people to whom s/he is speaking cannot escape the truth of the world of God. How does this happen?

Truth-entrapment might sound like a harsh term, but it is what Jesus did. If it was not entrapment, it was certainly confrontation. The stories he told brought people to the point where they had to address the truth about themselves.

No one likes to hear the dentist say, "You have a cavity. It needs a filling. Do you want Novocain, or would you like me to do this without it? Either way, it must be done. You will live in less pain if we take care of this now."

It will be no surprise to the patient when s/he hears, "You have a cavity." That person already knows what is wrong. The toothache causes experiential pain, and the patient is waiting for the glorious relief that is just around the corner.

The preacher must be there to lead the audience to the heights of the majesty of God and out of human suffering. As we behold the expanse and intricacy of the universe, we are caught up in the truth of the scriptures. We hear God say to us, "With man it is impossible, but not with God. For all things are possible with God" (Mark 10:27).

Scaffolding

In a sense, helping people understand the scriptures is what educators call *scaffolding*. One of the primary means in scaffolded teaching is using prior knowledge to help the listener construct new levels of understanding.

Traditional means of explaining the scriptures is often done by discursive points of logic, that is, sequential reasoning. This is one type of scaffolding but requires that the learner has the mental energy to follow point-by-point argumentation.

Imaged delivery, stories, and parables provide a different kind of approach, one that appeals to several other domains of personal experience and prior knowledge. Figured speech, whether images, comparisons, or full-blown stories appeal to the imagination, to relationships, to feelings, and to chronology.

An overreliance on abstraction in preaching may deny the fundamental component of Jesus' methodology. He scaffolded by using concrete correlations that involved comparison.

Argument by Analogy

Analogy is more than correlation. Analogy has by its construction an implicit argument.

Were I to say to my wife, "Honey, your hair looks like a tangled mess of fishing line, like a bird's nest after a hurricane," not only might I not live to see the light of day, but I am perhaps going to be sleeping on the couch.

Analogies have argumentative force. They are not neutral. They imply a host of contingencies that the listener knows implicitly. Hurricanes destroy homes, uproot trees, and leave people homeless. We all know this. The hair style is more than not working; it is a disaster.

Jesus' method was not one of explanation. In fact, He preaches no expository messages like we know them today. Our sequentially ordered method of points developing meaning from the Old Testament with evidence was not the way of the Savior. He preached to the experience of the listener.

This is not to say that we should be preaching something other than expository sermons. I am definitely not advocating Narrative Theology or some 'Storyesque' sermonic form. I am simply saying we can vastly improve our connection with people if we stick to Jesus' method of argument by comparison.

The Supernatural Nature of Preaching

Some authors of late have advocated that we deliberately *not* follow Jesus' method of parabolic delivery because they say Jesus was the only one with the authority to supernaturally reveal and conceal saving revelation (Mark 4:10-12).

Methodologically, Jesus set an example that we must follow. We should not only replicate His life but also His teaching method. Otherwise, we make void the power of God by maintaining a weak tradition of discursive and complex subordinated preaching, more suitable for high-literates capable of following sequential delivery. Jesus did not do this, and we should be careful in what contexts we use highly complex rhetoric.

It is possible in some instances that complex speech feeds the pride of man and denies the supernatural nature of preaching. At one point in Jesus' ministry and in a moment of jubilation, He prays out loud in front of the crowd, "I thank you, Father, Lord of heaven and earth, that you have hidden these things from the wise and understanding and revealed them to little children" (Matt. 11:25). This was Paul's clear point in 1 Corinthians chapter 2.

> Now we have received not the spirit of the world, but the Spirit who is from God, that we might understand the things freely given us by God. *And we impart this in words not taught by human wisdom but taught by the Spirit, interpreting spiritual truths to those who are spiritual.* The natural person does not accept the things of the Spirit of God, for they are folly to him, and he is not able to understand them because they are spiritually discerned. (1 Cor. 2:12-14).

If sharing spiritual things is a supernatural act infused with the supernatural gospel and empowered by a supernatural God, our method cannot be from the perspective of logic and subordination. At this point, we absolutely must take a lesson from Jesus.

Typically, we tend to preach like Paul wrote, full of subordinations and print-based explanations. We justify our delivery style by appealing to the epistolary writings. However, when people preach like Paul wrote, they create not only verbal distance through complex vocabulary but also spiritual distance by mistaking human logic for spiritual illumination.

Paul elaborated to the Corinthians that he did not employ lofty speech or wisdom because he knew that a message of a crucified Christ through a weak and trembling messenger was Spirit-infused and powerful. It also produced clear faith in God. He did not want a human method, well executed by Paul-the-lawyer, to move people from a reliance upon the power of God toward some kind of human wisdom that does not produce results (1 Cor. 2:1-5).

There is a decisive shift in communication method when we accept the supernatural nature of preaching. Logic becomes subordinated to revelation. We must humble ourselves before the text to receive its meaning. As schooled and educated people, many of us have a hard time accepting this. This is not about grammar. It is about God.

We somehow believe that if we are incisive, declarative, and clearly logical, we will have good, spiritual results. If we have consistent bodily motions that are not distracting, people will focus on the words we are saying, and God will bless our delivery. This is, however, only a very small part of preaching.

The reality is that the message we proclaim is a supernatural one. We should be arguing and pleading with the eternal destiny of the listener in the balance. Unless we are Jonathan Edwards, Charles Spurgeon, Henry Ward Beecher, or someone spiritually gifted to teach with an innate rhetorical ability, we should boldly preach the words God gives us in our weakness and in our trembling.

God uses the weak vessel, with both inherent flaws as well as its dynamic personal experience. Each one of us has this incredible power of spiritual comparison, drawn from the well of life experience.

We will here attempt to foster that capacity to validate the eternal truths of the scriptures from what God has already shown us in everyday happenings. This book is about extracting biblical lessons from that precious journey and sharing them with others in dynamic ways.

Questions for Engagement

1. How does the idea of comparison change preaching strategy?
2. In what ways did Jesus teach by comparison?
3. What is the connection between exposition and application of the scriptures?
4. How does the idea of scaffolding relate to comparison and/or analogy?
5. How is an analogy an argument?
6. What are some of the factors that make biblical application supernatural and what might make some application informational or even carnal?

2   An Explosion of Common Ground

Before I revised the text you are now holding, my son read the book and asked me, "Dad, what kind of book is it? What is it that you want to accomplish?" I was shocked. I thought it was obvious.

People that love each other communicate. It is the nature of relationship. Within the framework of the universe, the concrete stuff of human living on this earth, there is this shared experience of God-talk and common grace. That shared communicative exchange is supernaturally explosive. It is a living and volatile common ground.

The specific revelation of God's word is complemented by the concrete world. God uses all of it to speak to us. Jesus showed us that in the way He communicated.

God is filled with love for us; after all, He sent His Son, the Word of God, to earth to reconcile us to Himself. The magnitude of that care is unimaginable. That singular act speaks loud and clear.

Preaching must be filled with that same voice of love, a love that embraces others with force and subtlety. Our task is not simply cognitive exchange. It is mirroring the great compassion we have experienced. It is being filled with the fullness of God and learning to pour that out to the people we serve.

The older I get, the more I want to learn the task of communication because God is talking in such a magnificent way. It is my call to be captivated with His word and His world.

What is so clear to me and other preachers of the Word of God seems to be hidden to a lot of people.

God is excited to speak. We need to be eager to listen, and when God talks to us, we then have something worth communicating to others.

The physical universe is not in competition with the textual matters of specific revelation, that is, of scripture. The two components of text and world function in harmony, calling and calling and calling.

Learning the ways of the connecting language of God is sometimes difficult because of fleshly and demonic forces. The spiritual components of a world ravaged by sin are massive and prohibitive. Yet, when I am possessed of the majesty of the Almighty and am also willing to be wooed into His presence of love, the text of the word of God then becomes clear, open, and magnificent. He shows me how this world correlates in complete congruence to His sovereign and providential workings, both in His wrath as well as His love. He gives me inspiration and reason to communicate that message to others. Sermons then become powerful and living.

This common ground of human experience is the chosen framework of the God of the universe. It is the carpet on which we walk when we read His word and observe His world. It is a shared platform for experiential wonder and learning. It is the place where God gathers us up to listen to His voice.

The world and how we are educated in it are jam packed with filters, sifting and screening how we understand the spiritual frameworks that God has infused into the atoms of the universe. As much as humanity tries to avoid the common language of God, they still tread on that ground. It is unavoidable.

That common ground is why we preach by comparison. The universe is filled with bridges to the hearts and minds of people. Let's unpack them in all their wonder and usefulness.

The Nine Bridges of Bible Application

To communicate God's voice, we have to speak in a language that people can understand, so we compare the Bible to what they already know. If I go to a tribal community in the Amazon and speak English to them, there will be very little meaning-transfer. If I switch to French, I will not do any better. However, they will understand me, if I speak *their* language.

Preaching is unfortunately like this sometimes; the preacher is speaking another language. People suffer the accompanying bewilderment.

The Spirit-filled and often educated Christian leader has to accommodate the aural frameworks of listeners. We must do what Jesus did, speak to common people in a way they can understand. "And the great throng heard him gladly" (Mk. 12:37).

Because Bible application is sometimes elusive to those that teach, I have attempted to outline a common grammar and structure to frame speaker-thinking *for the sake of the listener*. Without making things too complex, at least not yet, let's just picture this framework right now, so you, the reader, can see where we are going.

I have identified nine bridges, or connecting points, for capturing the minds of listeners in a language they can understand. These will be the frameworks for common-ground-applications, explained in detail later in the book. The nine components are relationship, emotion, movement, moral human behavior, desire, fixed objects, abstraction, story creation, and parables. They can be pictured like this:

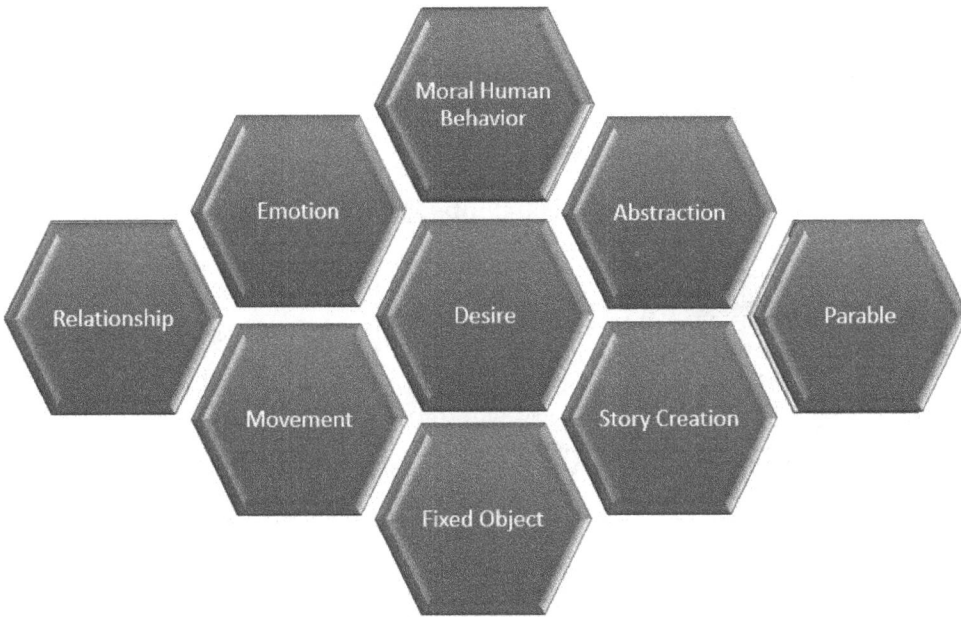

Each bridge above has its own qualities and subgroupings. Applications are formed from identifying component comparisons within a chosen text. It may sound strange at this point, but frequently a student of the scriptures knows that there is something in the text, but s/he cannot exactly identify the reason for the inclination or feeling that is generating the observation. The ensuing chapters will help you locate those details.

Ultimately, we want to develop an application reflex that is not dependent upon processing through these domains. For example, once you learn to use the hammer, you can build a house or a boat or whatever else you want to construct. You don't consciously think, "Okay, now how do I use the hammer again?"

It needs to be noted that in terms of parallel form, I self-admit that the foregoing items are not congruent. Their syntax and parts of speech are not the same. They are presented as useful bridges or windows to auditors.

To continue my previous analogy, a hammer and saw have different purposes, but both are tools. In the same way, movement and parable are different in form and function, but for our purposes, they are both tools. A hammer is not the same as a doorway, and a saw is not the same as an architect's blueprint. The foregoing bridges are not grouped for likeness or function. All are necessary to construct an application-house.

Again, these different bridges are simply pathways to the audience. Each will be treated individually with examples as we progress. Some are simple and some are complex.

For illustration purposes, we might look at a short passage to outline by example how this will play out in practical terms.

Fixed Object

The door represents salvation, the point of entry, a barrier, inability to traverse.

Moral Human Behavior

People are inclined to find illegal and alternative ways that are not right.

Abstraction

Leading sheep 'out' to pasture, to be fed, to migrate, to move.

Movement

Opportunity, clearance, vetting.

John 10:1-5

"Truly, truly, I say to you, he who does not **enter** the sheepfold by the **door** but **climbs in by another way**, that man is a **thief and a robber**. But he who enters by the door is the **shepherd** of the sheep. To him the gatekeeper **opens**. The sheep hear his voice, and he **calls his own sheep by name and leads them out**. When he has brought out all his own, he goes before them, and the ***sheep follow him, for they know his* voice.** A stranger they will not follow, but they will flee from him, for they do not know the voice of strangers."

Movement

Entering and coming in represent opportunity, shelter, protection, and welcome.

Emotion

Stealing generates feelings of improper motive, fear, or injustice.

Relationship

People know when they are cared for, protected, and led.

Desire

Heart-felt sense of submission, leadership, familiarity, recognition.

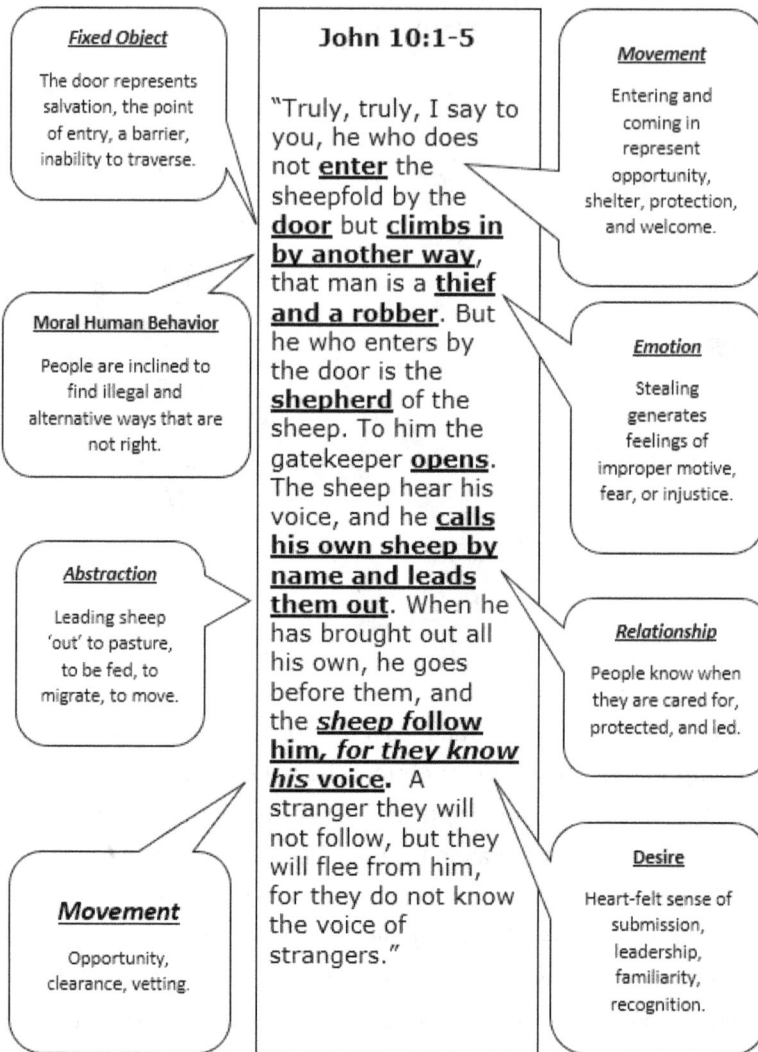

Naturally, this is a highly simplified sample. Each component listed here can also represent other categories. For example, following the voice of strangers is 'movement' as well as 'desire.' It can also be an 'abstraction' for following the call of others or being in 'relationship' with unhealthy people.

When bridging to the audience, the speaker uses simple categories to create connections with the listeners. For example, when we see relationship in a text like John 10, where Jesus calls sheep by name and leads them out, the parallels in the contemporary world are numerous: a mother calling children by name, a coach calling players by name, a teacher calling students by name, a secretary calling people in a waiting room by name, etc.

This same type of extrapolation can be made in every component above: opportunity in following someone, vetting the voice before moving, the emotions we have when seeing stealing, someone jumping over a wall to break in, the desire to recognize a voice of one we love, etc. The examples go on and on.

Not included in this above diagram are story and parable construction. These narrative forms are a bit more complex and need time and space to expand. Narratives, with all their subsets, are varied, and may be as brief as a pictured image or a lengthy example-story. They need to be addressed at length and will be quantified in detail and by example.

The Connecting Language

Before we get into the mechanics of multiplying applications and illustrations, it is critical that the spiritual components and rationale for this process are abundantly clear. The 'why' must precede the 'how,' otherwise we do things by formula. This is not in the heart of God.

Each move in a sermon should be purposeful. The points should be God-inspired and others-oriented. To do this, we find the heart of God as well as suitable language to reach the hearts of our audiences.

The task of the preacher is to find a connecting language, moving from the words of the text to the language of the people. If God is talking, what is He saying, both in His word and His world?

The preacher is himself a conduit, or as Paul put it, an ambassador, pleading with people to be reconciled to God (2 Cor. 5:20). That reconciliation implies alienation of men with their Creator; it is an alienation we must help others to overcome. That struggle is much easier when we truly understand the magnitude of the Messenger and His message.

When I am possessed of the majesty of God, there is an inspiration and natural, attractional warmth that others sense. Consequently, it is imperative that I as a preacher am filled with a sort of Christocentric glory.

In the Mount of Transfiguration in Luke 9, Peter in his excitement wants to erect a monument to the presence of God, a sort of memorial moment. However, the voice of the Father cuts through the cloud and says, "This is my beloved son, hear Him!"

The export is this: If I see and hear spiritual things, I must be more attentive to listen to the voice of God and be enamored by Jesus Himself. If I understand and feel the majesty, I will be the person whom I need to be and want to communicate the truth that has become so clear. That speech will have a supernatural quality.

The Challenge and the Solution

Some advocates of biblical exposition create an artificial tension between the world and the biblical text. However, the careful observer can see how the natural world mirrors and elucidates the truth of the scriptures. Jesus, the living Word of God, used creation in all its fullness. He was not afraid to illustrate. He had a decisive application-focus that centered around examples from life.

How can we do what Jesus did? For most individuals who preach the Bible, the critical question they ask is: What do I do after I understand and interpret the text? How will this central idea strike home in the ear and spirit of the listener? How do I transform notions and advice into relevant, orally delivered nuggets that have worth to others?

The answer is this: communicating key ideas from scripture to an audience by the power of the Spirit requires that the speaker understands the capacity of language for resonance in the hearing of a listener. Communicated words must capture the mind and heart of the hearer as s/he has experienced life. The sermon must answer a question, fulfill a need, or rattle an emotion. This is how Jesus rolled out His teaching to the common people of His day.

It is entirely possible to replicate some of Jesus' methods of engagement with a little practice. Often, we use modern parable scholarship to explain, interpret, or analyze Jesus' use of speech figures. However, preaching should move from text-observation to a spoken narrative agenda that replicates Christlike resonance with an audience.

Human resonance is something that we will deal with at length in the pages that follow, but for now we can just say that it is a type of experiential harmonic between speaker and listener and happens when the preacher creates a correlative idea that is known to the auditor.

Finding the path toward resonance is sometimes a struggle. Many expositors battle for illustrations and applications. They resign themselves to a discouraging falsehood that illustration is just not their gift. Even Aristotle was under the false assumption that mastering metaphor was impossible for those to whom it did not come naturally.[1]

For the communicator of the biblical text, it is both important and easy to make proper use of the globe we live on. The following pages function on the premise that general revelation and natural revelation, namely the world and all that is in it, are the tapestry on which we can unfold special revelation, the Word of God. However, getting from textual grammar to a supporting story or image can sometimes be like making a quantum leap into ambiguity. It does not have to be that way, however.

Jesus' Method of Engagement

Jesus' parabolic methodology made detailed use of the natural world to build bridges and span cultures. In fact, He did this much more frequently than citing the Old Testament or employing what we might know as 20th century expositional preaching. Why did He do this? We might also add an additional question of whether or not we should copy His approach, and if so, when?

As one observes the audience of Jesus' ministry, that is, common folk, it stands to reason that He was very interested in bridging spiritual realities to the everyday life of His listeners. He was interested in taking them from where they were to where they needed to be. Since they were in fact familiar with life's trials and were generally simple, worldly people, He used the tools of the everyday context to speak to His audiences.

This difference between Jesus' style of delivery and modern-day evangelical approaches haunts many of us who preach on a regular basis. Not all teachers of the scriptures work at using the physical world to reach their audiences. When they use speech figures or stories, often their illustrations have problems matching the exact biblical meaning. The correspondence between text and illustration is frequently weak or non-existent. I am, of course, also one of the chief rule-breakers. It is a hard reality to avoid.

In studying this problem over many years, I approached this curious dissimilarity from different angles and eventually decided to attempt detailing a method for bridging the Word of God to the uninitiated, the unchurched listener. In struggling to come to grips with the practical side of creating and using images, stories, and parables, I came across some foundational concepts of figure theory.

During my journey, I was trying to understand the mechanics of parable formation and stories in general. I wanted to know the historical foundations of Jesus' approach to sermon delivery in Jewish tradition. Additionally, I was also looking for some keys to creating illustrations and parables from scratch because Jesus never taught us how to duplicate His method.

Much of the scholarly work written on parables has addressed interpretive issues, but I was much more concerned about duplicating what Jesus did. Unfortunately, there is very little that renders clarity on the subject, and I could not find much helpful information about the theory or practice of parable construction.

Matching Textual Export with Real Life

At a broader level of application is the frequent problem that concrete illustrations sometimes do not exactly match the meaning of the textual content from which they are drawn. It is not uncommon for there to be significant correlation issues between text and application, but for lack of alternatives, the speaker uses weak word-pictures.

When the preacher rises to the task of analogizing the Bible to real life, things need to be accurate or they do not work well. Conversely, when the illustration has strong correspondence, the listener intuitively knows the truth of the message. If the image, the similitude, or the story does not correspond closely to both the textual idea and the real world, the meaning is mutated and the people who are listening miss the point or feel a sense of puzzlement.

Upon researching the theory of illustration and figures, I discovered that there were implicit rules for creating figures, rules that speakers often ignore or violate intentionally. It is helpful to know how sermonic development can easily move from textual ideas to figured applications appropriately.

Ideas are formulated through a process of '**symbolic extrication**,' and formulated by taking a hard look at the words of scripture and making sure they follow the '**analogy of intrinsic attribution**.'[2] These ideas are detailed later in the chapter on "Capturing the Ordinary." However, let's look briefly right now at what this means.

When dealing with the main idea of a biblical text and attempting to associate that main idea to the concrete world, the idea-formulation sequence is very important and comes with principles and implicit parameters that control meaning-transmission. In other words, there are innate qualities in language that encourage or discourage imaging; this is the analogy of intrinsic attribution. The process of finding the universal or extracting an idea is symbolic extrication.

The speaker cannot play fast-and-loose with the text because words export precise sense. The associations we make between biblical, textual meaning must correspond properly with the illustrations we create.

For example, in preaching on the 'pearl of great price' in Matthew 13:46, the intrinsic attribution might be, among other things, that a singular piece of jewelry or gem has supreme worth. I can analogize to diamonds, a valuable antique, a priceless or rare coin, or a small painting by a world-renowned artist. Words have intrinsic meaning.

Understanding this led me to codify principles for creating analogy, and I began to feel more settled in coming up with a simple method for application and illustration mechanics. I also became more and more motivated to outline my thoughts, since preachers struggle at finding suitable material to apply the scriptures.

Good sermons, like good songs or poems, capture an idea in simplicity and profoundness. For a preacher, this should be a common reflex. It is the habit of delving into God's majesty, in a sense, and makes the Bible live for people.

When I use the metaphor of 'the Bible living for people,' what I mean precisely is that the Bible connects to their personal experience. They know it is true because they have already lived it.

Resonance and the Power of Comparison

In figure creation, whether one is talking about images or extended narrative, the underlying connection between the communicative idea and the concrete common reality is called **analogous correspondence**. This idea is central to healthy application and will be treated in stages throughout the book.

The validity of the communication success is measured in true or false resonance in the ear of the listener. Do the people 'get it'?

To explain this in a scholarly way, fully understanding the real danger of becoming too technical too soon, I would say this--the health of any correspondence between two things or ideas is a shining combination of components: textual idea, created story or figure, the exact syntax of the oral language, and the real-world reality to which that language points. Does the created convergence work for the hearer?

What this means practically is that one cannot simply create something that resembles a good illustration and hope that people understand what one says. Rather, it means it is important to learn the precise principles and rules of figure creation as well as how audiences decode language.

Preachers need help in this area; they need to know how to create illustrations that rattle, so to speak. Additionally, those creations should not just work for them but also for their audiences.

For the most part, the preaching academy in the English-speaking world has been slow in producing material concerning the science and theory of sermonic application, principles and techniques that help the average preacher. When it comes to illustration, we have been more deliberate in collecting and cataloging illustrations. I will say in passing for clarification that **illustrations** are specific examples with implicit application.

Rules for figure creation or even sermonic suitability of illustration are rare. These pages explain the theory and implementation of the text-to-audience process; they do not attempt to differentiate illustration from application, two terms that are impossible to differentiate for reasons of overlap.

I am certainly not saying that everything that follows will be simple or easy to employ. However, I do know that with a little focus and practice, the applications will flow like water.

Doing What Jesus Did

Before one can develop and learn the mechanics of figure formation, that is, a sort of analogy-producing reflex, it is important to understand the theory of audience reception. Think about the preachers that you listen to on a regular basis. Can they capture real-life images and stories at any moment to drive home the biblical text in a way that the listener can grasp with clarity? Jesus did this.

When I speak, I want the listeners to be like the officers who could not arrest the Savior in John 7:46. They replied to those that sent them, "No one ever spoke like this man!" Their intent to do evil was thwarted by the quality of Jesus' language. I want so desperately to turn people from their sinful intentions. It should be an outcome of what I am proposing in these pages.

Beyond this is an even harder question. When was the last time you heard a sermon filled with parables, those short wisdom-analogies or stories that force a truthful confrontation? To this day, I have yet to hear a parable-driven sermon.

It seems very strange to me that we are not doing what Jesus did. Some preachers even say we should not do what Jesus did because of the condemnatory nature of the parable as detailed in Matthew 13 or because Jesus' role as a judge is not ours, separating out the listeners to isolate those with hardened hearts. We have to be careful that we do not make void the law of God through our tradition.

I believe we should follow Him in His most fundamental delivery modality, otherwise, we treat certain types of illustrations as out of bounds, somehow wrongly assuming that the preacher is in the place of God. Yet, positioning ourselves between God and man is exactly where Paul says we are: "Therefore, we are ambassadors for Christ, God making his appeal through us. We implore you on behalf of Christ, be reconciled to God" (2 Cor. 5:20).

Such thinking that forbids the use of parables is seriously flawed and even dangerous. In fact, the power of the medium to convict is the very reason why we should be preaching using parables. As Paul states in Romans chapter 1, natural revelation condemns us. There is a judgmental quality in illustrating, even when the image communicates something positive. There is implicit indictment woven into the fabric of creation. This convicting power paves the way for redemption and the blood of Christ.

Ultimately, it is my hope that this book teaches communicators how to correlate the Word of God with that living language of God's creation. Most preachers who teach expositorily claim that they preach the Word. But the question is how? Do we use creation as Jesus did? How do we paint on the tapestry, and do we do it well?

This book outlines a journey, not only for me, but also for you the reader. It is one of possibility. You will not be an expert illustrator next week. As you will discover, this is sometimes a complex process that will take a lifetime to master. However, you will learn many of the fundamentals in a few short pages.

Picture yourself addressing people with the Bible *and* with illustrations. Imagine saying, "The Bible says this. Let me illustrate what that means." Imagine looking out into the audience and the heads are all looking intently at you with smiles on their faces! This is the power of Jesus, so why not try to do what He did?

How Do We Get There

When someone hires a carpenter to build a house, the owner not only wants a professional who knows how to follow the blueprint, but the homeowner also wants a creative person who can figure out a captivating vision of what life will be like once the client lives there. This is the challenge of preaching: we take what the Architect has drawn in blue-prints and put nails and wood to them.

Some might look at this book and say it is a work about illustration skills; however, it is much more than that. It is about creating a Spirit-infused, creative mind, captivated by the word of God and a love for the audience, an audience that lives in a thoroughly concrete world, not a world of abstraction.

If the speaker is possessed by God, that person will be immersed in the joys and sorrows of material living. This seemed to be the way of Jesus. He embodied what he was talking about, so it was only natural to reflect material truth with words.

A speaker must have a vision for a habitation that is unique and special, one that emerges from his or her divinely possessed soul with a mind and tongue, wholly yielded to an omniscient God who knows what the audience needs. He creates a sermon that demonstrates that the Savior is sovereign in the preaching process.

I am categorically against the idea that we can simply teach method, and out will come a Spirit-infused, captivating preacher. If the Spirit of God does not possess the verbal carpenter before that person takes up the hammer, all this is in vain. The sermon or teaching will be lifeless, and in human terms, dry or fleshly.

So many great men of God were ruined by preaching classes that presented a method that destroyed what God was doing in them. This is what I hope to avoid.

The 'Love' of Application

Our job as people who preach the scriptures is to talk about implications. We are here to grab people by the metaphorical hand and walk them through the forest of the mundane into the presence of God and show them how ideas, principles, and behavioral mandates are infused with God Himself and His love for people.

It is imperative to unashamedly embrace the human side of preaching. It is incarnational. After all, "the Word became flesh and dwelt among us" (John 1:14). His life was a walking parable, a concrete representation of spiritual truth, and "from His fullness we have all received" (1:16).

There is something uniquely simple about this and demands a certain mindset in preaching, one that neither lets go of the text nor the people on whose ears the articulation lands. For over forty years, I have been on a journey of joy and discovery, learning how to connect the scriptural text to the dust of humanity. In theology, this is called Divine concession--that is, 'accommodation.' The Savior bowed. He stooped low to redeem us and show us His hands and feet.

Scriptural illustration and application are, in fact, verbal concession. The longer the biblical scholar reflects on the magnificence of God, the more s/he may tend toward abstraction. However, God Himself showed us in His preaching that imaged and storied concreteness is the endgame, the highest form of love for broken people.

Mankind is steeped in sin and preoccupied with life on this planet. The audience moves in a world of clutter and voices, a postmodern barrage of stimuli.

Amid the endless cacophony of competing agendas, the stuff from which sermons are illustrated is right there where people live. It is this *stuff* that grabs people because they have already experienced it. Yet, for the preacher, seeing it and accessing it can be quite fatiguing. We know it is there, but we often grope around in the dark trying to grab it and ultimately come up empty.

Let's begin to access all that fodder that makes preaching real, like Jesus' own spoken words to the broken world He loved so much. There is nothing trivial about accessing little things and making them plain. In fact, I believe it is the highest form of art. Capturing the universal truth of the scripture and placing it amid the details of life is essential to being an effective Christian.

I would be honored if this book drew wider access than simply the preaching community. It has tremendous value for homeschool parents, for Christian school teachers that share from the Bible daily, for Christian workers, and for parents who want to show their children how the Bible speaks in relevant ways to life.

First and foremost, we are Bible readers before we are Bible communicators. We must learn first to capture the sense of the text before we can communicate its relevance.

It may shock you, but what you are about to discover is a journey of tutelage in reading, not in speaking. If you discover gold, then you will shout it from the hills.

If the restaurant is good, you will tell your friends about your discovery. If you watch your son hit a home run, you will post it to social media. When you see God clearly in His majesty, it will be so much easier to glorify Him to common folk in common ways.

The results are harvesting, laughter, smiles, questions, and wonderment. When you arrive there, you will be doing what Jesus did.

Questions for Engagement

1. Why should preaching the Bible be illustrated by the physical world in which we live and not simply be an explanation of the text of scripture?
2. How do the nine bridges create different types of connections between speakers and listeners?
3. How does Jesus' parabolic methodology make detailed use of the natural world to build bridges and span cultures?
4. When dealing with the main idea of a biblical text and attempting to associate that main idea to the concrete world, why is this subject/idea-formulation sequence so important?
5. What is analogous correspondence and what are some of the features of a healthy correlation?
6. What is symbolic extrication?
7. What is the analogy of intrinsic attribution?
8. In what ways is Jesus' life of accommodation an example to us in Bible application?

3   The Holy Spirit's Power in Bible Application

The Holy Spirit's role in applying the Bible is rarely visited in textbooks. Preaching and evangelism books are filled with formulas, but the process of reaching the hearer is a supernatural one. God uses language to expose the human condition and provide a positive way forward.

The prevailing method for sermon construction or even speaking to lost people at a casual level often takes place out of a perspective of denial concerning the details of the listeners' lives. We teach and employ formulas rather than begin in a spirit of dependency on the Holy Spirit of God to teach us what the hearer already knows to be true.

While the reading of the text is a grammatical endeavor, applying the text moves from grammar to life-realities. The speaker needs to ask, "What things does God want me to bring up to the audience?"

In Bible interpretation, there is a supernatural component. The Psalmist declares, "Open my eyes, that I may behold wondrous things out of your law" (Ps. 119:18). Unless God opens our eyes and ears, what we 'see' and 'hear' might not be what the audience needs at any given moment.

The idea that we can master the content of scripture through grammatical examination is false. In this idea we must recognize the difference between the flesh and the Spirit. "The secret of the LORD is with them that fear him; and He will shew them his covenant" (Ps. 25:14).

Just before Jesus left this earth, He gave His disciples supernatural power to have clarity about the Old Testament. Immediately prior to the Ascension in Luke 24:45, this is what we are told; "Then He opened their minds to understand the Scriptures." Until there was supernatural illumination, the scriptures were fogged to the apostles.

Without the Holy Spirit's empowerment to clearly see and apply the Bible, our efforts are mechanical and will receive mechanical results. This is why Jesus over and over again tells His listeners, "He that has ears to hear, let him hear" (Matt. 11:15; 13:9, 43; Mark 4:9, 23; 7:16; Luke 14:35, etc.). So clear is this principle of Spirit-protected meaning in the scripture, that Jesus, after giving the interpretation of the Parable of the Sower, shouts out the same phrase, "He who has ears to hear, let him hear" (Luke 8:8).

Power in Weak Dependency

There is a broken dependence that comes over the communicator of the gospel when s/he embraces specific weakness. It is no longer the power of man's ability to carefully orchestrate prepared illustrations. It is a matter of the Spirit's precise leading in application that makes the difference.

I know that there are many who feel that illustration is a mechanical process, even to the point of advancing that guidance of the Spirit is a pagan notion. However, the Bible is more than clear about this.

Paul said, "I did not receive it [the gospel] from any man, nor was I taught it, but I received it through a revelation of Jesus Christ" (Gal. 1:12). So shaken was he over what he received, he isolated himself and did not seek human counsel about it for years (1:16).

If we have resistance to the supernatural application of the scriptures, it puts us in an awkward place with respect to God Himself. God is the revealer of secrets (Dan. 2:47).

Fleshly resistance to Jesus' own audience was the reason He rebuked them often at this precise point. "Let these words sink into your ears" (Luke 9:44). Peter repeated the same approach: "You stiff-necked people, uncircumcised in heart and ears, you always resist the Holy Spirit. As your fathers did, so do you" (Acts 7:51).

Audience resistance is one side of the equation. It is not the same as a preacher-laziness that results in failure to make ideas spiritually powerful.

Picture for a minute a pastor pouring over the Bible without care for listener reception. The individual is like a mother preparing liver and spinach for kids who refuse to eat them. She could be making Alaskan salmon filets or even fish sticks. At least the audience would pull out the ketchup and go at it.

To believe for an instant that scriptural understanding without the Spirit of God can produce a godly Christian is to make our preaching cultish and powerless. Our knowledge of Christ is a supernatural phenomenon, totally dependent on the revelation of Christ. Jesus reiterated this idea when He said that, "All things have been handed over to me by my Father, and no one knows the Son except the Father, and no one knows the Father except the Son and anyone to whom the Son chooses to reveal him" (Matt. 11:27).

There is a categorical difference between someone who knows the Son intimately, communicating Him with passionate knowledge, and someone who has no intimacy with the God who answers prayer. When a preacher only has a grammatical understanding of the text, it is like hearing someone read about a colonial mansion, rather than taking a tour with a passionate owner of a classic property.

It might be offensive to think that a man with higher education is powerless at scriptural communication unless God Himself enables him, but that is exactly what I am saying. We cannot deny that He reveals His will and secrets to those who are possessed of Him (Amos 3:7).

The plea from David is that he was a sojourner on the earth, so he cries out, "hide not your commandments from me!" (Psalm 119:19). Of course, he knew the commandments. Yet he recognized it was possible that even in spite of his knowledge, God might possibly conceal their meaning. This was the case with the fleeing Israelites. "But to this day the LORD has not given you a heart to understand or eyes to see or ears to hear" (Deut. 29:4). They knew the commandments and had them written in stone, yet they did not have eyes or ears for the supernatural understanding of them.

The truth of this reality is a humbling one. The result is dependency, first for understanding and then for how that understanding might be applied precisely to particular circumstances or audiences. Imagine David's passion for application. "My soul is consumed with longing for your rules at all times" (Psalm 119:20). Did David not know God's statutes? Yes, he did, but he longed to apply them in his personal life.

From a Weak Preacher to a Supernatural Church

It seems that God finds delight in revealing spiritual truth to those with a childlike spirit and hiding it from those who are wise or think they are. This was Job's assessment in Job 28, when he discourses on how men find revealed wisdom through the fear of the Lord (28:25). All the fleshly digging we do cannot compare to the supernatural illumination by God's Spirit.

The supernatural nature of church life is expressed by Paul when he tells the Corinthians twice to have a specific desire for prophecy (I Cor. 14:1, 39). It is entirely possible for a whole congregation to enter a pharisaical mentality when the pastor believes that exposition is not a supernatural calling.

Collectively, a church can learn a poor model of reading of the word of God, one without a spiritual lens and without dependency. In Matthew 12, the Pharisees saw Jesus picking grain and did not know He was Lord of the Sabbath. They just had superficial, Sabbatarian legalism because their eyes were blinded.

The conclusion for us is that we might read something but totally miss the point of how the scriptures apply. The Pharisees missed the application. They created a community that was largely blind when the Creator walked in their midst. He was right there in front of them.

It may even be that a person can ignore the obvious reading because the message is painful and requires adjustment. Jesus showed the Pharisees this, but they sought to kill Him for it.

Powerful applications of the word of God are vast, and it should not go without saying that two people can read the same passage and come up with different applications. There may even be several primary or tertiary meanings, and certainly many applications from each. A gold mine can produce nuggets from every shaft. This is where it is necessary to have the Spirit's direction.

The Spirit's Role in Teaching Applied Truth

When Jesus was concluding His ministry, He clarified these principles to His disciples. The following passage is very comforting. It resolves the ambiguity of how we need to approach this discipline of preaching and illustration:

When the Spirit of truth comes, he will guide you into all the truth, for he will not speak on his own authority, but whatever he hears he will speak, and he will declare to you the things that are to come. He will glorify me, for he will take what is mine and declare it to you. All that the Father has is mine; therefore I said that he will take what is mine and declare it to you. (John 16:13-15)

The witness of the Spirit, however subjective, is a reality (1 John 5:6). To deny this moves us to the realm of mechanical religion. Our exegetical process would, at that point, be no different from a lost person reading the scripture without understanding.

Later in this study, we will emphasize the importance of grammar and accuracy in getting suitable applications. Grammar is not only important; it is critical. Jesus Himself had a view of inerrancy that is undeniable. "For truly, I say to you, until heaven and earth pass away, not an iota, not a dot, will pass from the Law until all is accomplished" (Matt. 5:18). He said this to preempt the idea that He came to destroy the law and the prophets.

Posture is central as we seek to know how to apply and illustrate the scriptures. We learn from Him; He teaches us, not the other way around. This is not just a grammatical exercise.

In a sense, teaching the Bible is a protected, spiritual relationship, not an impersonal textual process. We have to have a foundation of faith in our discovery and delivery. We cannot model faithless mechanics in scriptural communication. Not only will it leave us in a spiritual wilderness, but we will become like the very lost people to whom we are speaking, where the message is foolishness (Heb. 4:1; 1 Cor. 1:18; 2:5). If the message is not living for us, how will it live for our hearers?

There is not some super-spiritual eligibility requirement for scriptural application and verbal power. In fact, a Christ-centered dependence seems to be the prerequisite, a spiritual clothing found among the lowly (1 Cor. 1:18-29). This was Jesus' point in the beatitudes. The kingdom of God belongs to the poor in Spirit (Matt. 5:3).

Paul is very precise in his application strategy and gives his personal assessment, as he reflects on his work in Corinth. It was not carefully prepared oratory or sermons delivered with human skill. It was a demonstration of the Spirit and power, deep things that the Spirit taught him as he applied the Bible to his hearers (1 Cor. 2:1-13).

The Practical Side of Supernatural Application

Although we have a supernatural dependency as we examine the text, there is a certain practical nature to the process as well. We learn this from Ezra. He opened the scriptures in full view of the people, read the text "clearly, and they gave the sense, so that the people understood the reading" (Neh. 8:8).

Ultimately there is a tension between understanding the text and moving to the application of it. This requires grammatical skill but also spiritual discernment. Paul reminded Timothy about this. He said the word of God needed to be 'rightly handled' (2 Tim. 2:15).

There are some severe warnings about playing fast and loose with the scriptures. In Proverbs 30:5-6 we are told that we should "not add to his words, lest he rebuke you and you be found a liar." It is only the Spirit of the living God that provides applicable meaning to the text (John 16:13).

If in fact "it is the Spirit who gives life," "the flesh is no help at all," and the words that Jesus spoke are both "spirit and life," then there is a precise spiritual quality to biblical language. We need to be careful not to tamper with it by decontextualizing it to make a point that God does not make. The word of God is a sword and even more than a sword; we have to be careful how we wield it (Eph. 6:17; Heb. 4:12).

The abiding nature of careful preaching has enduring value. It does not pass away because it stays close to the heart of God through textual accuracy. (Mark 13:31).

Audience Reception of Spirit-Led Application

So, how does the audience's attitude and spiritual condition affect the way we communicate what God reveals to us and the way it is received by hearers? Our speech has to be simple, as if we are speaking to fleshly and infantile people (1 Cor. 3:1). This may sound cruel, but Paul says that his audience could not handle any more than that.

Additionally, the audience should not see any pride in us. God multiplies our efforts with His own blessing when we have a spirit of dependence. After all, we are stewards of God's mysteries, something for which we need divine illumination. We are not masters over those mysteries and there is absolutely no place for pride (1 Cor. 4:1, 19).

The more we meddle with the scriptures and move away from careful, contextualized meaning, the weaker our message, at least from the Holy Spirit's perspective. If the audience has a reception problem, that is up to the audience. However, if the problem is with us and our embellishments to the text, something that does not reinforce central or secondary meanings, we can fully expect our results to be in proportion to how far afield we are and how much we have watered down the word of God.

We should inspire the audience to examine the scriptures, as Paul did for the Bereans in Acts 17:11. Sometimes the scriptures are difficult. We can't expect everyone to always understand the deep things of God. That was even apparent for Peter, when he said he had trouble with understanding Paul's letters (2 Pet. 3:15-16). Peter warns us that if we twist the scriptures, we are "untaught and unstable," perhaps in a sort of spiritual psychosis.

We must implore people to examine the scriptures carefully, otherwise God will be their judge (John 12:48). It is possibly a faith issue when we cannot see scriptural meaning clearly. It is not always a matter of better exegesis.

Results of Spirit-Filled Application

Jesus was rather brutal with those that had a sectarian understanding of the scriptures but missed the heart of things. He addressed them in Matthew 22:29: "You are wrong, because you know neither the Scriptures nor the power of God."

We must move beyond a tacit reading of the Word of God to one of dependency. God's power needs to flow through His word to us.

When the preacher abides in Christ by the power of the Holy Spirit, the result is fruit. Jesus provides us with a very long discourse about the positive nature of abiding in Him and the negative results of not being connected (John 15). Abiding results in people being born again.

Listen to how Peter phrases this: 'Since you have been born again, not of perishable seed but of imperishable, through the living and abiding word of God" (1 Pet. 1:23). The Psalmist says the same thing in Psalm 12:6-7 when he says that the words of the Lord "convert the soul." Paul told Timothy that the scriptures make people "wise for salvation" (2 Tim. 3:15). We don't save people; God does. His words have a moving spiritual force.

The word cleans up people's lives (John 15:3), supplants wicked filth (James 1:21; John 17:17), and sets people free (John 8:31-32). It is our very life, and we cannot live any semblance of a spiritual life without it (Matt. 4:4; Deut. 8:3). It gives us direction and protection in every facet of our existence (Ps. 119:9, 105, 130; Prov. 30:5).

The number of times that the Bible refers or alludes to the word as bread, that is, sustenance, is amazing. Jeremiah even goes so far as to say, "Your words were found, and I ate them, and your words became to me a joy and the delight of my heart, for I am called by your name, O Lord, God of hosts" (15:16). Job treasured God's word more than food (23:12). Paul tells us to have a rich abundance of Christ's words (Col. 3:16).

If such is the case, why would we deviate from the essential meaning of the text? We would not because the Holy Spirit would not endorse illustration and application that go beyond scriptural intent.

There are many temptations that risk taking us away from scriptural focus. We can become overly concerned with grammar, have a desire to entertain people, or simply focus on a secondary idea that has little bearing on our immediate audience.

Our task as scriptural communicators is to stay as close to the meaning, intent, and implication of the scriptures as possible. That is why it is necessary to have a grammar of illustration. It creates an accurate transmission of the word of God to an audience that needs to stay connected to Him.

Staying On-Script in Preaching

Teachers of the scriptures often believe that they can go off script and take illustration and application in whatever direction they find suitable to their homiletical ideas. However, there is an enduring quality to God's words that we want implanted in the minds and ears of the listener. "Heaven and earth will pass away, but my words will not pass away" (Matt. 24:35; Ps. 119:60: Isa. 40:8).

There are severe warnings in the Bible against those who add to the word of God. Ezekiel is commanded to severely chastise the prophets for preaching a message other than the one God gave them (Ez. 13:1-23). God tells these men that He is against them. Paul told Timothy to be on the lookout for people who fill the air with their own opinions (1 Tim. 4:1-2). He calls their preaching content the "doctrine of devils."

This is why we need to stay close to the scriptures. In fact, "the LORD gives wisdom; from his mouth come knowledge and understanding" (Prov. 2:6). If we accurately preach and apply the words that God has given us, we provide a rock-foundation for listeners and don't end up incurring the wrath of God for distorting His word (Matt. 7:24)

Our preaching needs to be strong on the word and minimal in explanatory discourse that wanders from textual meaning. If the power is in the scriptures, the Holy Spirit will endorse what He has already said. When we say inappropriate things, invent sidetracked discourse, or fill the sermon with material unrelated to the scriptures, how can we expect spiritual power?

There is efficacious, life-changing power that goes out when we stay close to the actual words of the Bible and their meaning. Isaiah hammered this home when he stated, "so shall my word be that goes out from my mouth; it shall not return to me empty, but it shall accomplish that which I purpose, and shall succeed in the thing for which I sent it" (Isa. 55:11).

Even healing power is dependent in part on our implementation of the scriptures. The Psalmist said that God, "sent out his word and healed them, and delivered them from their destruction (107:20).

We implicitly doubt the healing power of the word when we fill our teachings with human discourse that does not contain biblical accuracy. If a preacher or teacher gets up and does not refer to the scriptures with utmost accuracy, there is a denial of the power of the word to heal. On the one hand we profess that the scriptures have the power, but our delivery process denies the very value we profess to espouse. We fill our time with our own words rather than God's.

It is with this understanding that we can now move forward with a discussion of illustration. Application of the Bible is, after this supernatural beginning, a grammatically-tied discipline. When we move from the supernatural to the textual, there is a connective process by which the Spirit of God cries out to the modern listener and applies the scriptures with power. "Is not my word like fire, declares the LORD, and like a hammer that breaks the rock in pieces?" (Jer. 23:29).

Questions for Engagement

1. What is the connection between the text, the Holy Spirit, and the listener?
2. What is the supernatural quality of Bible application, and what are the habits that foster Spirit-infused empowerment in teaching the scriptures?
3. According to the Bible itself, what is the role of human weakness in communicating eternal truth?
4. What potential dangers exist when someone is theologically trained and attempts to teach the scriptures?
5. What is the role of Spirit-dependency in explaining the text, and what Bible verses support that opinion?
6. How is Spirit-directed, Bible application dangerous for the listener?
7. What are the implications of Jesus' teaching in John 16:13-15 for our application of the Bible, and how does that relate to Matthew 5:3, when Jesus says that the kingdom of God belongs to the poor in Spirit?
8. How does the audience's attitude and spiritual condition affect the way we communicate what God reveals to us and the way it is received by hearers?
9. What should be the result of the preacher abiding in Christ and speaking by the power of the Holy Spirit?
10. Why is it necessary to have a grammar of illustration?
11. How is healing power related to the right interpretation of scripture and what scriptures support your answer?

4   Application is War

If understanding the Bible is a byproduct of spiritual dependency on the Holy Spirit of God, then applying the meaning of scripture to yourself and then to others is a matter of spiritual warfare. It is one thing to map out the battles; it is quite another to gather the armament, organize the troops, and face the enemy.

When there is truth-transmission at stake, you can be sure that the devil is involved in hindering what is happening. We have to remember that not only are we wrestling spiritually (Eph. 6:12), though the congregation is physically present, but we are also waging war in the heavenlies with a triumphant Christ (Eph. 1:21; 2:2; 3:10; Col. 1:15-20; 2:10, 15; 1 Pet. 3:20).

Not only is the application personal in the sense that the speaker strategically and lovingly speaks into the life of the listeners, but also there is satanic resistance to the entire process. Our victory is already established, however, and we need to preach in that confidence.

While there are demonic hindrances on the creative side of speaker thought-construction, there are also receptor struggles. These are not just practical but are rooted deeply in the spiritual frameworks of listeners' minds, representing a culture of thinking that is tied to their contextual world.

Being sensitive to the spiritual struggle that is taking place all around us is not really the first reflex when we are in conversation or teaching. We are often too worried about what we want to say and how we want to say it. Yet the spiritual life with its accompanying distractions is warring against the speaker as s/he delivers the message.

We tread on the precipice of countless diversions, countless obsessions, and countless distractions in the speaking process. We are consumed with fleshly objectives and human factors. Often, the last thing on our minds is spiritual warfare, but that is our lot.

The more precise and intentional we are in our personal engagement with our teaching, the more we can expect demonic resistance. We can generalize and speak in theory and platitudes, but our task is to incite positive change at every level through relevant instruction.

It is helpful to ask if our biblical application is surgical in nature? Does it have a very laser-directed purpose, and can we state what that is? The speaker must ask, "Am I generalizing?" If so, there must be a change in one's approach.

If the application is precise, the reaction will be eternal. This is not to say that God can't use our generalizations, but the Holy Spirit of God deals with us in personal ways. Teaching that is spiritually designed with very precise godly intentions results in a spiritual assault on the kingdom of darkness.

Charles Finney was fond of quoting Isaiah in saying that he saw his role as one of dismantling the 'refuge of lies' in the audience (28:17). Once we start approaching the strongholds of spiritual resistance, the war is on.

Let me give an example from Acts 28:3. Luke tells us, "When Paul had gathered a bundle of sticks and put them on the fire, a viper came out because of the heat and fastened on his hand." If I am preaching this text, I must talk about leadership service. Paul was gathering sticks for the fire after his shipwreck. He was the victim of the naval and military leaders' poor decision-making and the failure of these men to heed divine warning. Nevertheless, he was gathering sticks for the fire. The apostle Paul was picking up sticks for the wet and cold prisoners.

Were I to preach this in a church, I would have to ask, "You leaders, you deacons, you elders, you bishops, do you do the menial and the mundane jobs of this ministry or do you think that you are above Paul who lived to serve? By the way, if you are like Paul, you may be bitten by a viper in the process."

When we allow the Spirit of God to direct us in application, we cannot help but land in some hotbed of implication. This is the example of Jesus and the authors of the New Testament. We also need to live consistently in this same manner and state what needs to be stated. There will be a solid response to what we say, and it won't always be pleasant.

Early Battles

Typically, application is seen at the end of the sermon-preparation timeline; however, it needs to be one of the earliest things we do. Here is my logic.

When an architect knows how to design a house, he has all the skills he needs to move in countless directions. Yet, he does not draw a picture of the prototype of the final product until the client comes in with a picture or concept of the outcome.

We must approach the text with application outcomes *as we formulate a main idea and outline.* In theory, we assume application comes once we have interpreted the material. Yet the text screams out its implications from the beginning of examination. All the time we prepare, the Spirit is inspiring us with the outcomes.

Prayer about application implications of the text must be at this initial part of our posture *before* we begin exegetical analysis. If not, we will miss the Holy Spirit's clues along the way, as He speaks to us during the process of sermon formulation.

Failure to prepare our spirit to receive practical outworkings of the text may be oversight, but it might be pride as well. We wrongly assume that we accumulate all the interpretive details and make the transition in the end to speaker reception. Nothing could be further from the truth.

Our entire sermon needs to be constructed with the end in view and with the reality of how we will apply and illustrate the truth of the message. We cannot assume that we know the mind of God and how to apply the scripture to a particular audience. That is a supernatural work of illumination, something the Spirit of God gives us as we process words and meanings with humility.

There are some that assume sermon preparation does not include divine illumination about contextual application and precise need. However, we must respond to the Spirit who is constantly speaking and who loves people more than we do. He provides the overcoming power in our language. Our intellect often yields the wisdom of this world, and the preacher who depends on his own intellectual abilities will harvest the fruit of his own efforts.

A similar flaw exists in the idea that commentaries, Internet searches, and illustration files can replace prayer. Divinely given application comes through a humble connection to the Spirit of God. "But we speak the wisdom of God in a mystery, even the hidden wisdom, which God ordained before the world unto our glory" (1 Cor. 2:7).

There is a certain Spirit-led speech. Paul addresses this type of divinely given, analogous language in 1 Cor. 2:13 when he said, "...which things also we speak, not in the words which man's wisdom teaches, but which the Spirit teaches, combining spiritual ideas with spiritual words." The Spirit of the living God is the teacher, even to the point of giving us applied correlations and their words.

The Preacher and Mind Issues

Internally, there are a host of mind issues that plague the person who hopes to apply the Bible in a powerful way. That person can easily move from trying to help people to trying to impress them.

The confusion between valid desires that come with humble intentions and those selfish motivations that happen when we move in our own power are not that far apart. We genuinely want to do a good job when we preach, but pride and arrogance follow like army ants.

Feeling good about delivery is on one side of the coin and the desire to impress people is on the other. We should only be satisfied when we have said what God wants us to say in a way that transmits the biblical meaning by the power of the Spirit.

Additionally, occasionally the preacher confuses personal issues with audience issues, confounding the idea that my problems are their problems. This is a type of projection. There is obviously some shared experience, but speakers can be trapped in their own minds, providing answers for questions that no one is asking or sharing stories that land dead on the listeners' ears. Likewise, the preacher can be fenced in by a myriad of matters of conscience. This is not always helpful when the sermon should be audience-focused.

There is a need to know the difference between our personal concerns and an audience's need. These are sometimes identical, sometimes similar, and sometimes light years from one another.

Circumstantial Factors

People who speak to audiences frequently can become casual in their consideration of listener application. There is a clear need to examine audience demographic, setting, history, distance, etc. Ignorance of circumstantial factors may result in application failure.

For example, if I use a football analogy, I might reach a percentage of the audience but will likely lose an equal percentage of those who cannot associate the text with the illustration meaning. I might have to make up for this by using an additional illustration for those that hate football.

Failure to account for, or respect, audience realities will surely have trouble reaching the target of mutual understanding about textual export. I have a responsibility as a speaker to identify doors or barriers in the audience that will facilitate or impede reception. If I don't, my application might fall on deaf ears.

Beyond this, it might be even worse. The battle of spiritual warfare that I hope to win by exactly identifying the problem or fingering the solution to the battle warring among the auditors will be lost by my obsession with my own agendas. It may mean I have failed to love the listener as God does.

Application that Conquers Fear

Making precise applications can be a fearful thing. It requires careful consideration at every level. For example, if I am preaching about marriage, I need to be careful about offending divorced people in the audience, or those that are going through rough spots in their marriages. However, I cannot let fear dictate my delivery content. It just must be done with care and reflection in tone.

There are countless other fears. I can look at the audience and see that my example might only appeal to 30% of the people. However, that does not mean I should not employ it, simply because there may be listeners with whom this illustration does not connect.

Speakers are sometimes crippled by fictional or real ideas of how the audience might respond to an application or illustration. However, application is war, and we can fully expect a reaction. We have to be prepared for that. If we assume that our message needs to always be gentle and kind, we will not get very far, since the role of the Holy Spirit is to convict us of "sin, righteousness, and judgment" (John 16:8).

On top of these factors that make us reluctant to apply the scriptures with precision, most of us also have a subtle fear of failure, a fear we have not prepared enough, that we are weak and fumbling speakers, or that our past mistakes will follow us. It is for these reasons that speakers sometimes retreat into outlines and word meanings. We yield to the enemy and refuse to fight the battles of heart-application and practical implications.

We must exercise boldness, knowing that the elements of the text correlate absolutely and reflect the experiential realities of the listeners. We must know with some degree of certainty that God is pleased with how we are elucidating what He has already said.

What results as a byproduct of working through these inhibitions, fears, and mind games is that we engage the audience with love, force, and authority.

I will go one step further. Our very lives feed advanced application planning and strike the heart of the listener with force that brings about cognitive, emotional, and behavioral change. Because we are convinced of the truth of the text and have reflected on how that connection is made, the Holy Spirit confirms the intention of our words as we surgically lay down the implications to our hearers. The word of God, its meaning, and its connotation are powerfully received.

Naturally, this kind of result implies that the listener is, first, convinced of the truth of the text. The speaker herself must be gripped by the meaning and purified by its export.

A heart filled with love greatly aids the preacher to reach the ear and the heart of the auditor. When we are so overwhelmed with passion for God and His people, the application can be delivered with the heart of the Savior.

Students of the preaching discipline should ask how much they have grasped their role as a warrior. Generally, preaching is not seen as requiring battle armament. However, we have to remember that the listeners of Jesus' day not only wanted to kill Him, but they also succeeded. His message had both comforting and cutting effects. We must be prepared for both.

When we speak, the spiritual forces of darkness are in the way, especially when we correlate biblical material to the strongholds of our society. This requires that we have our textual analysis right as well as the implications of those texts. When all the components are firmly established, it is possible to drive points home with the confidence that is supplied by the Spirit of God.

Questions for Engagement

1. In what ways is the application of the Bible war?
2. When it comes to Bible application, what is the difference between generalization and having a laser focus?
3. In what ways do you personally struggle to arrive at the implications of a text before you speak in a formal, teaching setting?
4. Why are prayer and divine illumination essential in arriving at a contextualized application?
5. What is the difference between our personal concerns and an audience's needs?
6. How does the reality of fear weaken Bible application?
7. What happens to our choice of words when love overcomes fear in speaking?

5   Identification with the Audience

In day-to-day conversation, I have noticed that if I bring up a topic about which my conversation partner is conversant, the dialog explodes. For example, if I talk about coffee to a barista-type connoisseur, I get the latest on Burundian coffee or lattes.

In the same way, identification is at the core of God's way with man. Jesus became man, and it naturally follows that we are drawn to God-in-Christ because He became like us. As I have already stated, experiential identification brings human resonance.

Jesus was the Word made flesh. God was motivated by love to come and identify with us. The Creator became like His creation.

There is relational correlation in identification, something that brings along with it the very best of human experience–passion, empathy, excitement, and elation. Similarly, when we speak to others, regardless of the context, we communicate in language that the listener recognizes. If our experience is superior, we dial back our vocabulary and don't overwhelm the other person.

Beyond this, we typically might picture our conversational objective by throwing in descriptions with vivid language. We frequently also include a timeline. "I walked into the Starbucks at the airport under their green and white sign, and while I waited in line, I noticed the person in plaid in front of me paid for a $9 Mocha Latte Grande. It looked awesome with all that whipped cream. I caved and ordered the same thing."

Chronology and descriptors are helpful. They make the story live. They are not embellishments; they are necessities to capture the imagination and make a story reflect real life.

This should be a standard habit when we speak to others, especially if we are teaching eternal things. When we preach, we detail our language and even stoop to accommodate. This is love.

We must come out of the lofty tower of someone who already knows something to the lowly place of taking the listener on a journey. We must capture the minds of a preoccupied audience, that group of people normally scurrying about with a list of agendas, who happen to be in our presence at any given moment.

We open our mouths full of compassion, fully intending to rattle the cages of distraction, complacency, and misunderstanding by clarifying just how much Christ loves the listener. We do this simply and concretely.

Reflecting the Incarnate God

If we are to adopt an incarnational model of preaching, we mirror the intention of the Father. In Colossians 1:15, Paul tells us that Jesus "is the image of the invisible God." His journey on earth was a reflective one.

How do we share truths about the infinite, glorious God of Eternity? How do we communicate Him to a hurting world? It is of utmost importance to have a way to see Him and a way to show Him, a way that speaks identification, wonder, and love.

In Christ's image, we see the Father (Col. 1:15). He is the incarnate Creator and Savior of the World. As we discover Him in the scriptures, we grapple with how to communicate those realities we find with an audience perhaps less sensitive to eternity.

The preacher is faced with a dilemma of how to concretely represent eternal truths to people along a broad spectrum of intellectual abilities and experiences. Here is where a principle of identification is very helpful.

As already stated, human resonance between speaker and listener happens when the preacher creates a correlative idea that is known to the auditor. The ear on which the language falls is not the ear of the someone who just stepped off the turnip truck, so to speak, but someone who has a boatload of experience.

We must assume that God has already been speaking to the listener. How has He done this? It is probably through sickness, employment, money struggles, relationships, and a lifetime of choices.

God has already used life experience to teach the listener. You are certainly not the first person to communicate biblical principles to that person. The eternal things of God are everywhere present. That is the conclusion of Paul in Romans 1:20: "For his invisible attributes, namely, his eternal power and divine nature, have been clearly perceived, ever since the creation of the world, in the things that have been made. So, they are without excuse."

Every audience member is an expert in failed decisions and also a specialist in overcoming obstacles. Problems are endemic.

Who has not suffered from whispered secrets or work injustices? Who is not versed in chores, in workplace ethics, in abandonment, in betrayal, or in correction? The preacher must assume that a relentless God has already been at work.

Preaching is not always sharing something new, but clarifying what the listener already knows. In this endeavor, tone is very important in our delivery. If the audience already has experience with mistakes, family failure, language struggles, or some common problem, we cannot come to the conversation table as if the listener is a debutant. In fact, more than likely, the listener knows more than we do about life.

That vast pool of experience is the feeding trough of God's making. That person has a host of lessons, already learned, which need to be brought to the surface. What that person may or may not know is that the knowledge base s/he already possesses is a journal of God's dealings with him or her. It is our job to read it back to them out loud. How do we do this?

Bridging the Text to Ear and Eye

As was stated in a previous chapter, we live in a world of concreteness. We move, touch, and journey through the physical world. This is the kindling for teaching the scriptures.

It is from that concrete world that we build abstractions, generalizations, and principles. We all do this without knowing it. "Fires are hot. The stove is hot. I should be careful when I work around the kitchen or campfire." We are, in fact, a walking library of generalizations.

The Bible is not only full of these concrete stories and abstractions, but it is also the benchmark for understanding our environment. It is up to the preacher to capture those human details and moments and place them in proper perspective to God's covenant love.

People know intimately or intuitively both the concrete and the abstract. They do not always see how those component observations of the universe make sense in relation to their Creator. The teacher of the Bible must bridge the text to the concrete world and to the receiving audience. It is of supreme importance to understand that the audience is not ignorant.

We honor the listener when we recite a story or throw the biblical concept into an imaged delivery. When we do that, we say, "Let me show you how much you already know."

This bridging process can be done in so many ways, and the rest of this book is about exposure and mastering these processes. Again, let me say that you are an experienced veteran, even if you do not know it.

It is my firm conviction that almost all human beings are experts at similes, similitudes, and metaphors. They teach daily by association, by equating, by narrative, by association, by image, and by question every day of their lives.

The Path to Resonance

There are several sides to communicative resonance, the simultaneous connection between speaker and listener. Usually, however, the door through which we enter is not just cognition, it is one of emotion mixed with thought. We are highly passionate people, and we like to be moved. This is the way God made us. It is not entertainment.

Our association with the physical world is connected to our emotional center. If I brought up simple words in conversation, those words would generate feelings within you. For example, if I recited the words 'boat,' 'baby,' 'rocking chair,' 'stadium,' or 'whiteboard,' you would have an emotional resonance for at least some of these.

This reservoir of sensation toward the physical world is like a pool of affectation. We are moved by words, by stories, and by things we hear, touch, see, taste, and smell. In fact, smell for example, is fixed in our memory longer than other sensory stimuli. When we smell something like an odor we experienced years ago, that memory is brought up in our minds. We have a highly developed recall database when it comes to smells.

Beyond emotions, the minds of listeners already have refined cognitive structures. Some of them are defined by family, by faith, by society, by school, and by a host of other culturally forming teachers. Just bring up the topics of environmentalism, abortion, or immigration if you want to see people's cognitive frameworks. They will let you know very quickly.

Listeners are experts in love, protection, fear, and the vast array of human experiences. It is our job to touch their hearts with God's perspective on their accumulated pain and joy.

If we as speakers find the common ground of identification, we then might also find the door to biblical thought and behavioral change. People do not usually change as a result of being told they need to change. However, if they see in their own lives how God has repeatedly tried to break through in their past, they are more likely to connect the dots and embrace godly frameworks.

The individual experiences themselves that people live are not those biblical frameworks and should never be confused with scriptural principles and mandates; however, they do provide reinforcement for orthodoxy and orthopraxy, that is, right thinking and right practice.

Questions for Engagement

1. In your own words, how would you define the concept of relational identification with an audience?
2. What does it mean to bridge to the ear and eye?
3. How are emotion and cognition related to the discipline of identification with an audience?

6   Engagement to Encounter

Powerful application begins with powerful exegesis. However, the latter does not guarantee the former.

In my small sphere of influence, it never ceases to amaze me how unsettled pastors get when I tell them that the exegetical method as we practice it today in evangelical circles is almost totally foreign to the apostolic ministry of the first century. We seem to be centering the entire speaking program of the church around a view of 'preaching' that is actual scriptural teaching. Yet we call it 'preaching.' This is a definitional problem I will address later.

Bible students can misread the writings of Jesus and Paul, associating our four-walls-preaching with what we see in the pages of the New Testament, that is, powerful evangelistic miracles, encouragement, confrontation, and imprisonment. This is the nature of true preaching-- evangelistic proclamation. We must return to it.

Additionally, Sunday morning exegetical sermons must also improve, not just in their textual accuracy but in their illustrative precision. Today's ministers often speak from the Bible without textual referencing. Consequently, their illustrations and applications are also generalized without correspondence to the word of God.

Preachers typically speak within the confines of buildings and to audiences which are relatively static, and which may or may not include lost people. The consequence of this simple reality is a failed encounter because we relax and count on the sympathetic agreement of our hearers.

Beyond this, we can also impede meeting the living God when we approach preaching with excessive cognitive frameworks and word analyses, appealing principally to the mind. We must change this. Our task is larger than creating theological structures. It is ultimately about helping people meet the God of the universe with every aspect of their being.

Exegesis and Church Growth

It is entirely possible that poor handling of the biblical text can contribute to the emptying of a church. Few things are more disheartening than lousy exposition. Additionally, pastors can be Pharisees, and even among doctors of the Word of God, speakers can still be amazingly far from communicating clearly to the ordinary person.

In the same way that there is danger in exegetical neglect or overkill, there is a danger in illustrative malpractice and underkill. Just as a close analysis of the text is a discipline that every preacher must learn, casting a vivid picture is of equal worth in getting hold of people.

A broad look at the New Testament is a corrective lesson in priorities. Jesus did not teach His disciples literary analysis. He did not sit them down and show them how to parse

Hebrew verbs and dive into the rabbinical literature to get the meaning out of the text. Neither did Paul expend a lot of energy teaching his young protégés how to do textual analysis. The latter told his friend Timothy to 'preach the word' (2 Tim. 4:2). Again, biblical preaching is relevant proclamation to lost people, not exposition.

Paul's work at capturing the depraved will and wicked imagination of the first century pagan is no different than rendering captive a TV-saturated or phone-addicted person of today. The gradual decline and slow death of the evangelical movement in America is partially explainable by a preaching methodology that we find very little of in the New Testament. Jesus was an oral storyteller, constantly itinerant and associating with the crowds. He grew His 'church' on missionary preaching.

When Concretization is in Jeopardy

There is in current preaching a main-idea-hazard. We are on the precipice of peril if we think that formulating a main idea of a biblical text will win a lost world. Externalized preaching engagements require concretization outside the four walls of a church because people are not familiar with the Bible.

The value of a textual center lies in the preacher's ability to correlate it with the real world. The main idea is not just a generalization or an abstraction; the main idea is how the meaning creates connection between God and the listener.

A speaker can live by a smoke screen, thinking that once the plane has landed on the tarmac of a key textual principle, that he or she has grasped the heart of God. However, the heart of God is for that idea to land in the spirit of the listener with immense love.

Facilitating a spiritual connection of the words of a text of scripture with a thirsty hearer is the kind of heralding we need to be doing. "The Spirit and the Bride say, 'Come.' And let the one who hears say, 'Come.' And let the one who is thirsty come; let the one who desires take the water of life without price" (Rev. 22:17).

Our job is one of pleading for encounter, of introductions, and of reconciliation (2 Cor. 5:18). In God's presence is fullness of joy, and we need to propose to people that they must 'draw near' (Ps. 6:11; 73:28).

Questions for Engagement

1. How might we return to powerful, evangelistic confrontation in our current social contexts?
2. In what ways might our current concept of 'preaching' be unbiblical?
3. When is exegesis a positive method used for church growth and when is it unprofitable?

7   Crossing Cultures by Illustrating the Word of God

This is an unsettling book because it pays methodological homage to the greatest Preacher that ever walked the face of the earth, someone that was falsely accused and given a death sentence. He was a controversial man with cross-cultural and counter-cultural methods. His life ended with capital punishment.

In attempting to understand the making and the delivery of parables, I discovered that a parable can touch the hearts of eager listeners, but our instinct is not to create them. In constructing an entry point for learning to do what Jesus did, I discovered that I needed to teach the preacher how to bridge the cultural distances between the scriptures, the expositor him/herself, and the audience. Consequently, you have before you a manual on how to create analogies that tie the word of God to real life detail through illustrated delivery.

Part 3 of this book functions on the assumption that all communication is cross-cultural. It thrives on the reality that the preacher, or any speaker really, is both simultaneously *unlike and similar to* her listeners.

In our Western culture, the pastor is historically one of the most educated people in the village. S/he brings a different world into the pulpit and often distances her/himself from the people without even knowing it.

Let's face it. Preachers usually don't have much in common with bikers, with out-of-wedlock mothers, with postmodern teenagers, with income-strapped widows. We preachers are sometimes from another planet.

For myself, when I stand before people to preach, I must overcome a thousand cultural chasms. This book attempts to help the biblical expositor bridge the cultural expanse.

When a preacher talks to others familiar with the process of communication, when s/he mentions analogy or narrative preaching or image or illustration, it strikes to the core of the discipline and incites all kinds of emotion, from anger to smiles.

The simple reality is that picturing the word of God can produce similar results to those of Jesus and can even be dangerous. Our words can touch the ears of listeners and spark both controversy and healing. This is the power of application and the power of parables.

Listening Architecture

Resonance of the biblical message in the ear of the hearer on a typical Sunday morning delivery is a result of the prayerful, loving architecture of the sermon. It is the intentional construction that helps people correlate what they already know with what the Bible is saying *in its grammar*.

There is a simple process of bringing people into harmony with the grace and truth of the word of God. It involves showing them how the text of the Bible correlates with what they have already learned and observed. It is a way of reminding them of what the Spirit has already taught them.

Because preaching is a cross-cultural endeavor there is distance, but the land on one side (the preacher) and the land on the other side (the listener) is basically the same terrain. The roads are a little different, however. The landscape changes very little because essentially, planet earth is planet earth, and both live there. There is a common pool of experience and metaphor planted there for the taking.

So, while the preacher is from one culture and her audience is from another, they both put their experiential pants on one leg at a time. While it *appears* that people are very different, they are very much alike.

The arguments that audiences are homogeneous or heterogeneous are pointless. There is always common ground. There are always differences. It does not matter if the audience is all American, Latino, European, Black, Asian, or Amerindian. The real problem is in the mind of the preacher.

The most formidable obstacle is the preaching rut that produces endless boredom week after week. Discursive delivery and perpetual advice giving hardly resemble what Jesus did.

After overcoming this first problem of the preaching rut, the listening laziness of the 21st century audience may be even more formidable than the first. However, the preacher can't change this. S/he can only work on her/himself.

So, what is the bridge that spans the divide? It is the common ground between speaker and listener. It is the common lesson learned in everyday life. It is freezing an idea in space and time; it's that rare moment when you can serve up a spiritual truth to the pallet of a hungry, discouraged listener, however bored s/he may appear.

The task of preaching is certainly not principally a grammatical endeavor, although we are processing through a text, point by point, verse by verse. Those elements are the foundation. You would not feed people flour, would you. You need to mix it with a little shortening and milk to make biscuits. Unfortunately, many preachers serve up a bowl of flour to their hearers week after week and expect them to choke it down.

This is not to say that we are approaching entertainment, although what I am proposing is very definitely easy to hear. My job is not to amuse people. It is quite the opposite. Just as the parable divided audiences in Jesus' day, illustrations, carefully done, have a separation quality. The sound might be beautiful, but the results are not pretty.

Pulpiteering

Paul said that the wisdom of words makes the cross ineffectual (1 Cor.1:17). He essentially condemned the idea of 'pulpiteering' (2:1).

When I moved to North Carolina in 2005, I was talking to a member of the church where we settled. He was telling me about the Raleigh church-culture. He mentioned someone in the area that was the best Pulpiteer for miles around. I thought to myself, is that anything like an auctioneer, a bombardier, a pamphleteer, or a musketeer? The concept of pulpiteering is as downright unbiblical as it is bizarre. Our job here is not to produce Cicero or Quintilian.

We don't wield pulpits. We are the controlled, the called of God, the Spirit-led. When I stand before people, I am not Demosthenes. I am a simple man, led by God, desperate to grab hold of the heart of the simple person, the one who lives daily in the grind of the work world. I am the son of a lifelong Christian who humbly exhibited the power of God in the quietness of his powerful character and presence, not in his eloquence.

Speaking to people about the Bible is not really a wholly logical endeavor either. It is not principally about syllogisms, logical coordination, or reason. While we are explicitly commanded to cast down imaginations and every high thing that exalts itself against the knowledge of God, when one examines the Savior, He did this repeatedly using figures of speech. He was logical but not driven by rationality. He was impassioned about using common elements of life. He did this by picturing truth for people.

Because I believe American Christianity has hijacked the term 'preaching' and cashed in on several thousand years of accumulated rhetorical baggage, I have taken great pains in returning to a biblical definition of the word, particularly focusing on who the New Testament audience was when preaching was the matter of focus. This is the central task of the chapter entitled "Preaching is a Missionary Term."

Nor do I exonerate the guilt of expositional preachers who explain the grammar of the Bible in an arrogant, scholastic manner. It does not resemble the Savior and His method. Could this be the reason why evangelicalism is in almost universal decline in the West? Have we sanctioned complexity?

Ultimately, preaching in the Bible is a matter of simple, cross-cultural engagement of a burdened individual with a lost and needy audience. It is not a man behind a pulpit pointing out the meanings of Greek and Hebrew words to a group of saved Christians. This is not biblical preaching. Nor is preaching generalizing by excessive illustration or advice giving. These models are not what we are after here.

The man who communicates the word of God is, in one sense, culturally distinct; he is *unlike* his audience. He is on fire with the salvation of God. His audience is lost and headed for hell. He must overcome his own culture in a sense. He must evangelize wet kindling, dampened logs, and people burdened down with the crushing sin of life.

This fact alone is supremely important. We cannot simply be concerned about textual meaning, although the author believes strongly in clear and concise examination and sequential explanation of the word of God, word-by-word if necessary. Is there a way that the Bible, even its exact grammar, can cross the chasms of ethnicity, Postmodernism, age, gender, language, background, race, and socioeconomic segmentation? Yes, it is through properly correlated analogy from the scriptures to the material world.

Biblical preaching should be cross-cultural evangelism executed on the platform of the material world. What has emerged as 'preaching' in modern evangelicalism is in fact expositional teaching. It is not the New Testament, biblical norm. It should not even be called 'preaching.' What takes place in most churches is men addressing saved audiences with solid teaching. This does not even resemble what we read in the gospels. New Testament preaching is *heralding Jesus to a lost audience*.

The North American preaching model, and for that matter, the preaching model exported to the far corners of the world by Western culture for the last 1000 years before the introduction of Chronological Bible Storying, is one created by high literates for high literates. It is not reproducible in oral cultures. Additionally, it is pulpit-dependent, building-dependent, has an engagement technique that is lexical in the print-sense of the term, can falsely assume that grammatical accuracy is equivalent to effectiveness, is often short on loving application, is dependent upon abstraction, is not usually situational to a hurting audience, and can overlook the need for that speaker's circumstantial dependence upon the Holy Spirit.

Having said this, it is the word of God that does not return void. Not one jot or tittle will fall from it (Matt. 5:18). Consequently, however flawed the model is, it is still the word of God that endures forever (Ps. 119:89). Biblical textual referencing is non-negotiable. Our preaching model just needs strengthening to resemble what Jesus did.

Jesus the Preacher

Jesus was Himself a cross-cultural preacher. He left eternity and emptied Himself. The God-Man spoke to His creation from the vantage point of the Godhead.

Jesus' life was, in essence, a comparison. "No one has ever seen God; the only God, who is at the Father's side, he has made him known" (John 1:18). Jesus was the image of the invisible God, and whether or not people perceived or accepted it, He was in His every action, communicating cross culturally (Col. 1:18).

As He shared His life, He was communicating deep spiritual things concerning eternal truth. Because human beings are fleshly, they have to work at having a spiritual orientation.

When you stop and think about the communication process, every exchange between two or more people, regardless of their respective upbringing, is a cross-cultural experience. Only part of their human experience is shared.

The speaker must cross cultural barriers to make sure s/he is understood precisely, but the decoding process of the listener involves filtering. The hearer might not interpolate meaning in the same way that the speaker anticipates the words will fall.

There are fundamental similarities and differences between people that cause communication transmission to either resonate or fail. The rest of this book is a roadmap to help speakers communicate in ways in which the audience tracks in sync with the speaker. It is counsel on how not to enlarge the cultural divide.

The Bible is a Cross-Cultural Book

It may come as a surprise to you to realize that a large portion of the Bible takes place in cross-cultural settings, to my reckoning, about 60%. Most of Genesis and all of Exodus, Leviticus, Numbers, and Deuteronomy transpire in countries in which the main characters are foreigners. The same could be said for most of Joshua, Ruth, Ezra, Nehemiah, Esther, Daniel, Obadiah, Jonah, Nahum, Haggai, Zechariah, and Malachi.

By far, most of the New Testament is written in contexts where the authors were not native. The Bible is written by immigrant populations.

If one looks at Jesus' life as a cross-cultural ministry of a God-to-man redemptive mission, the entire New Testament is cross-cultural communication, with the exception of the first third of the Book of Acts and the Book of James. Even if one exempts the gospels from this idea, all the epistles and the entirety of the balance of the New Testament is cross-cultural communication.

The ramifications of this are astounding. God's purposes involve crossing cultural lines.

This has earth shaking ramifications for our communication process. God is intimately concerned with us crossing cultural lines and living our lives among the nations. We are not simply called to go into all the world and preach the gospel, as if we are to form mission committees in our churches; this call is a comprehensive lifestyle norm of living our lives on extension.

Who can argue with the fact that God worked in Joseph's life to secure a 400-year legacy for the children of Israel, or that Assyria, Babylonia, and Persia were the preserving incubation medium of God's people, in spite of their historic disobediences? What is the conclusion of this idea?

Of the 27 books of the New Testament, 22 are clearly cross-cultural. If we add to that number the 17 Old Testament books above, the result is that 39 of the Bible's 66 books are written to narrate believers' lives on international tapestry.

Although God firmly establishes His purposes in mission, this is not simply a geographical phenomenon, however. It touches on the divine desire for reaching beyond ourselves, especially from the perspective of communication. From the perspective of words, we see the entire Bible is an example of how we traverse language and culture barriers to communicate truth among the nations and communities around us.

This cross-cultural communication process is central to the Christian lifestyle. How we tell others about Jesus is a process that needs examination. The biblical model seems to be that we live our lives in an integrated manner, one that moves in and out of the communities around us.

Bridging the divide of culture and language should be a natural, daily part of life. We communicate the gospel to others. They are not like us. We must tailor that message to live by communicating it in a way that makes sense, not to us, but to them.

Preaching as Cross-Cultural Servanthood

If communication involves crossing cultural lines, regardless of how we might assume that the audience demographic is 'like us' or 'not like us,' then the preaching process involves translation, so to speak. What does this mean?

When we are before people, we assume a posture. That posture determines if we truly understand the task.

Some speakers wrongly believe that we simply need to explain the text of the Bible. This is a serious oversimplification. Secular teachers of the scriptures do that. Jewish rabbis do that. Cults do that.

Teaching the Bible assumes that we have a correct, Trinitarian theology that advances scriptural orthodoxy and a proper view of inspiration. Beyond this, we also must connect to a listener that comes to the communicative process with a boatload of assumptions, culturally conditioned behaviors, and strong opinions about life.

To be optimistic about these barriers, the very surmountable task of bridging to the listener involves preaching by comparison, that is, drawing connections between the text and the common experience of speaker and listener. This resonance brings about an aha moment. This is a very reachable objective.

Communicating the text of the Bible involves work at multiple levels. The first is understanding and interpreting the meaning of 2000–4000-year-old texts, originally written in Hebrew, Aramaic, or Greek. The second is presenting the meaning in understandable ways to 21st century people. For this latter task, we have far more capacity than we think.

We must address impediments with boldness, if we are to create solid connections to our audiences, be they composed of one single person or a thousand. Our ethos speaks to whether we are in a communicative exchange that serves the listener or serves some secondary motive that we create.

One of the most serious problems to speakers is that they create fleshly and artificial barriers to listeners, typically without knowing it. The most common is thinking that one must present oneself in a verbal clothing that is not natural to who we are in Christ.

If we are to be like Jesus, we are pursuing speaker-authenticity. We should not be pretentious in any way.

Killing the Preaching Persona

One of the greatest impediments to the communication process is the adoption of a preaching persona. So, what exactly is a preaching persona?

When someone stands before others to speak, that person can become someone else. It is entirely possible, and frequently visible, that the speaker is not communicating as s/he normally does. When this happens, that person is adopting a persona.

Vocal performance is almost like watching a football game. The players put on uniforms and for a period, dazzle the crowd with extraordinary skills. Everyone knows that that person is very good at what s/he does.

The problem with this performance is that the speaker creates communicative distance without knowing it. The cross-cultural divide is widened when the audience sees that the person adopts a rhetorical stance that is not natural.

The audience intuitively knows when the speaker is delivering a message differently from his or her ordinary personality. The ability of the speaker to incite listener change is diminished because the listener knows it is a performance.

Mentally, the listener will go through gymnastics that might sound something like this if we were to verbalize them. "The speaker is out of character. He is not like me. He has adopted an unnatural ethos that is polished and syncopated. This is not like me."

Contrast this with a simple testimony of someone who gets up behind the pulpit and simply and softly rolls out how God met him in his pain, healed her hurt, or showed up at a critical moment because of prayer. The listener says in a mental response, "If God did this for that person, He could do it for me."

It is hard to imagine Jesus adopting a preaching persona. The scriptures are clear that Jesus rarely raised His voice. This was Matthew's commentary: "He will not quarrel or cry aloud, nor will anyone hear his voice in the streets" (Matt. 12:19). John 7:37 seems to be the exception to this rule when Jesus cried out for thirsty people to come to Him.

Crying out in invitation, however, is not a preaching persona. It flows from a heart that is full of love. Consequently, it is important to know that raising our voices when we communicate is not discouraged. It is simply important to know when it is natural and inviting and not from a platform for showmanship, punishment, or anger.

The preaching persona is only one component that creates distance between speaker and listener. There are others. For now, however, we need to build bridges.

Questions for Engagement

1. In what ways can Jesus' preaching be described as a cross-cultural endeavor?
2. What is the nature of audience resonance and how can it be used when we apply the Bible?
3. What are some of the qualities that are involved in audience resonance?
4. How is the idea of resonance different from entertainment?
5. What is the difference between preaching with audience resonance and pulpiteering?
6. If I am unlike my audience in so many ways, how do I approach the communication task with a healthy concept of connection?
7. How is encoding and decoding always a cross-cultural process?
8. What are some reasons we can say that the Bible is a cross-cultural book?
9. What is dangerous about a preaching persona, and what are some of the habits and actions that you adopt when you start talking about the Bible that are not natural to your normal communication?

Part Two: Capturing the Ordinary in the Immediate

8   Capturing the Ordinary

We capture the essence of scripture through careful observation. There is no substitute for simply examining the text, looking at each word, and finding connections and meaning. It is in this grammatical process where we begin to build a pool of ideas to communicate.

Those observations have countless connections to the concrete universe and the world of ideas. How we organize those thoughts to bring resonance to the listener is a matter of bridging.

Every speaker asks, either intuitively or directly, how to bridge ideas to listeners. The process of taking words and thoughts and making those notions palpable to an audience is a complex phenomenon, one governed by countless variables, most principally, comparison.

Amid all the variables, however, there are rules that can help with invention and clarity. However, while the discipline of speaking is an ongoing process of creative art, it does have limiting factors and precepts, especially as it relates to illustration and application.

The very realities of the text and responses of listeners are, in part, a measure of our ability to capture the ordinary. It is in the common space of shared experience that we find agreement between speaker and listener.

Finding the Illustrative Crux

Within the analogizing process, we are capturing the ordinary. Once we have done this, we relate the 'stuff' we captured through formulated textual or homiletical idea.

This process of translating an idea to the concrete world is what we do when we use metaphors and similes. Love is like a rose. He's as strong as an ox. The kingdom of God is like a merchant looking for pearls. The objectified idea is cast into the material world.

In these examples, there are both ideas and physical corollaries. In metaphor theory, the terms are 'tenor' and 'vehicle.' Usually, we have fewer problems locating the tenor (the thing we are trying to illustrate) than we do the vehicle, the latter part of the speech figure. When we do find both components, however, the idea just sort of pops off the page or out of our mouths. Unfortunately, the vehicle, or the way to make that idea live for the listener, often drives away before we can get it in the passenger seat.

This struggle to find the appropriate analogy is largely the focus of the remainder of this book. The analogizing process begins by finding the illustrative crux. It can be a thing, an idea, a state, a movement, a relationship, and a host of other key items in a biblical text.

The illustrative crux needs to also be isolated in detail, and then it can be bridged to the listener through image, story, explanation, or any number of other methods. There is no substitute for accurate identification of the illustrative crux.

When we take an idea and fuse it with explanatory language, image, or narrative, we transform it and create corollaries that associate with the past of the listeners. These speech figures will create varying degrees of familiarity and resonance with the listeners.

The first step in finding the illustrative crux is to isolate the focus of your application. We do this by examining the biblical passage, isolating the main idea, and articulating that idea in some declarative form. There are many books that have been published on how to do this.

What we are about to articulate is a method that moves from the exegetical idea to a language of transference by comparison. There is no substitute for the joyful task of sitting before the scriptures and discovering clear, teachable points by an exegetical method. That is the prerequisite. Nevertheless, there is a dearth of help that can assist the speaker in moving from those ideas to an application that applies strongly to a listening audience.

The Rules and Limits of Analogy

To move from ancient grammar and historical realities to common experiences of contemporary listeners, we start with the words of scripture and the relationship of the words. We then move to generalization or abstraction, eventually returning to the concrete associations within the modern context.

Illustrative Crux → Generalization → Concrete Comparison

For example, if our text is Nehemiah 1:4 in which Nehemiah sat down and wept over the discouraging news of the destitute condition of Jerusalem (the crux), we might come to any number of generalizations. Broken facilities are indicative of broken people. Or, we might say that when we hear bad news from fellow believers, we need to be deeply moved to pray.

As was previously explained, this process of abstraction is called 'symbolic extrication,' an idea first advanced in the poetic world and popularized by George Whalley in his book on *Poetic Process.*[3] The speaker needs to extract an idea and see the universal components, perhaps in a way that others can find affinity.

The gospels frequently employ universals to communicate truth. Those universals were then often transmitted to the crowd by concrete images, narrative stories, and analogies. For example, in Luke 18, the chapter begins with the universal and then is followed by the story. "And he told them a parable to the effect that they ought always to pray and not lose heart." Jesus then goes on to tell the Parable of the Unjust Judge.

The progression in this process goes from universal truth to analogous, concrete realities. It is not a complicated sequence but requires precision of idea and reflection about the analogous correspondence between elements.

Detailing an idea is the first step in articulating the illustrative crux of a passage, and often, the ease at which we can find a suitable image or story to reflect the truth of the passage depends on the precision we use in our construction of a main point.

For example, to extend the core principle about prayer above, we can move from general to specific ideas. Early on in our examination, our principle might be just "prayer." We can move beyond this to "persevering prayer." Yet again, we could state our main idea as "persevering prayer in face of injustice." Finally, we can say that our idea is that the most vulnerable of people should count on a good Father to provide justice in the face of an oppressor.

To excel at this type of development, it becomes essential to ask: What is the symbolism of the key idea? Are there universal principles worth our focus? What is the abstraction to which most people will gravitate in this passage?

Symbolic extrication may seem like something complicated or fancy, but we do this all the time. A woman might remark about someone's hair being done up in a certain way. That will resonate with other listeners who understand hair styles.

All categories are, in a sense, universal. We talk about beach bums, jocks, Valley Girls, lowriders, nerds, etc. Abstraction takes place when we locate within a text the component that we want to post out in public.

Sometimes that idea is affected by context, both the biblical one and the audience context. Sometimes the historical context is hard for an audience. The elements in the text do not relate. That is why it is important to bridge our current circumstantial milieu with the one of two thousand years ago.

Resonance and Connectivity through the Ordinary

In spending time addressing how to bridge to the concrete world, I am asking the reader to look at preaching differently. From the perspective of analogy, we need to do what Jesus did in His practice of connectivity.

There is always meaning-making in our speaking. That is, there is some degree of corollary between what the speaker is saying and what is understood by the listener. However, we need to ask how strong the vibrations are between the two.

If the speaker can connect to the previous experience of the hearer, there is *resonance*. This activity of conceptualizing in advance how the auditors will receive the message is critical. If the listener has no prior knowledge or experience with our subject or the illustrations we employ, the results will likely be limited.

When we exegete the scriptures and explain them to listeners, we often assume wrongly that simply explaining the word of God will bear a lot of fruit. However, we have an obligation to explain the word of God as Jesus did, carefully constructing bridges between the exact *words* of the Bible and the exact *experience* of this listener.

This idea is quite different from the common concept of illustration. What I am proposing is founded on the biblical principle that the hearer receives from God in a spiritual manner. Jesus said, "If anyone has ears to hear, let him hear" (Mark 4:23).

The reality is that when Jesus was addressing large crowds, not everyone was listening closely. Their ears were not open. They did not hear the message.

When God is at work in someone's life, the word of God resonates with them through the work of the Holy Spirit. Just as harmonies blend in a pleasing way because the frequencies correlate, similarly, ideas mesh seamlessly when God is at work by His Spirit in the life of the open listener.

Analogy of Intrinsic Attribution

When we create stories, images, and figured explanations to help people understand the Bible, we must yield to the rules of communication. We don't shout things that should be communicated softly. We don't trivialize holiness. We speak as God would have us speak, taking care about both the subject matter and the hearers.

In saying that communication has rules, the export of that idea is that there are grammatical and social codes that permit clear meaning transfer. If we violate them, there is confusion or even anger. We also violate the scriptural export and the observational truth evident in God's creation.

In figured communication, one of the clear principles is the analogy of intrinsic attribution, already mentioned above. Certain word-constructions and analogies can help or hinder communication, depending on the correspondence of the elements.

The idea that figures of speech have rules might be foreign to the reader. I remember a teaching assistant in seminary making a joke about people who find an illustration and then go looking for a scripture to put with it. I fell under conviction. I was that person. That one-minute conversation changed my whole perception of the illustration process.

Historically, people used to call figures 'tropes' and their use was referred to as 'tropical' construction of language. We, of course, use images and stories every day. They are the foundation of a natural, God-given imagination for the wonderful world He created. However, we don't typically reflect on the rules of what makes them excellent, powerful, and true.

In the joy of parable creation, we discover that there are principles that make figures work. These are nuts and bolts of storied resonance.

Personally, I love to be captivated, especially when my life is shaken by a precise scriptural idea. It fills my life with wonderment, tears of repentance, and the peace that passes all understanding.

The word of God communicated in the Spirit's power by a clean messenger through an idea that is already owned by the listener is a wonderful thing. It cuts through the laborious process of explaining why, or at least provides a paved road to the heart of the hearer.

Surprisingly, not all analogies work because inside language there are inherent meanings in words that make sense to the listener. When I say that, "The table has legs," everyone knows what I mean. But if I said, "The table has hands," people would be confused.

Stephen J. Brown explains the *analogy of intrinsic attribution* as the innate qualities of poetic and storied language that affirm or prohibit correlation.[4] This is why I can say that the clock has 'hands,' but I cannot say the bicycle has 'legs.' The analogy in the latter example is not intrinsic.

I have found a very simple principle to measure my own preaching, teaching, and general communication. Does what I am saying correlate to the text and to reality, or does the listener have to make a leap across an insurmountable chasm to understand?

As we progress in this book, it is not just a manual on humility and submission to the scriptures. It is a way to force yourself to ask difficult questions about *how you articulate ideas and whether they will resonate with the listener's view of the concrete world.*

The Choice of Illustration

One frequently observed way that speakers often miss their ability to relate to the common person is their choice of figure. In preaching a text about the widow's mite in Luke 21, an illustration of a football professional giving an immense offering, for example, does not immediately resonate with most people, at the level of the textual meaning. The listener can immediately deny the corollary by saying to herself, "I am not a man. I am not rich. I do not have disposable income." The story is about an impoverished elderly woman in a society without governmental supplements. It was a real sacrifice for her to give to the point of total abandonment to God. The speaker should find an illustration that has intrinsic attribution and correlation to a typical audience that is financially and socially vulnerable.

In this way of viewing preaching, we impose controls on our language, ones that show deference to the listener. We must understand why people are eager to listen to the scriptures and construct methods of speaking that are decipherable.

In the Gospel of Mark, Jesus is portrayed as being surrounded by crowds and almost crushed (Mark 3:9), needing to get into a boat so He could address all the people who were before Him (Mark 4:1). The average person was eager to hear this simple preacher. Does our preaching generate that kind of enthusiasm?

As we move into methodology, I am not advocating a formulaic way of drawing a crowd. This is a series of reflections on how to love an audience and make the word of God applicable and palatable to a broad range of listeners.

Resonance is inescapable when it happens. It is something we feel, see, hear, think, and even smell. It fills our senses and captivates our mind. It makes it possible to make sense of God's world.

People come and listen to the word of God because they want to make sense of a complicated reality in which they live. They want to know God has a plan, and that His plan jibes with what they know to be true. They want to hear the underlying rationales for things and want to be affirmed that their prior spiritual experience is worth something.

This is not a lesson in graduate-level oratory. Success in application and illustration is accomplished by the broken man sharing the eternal, penetrating message of Christ in the power of the Holy Spirit in such a way that the listener affirms truth by her or his own reflection on life experience.

The Scope of Illustration

The journey into the text is like descending a mineshaft. In the words of Job, men carry out extensive searches of the hidden rocks through mining in hopes of finding something precious. Because true wisdom lies in the fear of the Lord (Job 28), a grammatical extraction from the text is not enough. That is only the first part of the process. Ultimately it is God that must show the preacher what and how to illustrate.

Once you are down in the mineshaft of the text, sometimes it feels like pure darkness. The preacher does not know how to communicate what is there. Sometimes the point of the text is not clear. Sometimes there seem to be so many points, it becomes almost impossible to decide what to preach on.

The preacher looks for the sparkling stone or gold vein amidst the grammar. However, it is not like navigating in darkness with a flashlight with weak batteries. It is actually quite easy to create a multitude of original illustrations using some very simple principles.

My own journey in trying to understand figure-generation took me to many ancient and medieval texts long forgotten. Back before the advent of paper as we know it, or even the printing press for that matter, scholars and clerics captivated illiterate audiences with spoken language. Orality, not literacy, was everywhere.

Over the last ten years, I have tried to simplify a means of extracting illustrative material in the easiest way possible. I want to explain that process in hopes that it will be helpful to the reader. I have created some non-traditional categories and combined others because I have found these things more palatable to the reader.

There are basically three steps to creating illustrations. Within those steps are several tools, some simple and some complex, that will be necessary to master to stay true to the word of God. This is an accurate science, not a fast-and-loose approximation game.

While in seminary, it was my habit to go looking for illustrations. When I found one that would closely fit my sermon, I thought I had hit the lottery. Even if the result and communicative nuance of the illustration did not exactly reflect the meaning of the text, I would use it anyway. It was simply too hard to find good analogies. I no longer have that mentality.

I feel guilty when the meaning of my image does not exactly fit the text of scripture, because I know from experience that there are hundreds and thousands of parallels that work like hand-in-glove. It is just a matter of processing through the work of finding the precise illustrative crux and concretizing it using life stories from the methods that follow.

While it can be an excruciating process just finding the right text to preach, or more commonly, the right elements of the right text, this is not the issue in this book. I am assuming you have found your text, found your main idea, and can substantiate the interpretation with some rationale from a biblical perspective or from the original languages.

The issue at hand is illustrating the meaning of the text in a way that people will understand. Many preachers resort to extensive discursive delivery, that is, explaining the text using logical connections and explanations that are grammatical. Though this approach is fundamental in the communication process, it is not the only way to reveal meaning.

Beyond this, it can be boring and disconnected from the realities of the listener. There are different kinds of meaning, some of which are helpful and appealing. Grammatical logic is only one essential ingredient upon which communication thrives.

Additionally, illustration also dances in the realms of the Spirit and in the emotions. Experience tells me whether or not what the speaker says is true. It does this by recalling what I have previously discovered in my own life. The speaker's words bring recall of memories and emotions that validate the message.

Questions for Engagement

1. What is the illustrative crux and how do we find it?
2. What are some of the differences between a textual idea and the illustrative crux?
3. What is the connection between teaching the Bible and capturing the ordinary in an application?
4. What are some of the rules and limits of analogy?
5. How does the analogy of intrinsic attribution keep us close to textual meaning when we make application to the Bible?
6. How might an image or story be used to 'explain' the text?

9 Exampling the Illustration Process

In the process of teaching preaching, hermeneutics, and Bible application, it has become apparent that students consistently overstate their understanding of chosen texts. The way I know this is that I ask them to create an illustration or application to a verse, and they crash and burn.

The odd thing about this phenomenon is that if you ask students to explain the text, they will stumble their way through with some degree of coherent sense-making. Yet, upon asking them to illustrate a textually precise component to a particular audience, the innate reflexes are just not there.

A sports analogy might look like this. You ask a friend if he or she plays tennis, and that person says, "Sure, I love to play tennis." When that person arrives on the court, the ball is all over the place. There is no control, and it becomes clear that s/he knows little about the game and played a few times back at the age of 12.

Skill mastery when it comes to meaning transfer is swinging the metaphorical racquet correctly. It is about control and precision. The distance between knowing *generally* what a text means and *exactly* what a text means *to an audience in a specific context* is as remote as two sides of the Grand Canyon.

Frequently people assume that seeing what is in a text is the same as the export of those words to others. It is not. Bible students often do not see how a particular text speaks differently to a kindergarten, junior-church setting as opposed to a men's group.

The ability to apply ideas to varying audiences is contingent in part upon both the recognition of the multifaceted nuances of a passage as well as varying reception frameworks of auditors. There are helpful ways to transform culturally sensitive ideas into contemporary settings. One's capacity to bring a point home to today's listeners may be in part based on the speaker's capacity to codify the implications of precise nuances of textual ideas.

Applying exact meaning to a particular demographic audience is not as hard as it might appear and begins with the frank acknowledgement that the speaker needs humble clarity about the exact components within the biblical material that need illustration. Let's outline what those are.

Component Parts of a Textual Idea

Illustration is obviously not the same as exegesis (critical textual examination) or hermeneutics (interpretation). *Illustration is a form of exposition and not a byproduct of exposition.* It also comes with its own set of very precise rules, as I have already stated.

Strangely enough, when Bible students move from exegesis to illustration, they are lost. Even the once-amazing-teacher often flounders around in generalities, telling the student in vague terms how to communicate the meaning of a verse to an audience.

Ministerial students are often not trained in illustration or application. Consequently, they look to the Internet for corollaries, not really knowing what they are looking for. They plug a random variable string into the search engine. It looks like this: "illustration about hope" or "story about anger." What comes out of that search might be somewhat appropriate, but it is more than likely not a good match for the precise textual meaning the expositor hoped to communicate. It is also not organic to the speaker's personality.

There is a solution to this. Once a student lands upon a verse of scripture that s/he has exegeted, there is a clear process for illustration-creation that is a different one from historical/grammatical method.

The approach articulated in this book forces the student to take a very close examination of how meaning is transmitted through analogous correspondence. The student looks within herself for a powerful comparison to real life that will resonate with hearers. It is not about meaning-acquisition but about meaning-delivery to a precise audience.

There are some people who can discover the meaning in a text without any difficulty. They might also be able to write about it. Yet, when they are placed in front of an audience, the results are less than stellar. The reality is that they do not understand mental common ground or meaning-reception from the audience's standpoint.

What follows is a series of modules describing how to look at a text of scripture in terms of thought units or illustrative components. Every attempt has been made to simplify the process into broad and repeatable steps that often bear fruit in the meaning-clarification exercise. Again, this is not about clarifying the meaning of the text, something we assume the reader has already done in the historical/grammatical method, but it is about delivery corollaries that are figured. The student must ask a whole new set of questions.

At the center of this illustrating and application process are a series of questions and answers that involve frequently repeated and practical components that are necessary in making the Bible live for an audience.

While the exegetical discipline brings meaning to the surface, application makes that meaning palatable to an audience. Yet, there is another step that is necessary in the communication process to bridge these two components.

Components of Illustration

Those of us who preach and teach on a regular basis interpret texts to audiences implicitly, often without even knowing what we are doing. Some of us get it right, at least most of the time, and some of us struggle, wondering why the illustration and application phase of the preaching discipline is so laborious.

The major components of illustration and application explained in this book are as follows:

1. Relationships
2. Emotions
3. Movement
4. Moral Behavior
5. Desire
6. Fixed Objects
7. Abstraction
8. Story Creation
9. Parables

An illustrator is typically addressing one of these areas or using one of these methods when s/he applies a text to an audience. In educational theory, many scholars reduce human behavior to cognition, affection, and behavior. However, in formulating illustration theory that is Bible-centered, there are many other things going on in the text/audience dynamic that are easier to isolate with additional categories.

The spiritual realm is much more complicated than educational psychology because it involves God and other people. It also involves explaining His word, the textual center of Christian thought. Within that text there are covenants, fixed laws, fixed objects, historical archetypes, evolving storylines, and a whole system of orthodoxy that cannot be ignored. Illustrating a text demands interpolating all these factors of textual meaning while at the same time dealing with audience factors and laws of language and interpretation.

Unraveling the complexities of contextualized communication after expository work is our current objective. It involves a micro analysis of texts *along with their implications to a precise listening demographic.*

The Process of Illustration

Any explanation of the Bible is not the Bible; it is talk about the Bible. We generally isolate precise meaning and explain texts using any number of approaches. Many of those ways are pictures and analogies. They are *figured*, something where we cast the scriptures into a new light using cultural explanations, parallels, word origins, stories, images, and figures of every kind.

Meaning-transfer to an audience happens through a commonality of experience and vocabulary. Apart from the physical reinforcement like dramatization, hand movements, or vocalization, words themselves export meaning in vast ways. But how do speech figures and stories correlate and embody precise components of textual meaning? That is another question altogether.

When an expositor attempts to use figured communication to transmit meaning, those characters and images s/he uses stir up a host of possibilities that are based in the audience's scope of experience. Those meanings might be solid and resonate with the listener. However, some might not be familiar to the auditors and might actually distort the intent of the speaker. In some cases, meaning becomes even further removed, and those stirrings in the ear of the hearer might not even approach the meaning of the texts we are trying to exposit.

Many teachers of the scriptures do not understand that figured communication has rules, and those rules facilitate or hinder meaning. Clarifying and facilitating the creation of clear meaning-transfer means following the principles of accurate correspondence. How do we assure that what we are saying to explain a text actually closely resembles the intent of the author?

It needs to be said that this work does not accept the theory called "the intentional fallacy," the idea that the author's intent cannot be known. The self-apparent contradiction of that idea is clear.

So, how does a speaker create resonance with an audience through figurative communication? Additionally, how does that speaker properly represent the text s/he is trying to preach?

The Illustrative Crux

I need to explain the idea of an illustrative crux in more detail. Without arguing the method or rationale for constructing main ideas or when it is appropriate to preach sub-ideas from biblical passages, I want to assume that it is important to illustrate any and every aspect of the scriptures. If a main idea involves several secondary concepts, as it often does, it may be necessary to illustrate sub-points. Consequently, nothing in the scripture is off-limits.

Sometimes it is very important to illustrate the most minor point of the Bible with utmost clarity to make the larger, more critical ideas clearer to an audience. Once the preacher finds the main idea within the text and isolates an element for illustration, it is important to find the *illustrative crux*. The illustrative crux is the aspect, or sometimes aspects, that need clarity.

The illustrative crux is the precise element or correlation that needs to be pictured. Often there are many, even within a very small passage.

As we stated previously, there are inherent qualities that permit or forbid illustration. This is Brown's argument stated above that the communicator needs to find the analogy of intrinsic attribution. The preacher asks this question, "What are the main qualities within this idea or text to which I can draw parallels from another domain?"

To simplify this thought, I would say this: every textual component that the preacher wants to communicate presents itself in a certain way, usually with movement, but not always. If the preacher isolates the movement, the state, or the pattern, it is then much easier to find similar pictures from common life.

Once the reader has identified the illustrative crux, illustrations are built around *analogous correspondence*, or the real-life corollaries. This will be explained in great detail in the pages that follow. First, it is important to understand how to break down words to find parallel ideas.

When approaching a text for illustrative purposes, the speaker must delineate exactly what s/ he wants to illustrate. There is a simple progression to follow. Each step involves separating out precise components.

If someone looks at a pie, or for that matter, eats a piece, it does not mean that the person sampling the product could reproduce the whole. In the same way, a person can hear a thousand sermons but still never be able to construct even one cohesive, well-illustrated sermon. I love smoked pork barbeque, but I could not reproduce the taste of well-made mesquite-smoked brisket.

When a biblical communicator picks up a text to preach, not everything in the text is relevant at that moment. There is likely a main idea. There is probably also the immediate call for application. Consequently, there needs to be a priority applied to the multiplicity of possibilities.

Every text has several inherent teachings that require illustrating. How does the preacher find illustrative material to clarify the meaning *after the textual idea has been isolated?*

A preacher usually plans in advance to connect with the audience by clarifying textual points. There is a process and progression in communication. Certain ideas are powerful and clear, begging for illustration. Others might create digression. Once the preacher separates out a preachable idea, it is then necessary to find an illustrative crux within that concept.

Finding the illustrative crux is not always that difficult. It comes into focus through successive stages, but this is where most preachers get bogged down. Where does the communicator find analogous material that will strike home with precision?

If a North American walks into someone's house in the Amazon, that person will almost always find a fruit basket on the table. More than likely, a North American person has never seen some of what is in there. If the visitor wants to know what those items are, which ones are edible and which ones are for show, it would be necessary to pick them out one at a time and say, "Do people eat this? Does this taste good?"

In the same way, biblical verses are often packed with multiple approaches and ideas. The speaker needs to separate out grammatical distinctives, and from those elements, it becomes significantly easier to make a meal that will not poison the hearer.

Finding the Illustrative Crux within a Text

Sentences not only have grammatical parts, but they also have various kinds of movement, state, communicative nuance, moral ramification, and emotion. Consequently, the would-be-communicator needs to separate the most prominent, non-grammatical elements clearly and precisely.

Grammar communicates ideas, so the exact grammar is preeminently important. However, the common mistake made by preachers is that they focus on the theological side of the grammatical export to the neglect of other critical aspects.

Emotion, for example, is carried by grammar. So, if the text speaks about suffering and joy, it is important to illustrate joy in suffering and not just speak emotionlessly about the topic.

It is very possible to help the congregation feel joy. It becomes integral to communicate emotion, process, cause/effect, state, etc.

Before one can begin illustration-generation, it is necessary to narrow the textual idea with as much precision as possible. In the same way a logician might isolate *stasis*, or the point of dispute in issue-argumentation, a preacher should isolate a critical textual component needing illustration.

In essence, throughout the process of sermon production, the preacher repeatedly asks: "What is the critical sense here to which the text is speaking?" It might not be immediately clear how the crux needs to be imaged, however.

The ensuing method is one way in which the student can isolate or generate analogous material. First break down the textual idea for illustration. Various preachers and scholars approach this skill differently. In the classical world, students were taught the disciplines of the progymnasmata. Rhetorical pedagogy sought to prepare the student for a broad range of communication disciplines, from narrative to trope generation. Much of classical rhetoric involved argument instruction and defense, and frequently, the individual was taught the breakdown and generation of ideas for writing and speaking.

What I seek to do here is much simpler and much more biblical. Since Jesus was an illustrator, how can we duplicate His method? This is not about parable interpretation or image entertainment. It is the science of textual analysis with a very particular goal of a sort of crisis-illustration. How can the speaker raise the importance of godly choices in a simple communicative exchange? What follows are some simple rules and generation techniques for helping create sermon illustrations.

The Nuts and Bolts of Illustration Theory

In this section, I will outline what will be addressed in detail in the ensuing chapters. In this brief overview, the reader will grasp the scope of correspondences that are possible and typically emerge from any given biblical text.

In the same way that a speaker wants to 'show' an audience an idea rather than simply 'tell' someone something, language innately possesses picture quality and should be exploited. Many words themselves are metaphors or are used metaphorically. They also generate images in the minds of listeners. In simple terms, each word inspires an image or a known action.

When a speaker says, "computer," the listener usually pictures a laptop, desktop, a CPU, a main frame system, or some other physical form. When the communicator says "eating dinner," the audience might imagine people sitting at home, in a restaurant, or actually eating in a particular way. They might be raising a fork, using chopsticks, or doing some active movements with particulars, maybe utensils.

This vast and varied pool of experience is one of the speaker's strongest support mechanisms. It becomes the actual means of getting a point across. If the speaker can identify common ground and marshal that in an argumentative fashion, the result is more certain and the listener is not left up to himself or herself to extrapolate meaning from generalizations.

Words speak expressly with experiential qualities. So, when approaching the text of the Bible, the speaker needs to ask how the grammar self-illustrates. There are forms, movements, causes, prerequisites, consequents, and a myriad of other elements that cry out for parallel illustration. These are easy to reference and engender strong emotions and conclusions without endless explanations.

Illustration theory involves two basic steps. The first is isolating the illustrative crux. The second is finding parallels or comparisons that have similar essential qualities.

In constructing illustrations, speakers generally complicate communication by inserting complicated allusions that have no parallel to a textual component. What I mean is that the biblical text speaks to an issue that might be quite clear, yet the speaker tries to do too much. Not only can an illustration say too little or miss the mark, it can also illustrate too many additional components. The result is that simple meaning is lost.

There are five general areas that are very easy to illustrate. To these five, we will add later discussions of desire and stories, but before moving on, it is necessary to explain the scope of illustrative sourcing by beginning with these components.

The speaker wanting to illustrate needs to first look at these essential elements and can usually find simple illustrative material without much work. Here is what the preacher should do:

1. Find the **relationships** between/among components.
2. Find the **emotions** being generated by the idea.
3. Find the precise **movement** in the text.
4. Find the **moral** implications of the crux.
5. See if there is **human desire** for or against the idea.
6. Find the **state** of the elements, namely, **fixed objects**.
7. Attempt to locate **abstractions** that help the listener generalize a core idea.
8. Create a **story** that corresponds to one or more of the above elements.
9. Formulate a **parable** that reveals where someone stands on a particular matter.

Itemizing a Web of Ideas

Let's take a minute to see how these fit together and overlap. In looking over this list, the idea of movement is critical but must be spread out, and you will see that it permeates all discussions of the text, even when we talk about things that cannot move. Additionally, almost all movements have moral implications. Relationships also have moral overtones.

In outlining an illustrative theory, isolating moral implication is a continual process and cannot be separated out from other aspects of the process because it is woven into the fabric of life. For example, waiting one additional minute in making a decision can have moral implications. Crying over something implies a moral connection.

Similar overarching comments can be stated about emotion. In a general way, it is important to analyze all the implications of the grammar of the biblical text, but in doing so, you will notice emotion almost everywhere. For example, if a preacher is speaking about the "wages of sin" from Romans 6, there are many emotions generated in the text. 'Wages' are generally positive and mean collecting a paycheck. However, the wages are surprisingly negative in this text. The payment slip in the envelope is a death notice, a terminal pink slip. The idea of death also generates sadness, fear, coldness, fire, and a myriad of other deadly or evocative feelings. The speaker may or may not want to include them.

Verses are not simply about factual conclusions. They are about the whole person. This is why verses need to be broken down into component elements like relationship, emotion, movement, moral export, and state.

So, how does this play out when analyzing a verse? Recently, a young preacher was talking to me about his need to illustrate Matthew 6:19-21. I found it a very easy beginning point to model an illustrative process. Jesus said this.

> Lay not up for yourselves treasures upon earth, where moth and rust doth corrupt, and where thieves break through and steal: But lay up for yourselves treasures in heaven, where neither moth nor rust doth corrupt, and where thieves do not break through nor steal: For where your treasure is, there will your heart be also.

Upon first glance, this is a very simple passage to understand. Jesus polarizes His metaphors. In good parabolic images, He forces the listener into one of two groupings: people who bank in heaven and those who bank on earth. But let's look at the passage according to the model above, asking four questions about movement, state, emotions, relationships, and moral nuance.

In attempting an extended illustration, I will approach this text out of order from the previous list. The reason is that I find the entry easier by analyzing movement. Follow along as this simple passage is unpacked in multiple approaches.

Illustrating Issues of Movement and Causality

One of the easiest ways to find illustrations for biblical material involves isolating movement in the text. Once the movement is pictured, it is possible to find parallels from other domains.

Movement is simple to identify. On the surface, there is action. However, upon close examination, there is a vast and complex matrix of causes and effects. Understanding this process of underlying motivation and consequent result will open new worlds to the illustrator.

Probably the single most productive illustration technique I have learned over the past ten years is how to isolate causes and effects. There are various ways of dissecting an idea, but the fruit is always there.

As a theory, causality is very complex, but quite easy to master at an introductory level. This is how it is done.

Things that move do so over time. In other words, action evolves across the clock. An act might take five seconds or five years. There is a process.

All processes have causes. A cue ball is struck by a cue stick and moves the pool balls to the pockets. The hand of the player held the cue stick and struck the ball. One player wins the game when all his balls are in the pockets.

I can isolate any individual action and find the causes and the individuals that preceded that action. In the same way, I can isolate the results of that action.

In preaching, identifying cause and effect is central. If I were preaching about Absalom fighting his father and ultimately getting caught in the oak tree in Ephraim, I could isolate causes and effects for illustration purposes.

What were the causes of Absalom's tree dilemma in 2 Samuel 18:10? Was it his hair? Rebellion? His choice to fight his father, David? His counselors, Hushai and Ahithophel? Was it his environment—the battlefield, the trees, the hill country of Ephraim? Was it the fact he was riding alone and did not have help? Was it God's sovereignty in taking his hand off David's son?

These are all causes. They are easy to illustrate with other circumstances. We can look for parallels of people with outward beauty but hurt themselves in their arrogance and self-will. We can search for people we know who rebelled against their father. We can look for people who fought their father. We can point to people who heeded the counsel of others or who surrounded themselves with the wrong people. We can talk about environments—about creating battlefields unnecessarily or of the need to be in Jerusalem submitting to our father rather than siding with distant relatives to avoid submission. We can remind people of a story where evil people end up alone because they did not fight the Lord's battles.

Cause is easy to spot; it just requires careful examination and a prayerful spirit. It is beyond the scope of this book to address the technical side of causality, which is, in and of itself, very complex. There is no reason to label efficient and sufficient cause, etc.

It is much more profitable and far simpler to address temporality and how an analysis of time helps us find an illustrative parallel. There are three aspects to analyzing action: before, during, and after.

1. What transpires before (cause)?
2. What is transpiring during the action (concomitants)?
3. What transpires after the action (effects)?

When dealing with cause, there are several ways of looking at cause. **Causal factors** can be broken down as follows:

1. Derivation—how an action emerges
2. Speed, delay, rhythm, or repetition—the timing of process
3. Process detail—the step-by-step mechanics of action
4. Relational causes—how people influence development
5. Volitional motivational--choices of participants

To illustrate the simplicity of this model, I want to return to the Matthew 6:19-21 passage. In attempting to isolate causal factors involved in making banking choices, laying up treasure in heaven or earth, the verses might be viewed in the manner listed below.

If the reader diagrams all these elements, namely the causal aspects of movement in the text, it makes illustration much easier. The passage is, like many parables, itself an illustration. It is really an illustration and an explanation about allegiances. Were a person to diagram this, the issues of movement might be as follows:

1. DECISION-MAKING about treasure storage (either heaven or earth)
2. The simple action of STORING treasure somewhere
3. The DESTRUCTION of treasure by animals (moths)
4. The DESTRUCTION of treasure by rust
5. The BREAKING THROUGH of thieves
6. The STEALING of thieves
7. Treasure STORAGE in heaven
8. PROTECTING treasure from beasts, decay, and other people

These actions can be further analyzed at a deeper level. In dividing cause into derivation, process, speed, relation, and volition, the vast number of illustrations become immediately evident.

Derivation

Derivation deals with how a process comes to be. In other words, it is often important to talk about what is involved in the emergent process. For example, if someone were preaching from Acts chapter 13 and wanted to talk about Paul and Barnabas leaving for the mission field, it would be important to address the prayer process of the leaders at Antioch. It may be important to ask if the text gives any clues about how this decision came to be—prayer, ministering to the Lord, a revived local church, listening to the Spirit's voice, etc.

In looking again at the Matthew text, a derivation analysis might look something like this. It answers *how someone might approach* the question about whether s/he should lay up treasure and where.

1. Since in this text derivation is IMPLIED, the preacher can speak to the issue of DECISION-MAKING and assess implicit factors involved in investment choices. It is important to deal with:
   a. Assumptions about the importance of material goods.
   b. Assumptions about corruptibility of earthly treasures.
   c. Assumptions about relative values.
   d. The person who is motivated toward treasure preservation based on unseen factors.
   e. Fears about the future, forced decision-making.
   f. Hope for a return or preservation of treasure storage.
2. How someone GOES ABOUT CHOOSING where to secure investments is critical.
   a. What are my choices?
   b. How many are there?
   c. Are there contingent factors that drive choices: a wife, a child, a boss, etc.?

Process

Another way to deal with causal illustration is to analyze the process in and of itself. In process analysis, the issue is *sequence.* The issue is not speed, for example. Order speaks to correctness. For example, were I to preach on Acts 18:8, it is very clear from the text that the next step after Crispus and the Corinthians believe is that they were baptized. The issue is not just baptism in and of itself, but it is a matter of establishing the foundational proclamation of faith *prior* to the act of baptism. Many verses of scripture address the issue of sequence.

Examine the breakdowns below. They all have cause/effect elements; however, the real crux here is between the two—the process itself. Using Matthew 6:19ff once again, the reader will note there are several aspects involved in the treasure keeping process—storing, destruction, and protecting. The illustrator can choose to focus on one process or several.

1. The process of STORING: How someone goes about protecting their investments on earth.
   a. Money
   b. Housing
   c. Possessions
   d. Stocks and portfolio investments

In explaining this to a congregation, the illustrator must create detail to strike home with parallels drawn from the listeners' experiences.

Experience in and of itself is a sequential process. When the illustrator pictures any process, remembrances and images are drawn into the listeners' minds. "I filled out my deposit slip at the bank and counted out the cash. I counted out the twenties, then I counted out the tens, then the fives, and then the ones. I put my money in storage. It would get corrupted in my wallet. What I did not know was that inflation was corrupting my cash with cost-of-living increases and depreciation."

2. The process of TREASURE DESTRUCTION AND CORRUPTION: How corruption processes are intrinsic to the fallen world.
   a. Insects (creatures--moths)
   b. Rust through aging (decay)
   c. Thieves (people—treasure stealers)

People cannot do anything about processes that are embedded into the world tainted by sin. In Jesus' illustration, the problem is that destruction is unavoidable. The process is permitted by God to demonstrate the transient nature of this world and its contents. Insects, rust, and thieves are just a sampling of the inevitable process of decay.

In focusing on process, the preacher is not really talking about motives or even ultimate effect. The target is momentarily breaking down steps. The reason for doing this is very important.

In suspending criticism or delaying making judgments about rationales or moral contingencies, the speaker attempts to create common ground. One of the best ways to keep people's attention is to remind them that they have had similar experiences. Most listeners have lost things to insects, rust, and thieves. This resonates with the common person.

Feelings accompany processes. In this case, the feelings are negative toward moths and rust. There is sadness in loss.

When Jesus gives His three short illustrations, a cloud moves over the speech and the listener is drawn in through personal experience. The simple rehearsal of a common process generates interest, both an interest in shared experience and the desire to protect one's investment.

3. The process of PROTECTING investments: This involves how we tend to build fences around material things and obsess mentally to hedge our substance.
   a. Physical protection: banks, fences, insecticides
   b. Mental process: worry about investments, safety, choices about who and how to protect

Jesus knows that people are tied to things and have a natural tendency to give eternal worth to this world. Our sense of time and value are not God's. Consequently, we protect our accumulated wealth. We want to guard the things into which we have poured our time and resources.

People want to preserve and guard against hostile forces—insects, rust, and thieves—essentially animals, decay, and other human beings. Jesus essentially attacks this value system at several levels.

Speed, Delay, Rhythm, or Repetition of Process

The viability or spiritual implications of any movement can be judged based on several other factors. A correct decision made at the wrong time or too quickly might very well be a bad decision. The same could be said for a decision that is repeated. It might be right the first time but wrong later, suitable for a toddler but not for an adult. Repeated movements may result in rhythmic process or even tradition. So, illustrating movement might involve nuancing the issues of speed, delay, rhythm, or repetition of process.

Jesus often deals with these elements. He says, for example, "Follow me and let the dead bury their dead" (Matt. 8:22). The issue is immediacy. Following tomorrow is not an option.

In the same way, in 'movement' there are explicit moral contingencies. In other words, actions have export. If I raise my hand, it could mean I am going to hit something, or I may just be stretching. If I am quick about it, it says one thing. If I am slow, it may say something else.

In approaching the treasure passage, speed and delay are especially important.

1. Treasure is constantly corrupting, so THE DECISION SHOULD NOT BE DELAYED.
2. If I delay my decision to store up in heaven, I could LOSE MY ETERNAL REWARD.
3. Also, my treasure is right NOW AT RISK of being stolen.
4. In terms of rhythm, this is a CONSTANT and DAILY decision. I may have stored up yesterday, but today am I storing? Consistency measures my obedience.
5. Repetition creates rhythms, habits, and traditions. These cycles about my treasure accumulation speak about my character and my relationship to God.

This type of thinking can be applied to almost any action in any biblical text, especially *commands*. When the Bible commands something, the preacher must consider what kind of timing is implied. If I am to love my neighbor, I might not be able to do it if I am working in the garden. But if I pick some vegetables, I can carry them to the neighbor later perhaps.

Universal commands have implicit expectations about timing. The Great Commission is binding on all Christians, but does my evangelical spirit get shelved today because yesterday I shared Christ with someone? Certainly not. There needs to be repetition of action.

By contrast, Phillip is commanded to go to the south, ultimately to meet up with the Ethiopian eunuch in Acts 8. This was a one-time event. There are precise implications in this text. The Spirit of God may command me to reach one person at one precise time. Speed is of the essence and repetition is not important. Delay is catastrophic.

In summary, in dealing with any text of scripture, the illustrator can ask if there is a process involved in the textual movements. Is there a sequence that should be highlighted? Is the problem in the process that the biblical character skipped steps? Is one step critical in the process, maybe avoided?

The speaker can choose to emphasize any aspect of the process that is important for understanding, even non-material components. Not all processes are physical of course.

Many times, the most important aspects of processes are mental ones. They involve conceptual order and decision-making. Therefore, it is critical for any speaker to break down the process into extensive detail to assess if some component of the non-material steps needs to be clarified for the listener. In this way, the audience can embrace the need for change and reorder whatever is lost, missing, or out of place.

Volitional and Motivational Causes

When Jesus says that our hearts are tied to our treasure-hiding, He is dealing with volitional and motivational causes. He is saying that we are *motivated and choose* to secure our earthly money and passions. Causality is almost always linked to desire in some way. While the issue of desire will be treated extensively later, here we want to address motivation in a cursory manner.

The preacher can address this common phenomenon by pointing out human choice and the things that motivate people to make the decisions they do. A teenager wants a new phone, so she saves her money and bugs her parents. A middle-aged man purchases a boat because he wants to go fishing on the weekends. People are driven by desire—love, hate, loneliness, fear, etc.

Temporal Issues and Moving Beyond Temporality

There are a host of issues that involve timing when one examines the scriptures. For example, what transpires before is a matter of cause. Also, there is the question of how something comes about. That is called derivation.

Whenever we deal with time, we also might ask what is going on at the same time, that is concurrent phenomena. In other words, when illustrating an idea with concrete realities, one might ask, "What is going on nearby or simultaneously with this action?"

What follows an action is an effect. A person might want to illustrate subsequent action when illustrating.

When it comes to movement, it might be important to move beyond temporality. One might find an additional matrix of factors that can involve the following. To illustrate this, let's look at the treasure passage above from another set of angles. Consider these possibilities for illustration:

1. The reality that I am actively laying up treasure AND MIGHT NOT EVEN KNOW IT
2. The self-interest in laying up for MYSELF treasure on earth
3. The INEVITABLE TREASURE LOSS because there are treasure spoilers
a. That there are LIVING forces that destroy our treasure (moths)
b. That TIME is against us (rust)
c. That DECAY is active even when I am not
d. That treasure is not safe from other selfish PEOPLE (thieves)
4. That people will VIOLENTLY steal the treasure
5. That treasure stowage TIES US DOWN

If these were not enough for the preacher, there are still a host of other ways to analyze cause and process in movement. One could talk about the quality of the action or its moral implications of motives for doing something. For example, is there joy or obligation in the impetus? One could talk about the competence or incompetence of the actor. Is there excess or speculation in investment?

Moral Human Behavior

As was previously stated, there are moral implications in ideas. These also need to be illustrated. They are not necessarily movement, state, or emotion. They might be assumed prerequisites, moral consequents, or ethical adjuncts.

To simplify this idea, the reader should ask questions of the text that involve right and wrong. What is the text saying about moral implications—before, during, and after—the isolated text under consideration?

When Moses tells God to "send someone else" in Exodus 4:13, what are the moral implications? By this, I do not mean the emotional implications, but the ethical concomitants. What moral causes and results swirl around this statement?

1. Moses obviously DID NOT REALLY CARE ABOUT THE CRY OF HIS PEOPLE, or he would have responded to God's initiative.
2. There is a LACK OF LOVE.
3. In chapter 3, it is apparent he was IGNORANT OF GOD HIMSELF.
4. He might have been AFRAID OF THE INEVITABLE BATTLE with a stubborn Pharaoh.
5. He obviously FELT POWERLESS and focused on his own abilities.
6. He DID NOT ADEQUATELY RECONCILE HIMSELF to his past murder of the Egyptian.
7. He was INSECURE about his speaking ability.
8. He was FAITHLESS ABOUT THE SIZE OF HIS GOD.
9. He might have FALTERED WHEN HE REMEMBERED THE ACCUSATIONAL ATTITUDE of the Israelite who accused him of killing the Egyptian.
10. He might NOT HAVE WANTED TO TAKE RESPONSIBILITY.
11. He was possibly OVERLY CONCERNED about his job, his sheep.

12. He possibly did not want to address his COMPLACENCY.
13. He might have been REBELLIOUS.
14. He likely RETAINED SOME BITTERNESS AND ANGER toward the Egyptians.
15. He presumably DISTANCED HIMSELF FROM HIS FAMILY.
16. He might NOT HAVE KNOWN THE WAYS OF GOD.

Enumerating moral ramifications is not a useless endeavor but very profitable for coming up with illustrations from other parts of life. The speaker simply needs to extrapolate from here to parallel circumstances. It is possible to process right down the list, identifying past or current *stories or circumstances that have similar moral parallels.* Can I identify a story or an image where, I or someone I know, did not want to respond to a cry or a command from a superior because of:

1. A lack of love.
2. Ignorance of the power of the one having authority to command the task.
3. A sense of powerlessness.
4. A failure to reconcile oneself to past failures.
5. A sense of insecurity.
6. A disbelief in the capacity of God to perform.
7. A lack of desire to help someone who criticized you previously.
8. A lack of desire to take on a large task.
9. A fixation with a current, less important job.
10. A sense of complacency.
11. A rebellious attitude.
12. A residual anger toward an ethnic group.
13. A desire not to be reconciled to an abandoned family.
14. An ignorance of the ways of God.

Moral crisis is universal. We all have neglect and hopes. We dwell in a world constantly battling over rightness and whether or not to initiate action against internal or external forces. The battle is in the realm of faith and of sin. For Moses, there were two choices: to remain complacent or to advance. Yet, while the choice was simple, the rationale was immensely complex.

Often the moral implications of a text are not clear. Even when they are stated, the reader cannot speak categorically about the broad range of implications. They usually must be qualified.

What do I mean by this? Well, many preachers don't like illustrations because they get away from the text. However, *any talk about the text is getting away from the text.* Some preachers never tell stories because they are adding to the meaning of scripture. However, all their preaching is in a sense, not scripture, so they are explaining the text in some way *using their own words.*

When addressing moral implication, there is a certain amount of exegetical care that needs to be taken. Sometimes the moral ramifications are clear. Oftentimes they are not.

For example, Matthew tells us precisely that Jesus "did not [do] many mighty works [in his own country] because of their unbelief" (13:58). But we don't know if Jesus was angry, whether or not He was teaching His disciples something, if He acted like this because He was grieved, etc. We also don't know the moral implications of unbelief: whether or not it was generational inheritance that the Jews received from their parents, whether or not they reached this state because of a comparison of Jesus with other miracle workers, if it was because of entrenched convictions about Judaism being a religion of law and not of faith, etc. We know only that Jesus made the decision not to do miracles because of the causal factor of faithlessness.

Preaching demands making sense from biblical culture and contextualizing it to modern day society by comparison. It requires that we make hermeneutical decisions and postulate applications that will meet the needs of listeners today.

Ultimately, illustration, no matter how good, involves the nuancing of the textual idea. It is impossible to move to any parallel story or image and not be in the realm of conjecture.

However, isolating precise elements from biblical grammar makes it easier to analogize to solid parallels in other parts of life. For example, we are told in chapters three and four of Exodus that Moses had precise issues with returning to Egypt, namely, his lack of knowledge about Yahweh, his speaking/communication inability, and his powerlessness. So, when we look for moral implications in the text, we cannot say for example, that Moses had a personal weakness for bowing down to other gods and that's why he wanted God to send someone else.

The text provides us with moral boundaries and implications. So, while they are largely implicit, they are often clearly in the text and should be illustrated with force. People need clarity about moral judgment and decision-making. Illustration provides the means to clarify the implications of biblical theology.

Illustrating Issues of State

Issues of state are different from movement but can also be illustrated. For example, in returning to Jesus' discussion about laying up treasure in heaven from Matthew 6, treasure does not move or decay unless there is a thief or moth. The illustrator can speak about 'treasures' without talking about the necessary requirement of storing them.

Treasure can be cars, money, family, boats, electronics, etc. It is important to illustrate what treasures are before one illustrates the implications of managing them. The actions within the verses address treasure management, among other things, but in an audience of young and old as well as rich and poor, it would be important to address what constitutes treasure, essentially a definitional question. Is treasure an iPhone, a social media account, a car, or a summer cottage?

Ultimately, the passage is NOT about movement. It is about state. "Where your treasure is, there will your heart will be also." The listener must address where one finds oneself. Sure, there is the issue of how the treasure got there (movement), but the real export of the passage is a question of discovery, of where the spiritual portfolio investments are located.

If a person only illustrates movement, often the deeper questions of *state* go unaddressed. The treasure must be somewhere.

If a person were to outline the illustrative possibilities of the previous verse, she would have to ask herself additional questions about state that involve:

1. WHERE I lay up my treasure (earth or heaven).
2. That the safe place is not TEMPORAL OR EARTHLY.
3. That heavenly treasure is not subject to DEVALUATION (corruption).
4. That heavenly treasure is not subject to LOSS (thieves).
5. That heavenly treasure is SECURE.
6. That there is a safe PLACE to invest.
7. That earthly treasure is TEMPORAL.
8. That treasure-keeping SHOWS INTERNAL ALLEGIANCES.
9. That our treasure IS actually somewhere.
10. That our heart and treasure OCCUPY the same place.

Issues of state are always evident or implicit. Illustrators should carefully consider the implications of conditions of states. It may seem like the preacher is noting the obvious, but that is the point. "Where your treasure is, that's where your heart is." This statement by Jesus is the conclusion of the discourse. It is not a command; if it were, He would have said, "Change the location of your treasure." It is not a moral summary like, "You are wrong about where you keep your treasure." It is simply a statement of fact. It is a commentary on the location of the heart. The implications are implicit.

Illustrating Issues of Emotion

Once the questions of movement and state are isolated, then the preacher can assess questions of emotion. Issues of emotion are a hotbed of illustration. If people do not recognize or are not moved by the factual export of the text, it is possible to reach people by touching on the emotions that are tied to the ideas.

In the previous passage from Matthew 6:19-21, the words and concepts are like a mine of illustrative material. It is important to precisely list the emotions generated by the text. In just a few minutes, it is possible to see:

1. The JOYFUL discovery that I actually have treasure somewhere.
2. The FEARFUL reality that my treasure is on earth.
3. The SELFISH SHAME of earthly treasure.
4. The ANXIETY of lost investment and time of treasure storing.
5. The DREAD of potential loss.
6. The INSECURITY of earthly treasure.
7. The SECURITY of heavenly treasure.
8. The FRUSTRATION toward moths and other animals.
9. The ANGER toward thieves.
10. The VIOLATION of someone or something taking my treasure.
11. The ENTRAPMENT of being tied to treasure.
12. The CRISIS of not knowing where the treasure is.
13. The FUTILITY of laying up treasure on earth.
14. The SADNESS of the short, temporal nature of life.
15. The emotional BONDAGE of tying a heart to earthly treasure.
16. The FREEDOM of eternal investments.

In the same way that it is easy to parallel movement for illustration, the same can be done through emotional analogy. In illustrating emotional entrapment of material things, I can easily think of ten or twenty stories of people I have known that were entrapped by their possessions. The same can be said for the dread of loss. I can immediately find in my experience times that I or others have been in crisis or disappointment over material losses. I can then convert those historical happenings into a good story that works to demonstrate the emotion I am trying to isolate. If I do not want to mention precise people, I can create a universal person: "Imagine for a minute a person who owns…."

The fruitful multiplication of images and stories through emotional parallels is vast. Because we live in a world of charged emotion, once the preacher can isolate the emotion generated by the text, it is possible to highlight the meaning of scripture by showing the truth from actual human events. The results are undeniable in the ears of the listeners. They know intuitively that what the speaker says is true. Why? Because they have *felt* it before; that's why.

Verses that possess less emotion and are more factual discourse must be probed more fully. For example, the verse, "The just shall live by faith" (Hab. 2:4; Rom. 1:17; Gal. 3:11; Heb. 10:38) is quite a bit more difficult, but not entirely out of reach in terms of emotion. Consider this:

1. It FEELS RIGHT AND GOOD to be approved by God.
2. Declared justice by God brings CONFIDENCE.
3. Justice is UNASSAILABLE from a human perspective.
4. Faith possesses an ADVENTUROUS ELEMENT.
5. Faith possesses WARMTH AND SIMPLICITY.
6. Faith UNSEATS law.

It becomes possible to draw even from propositional statements deep emotional reality for illustration. In this passage, one can easily turn to times of approval when a student was affirmed by a teacher for believing or taking a risk. There are countless examples of confidence from being declared right. It becomes possible to talk about feelings toward authority once there is approval, or how previous law requirements are fulfilled when someone exercises faith.

The illustrator must first isolate the feelings and emotions in the text. Parallels come quickly. Even if one takes this passage in a purely juridical sense, there is still joy in being declared not-guilty, by living with future spiritual optimism, etc. Emotions exist in almost every declarative statement. The preacher needs to isolate these in the text and exploit them. God wants His people to be exuberant about conviction and truth as much as He does about action and obedience, perhaps even more so.

Emotions in a text are as broad as human experience. It is the preacher's job to create the textual climate, not violate it.

Textual export might involve warm or cold feelings. The text might be formal or informal, open or closed.

When biblical characters are involved in the textual passage, the speaker has a special responsibility for capturing relational phenomena by highlighting the emotions by capturing a tone or a stance. It becomes necessary to deliver not just the content of the word of God but also the emotive force.

Illustrating Relationships and Relational Causes

In this particular passage about treasure preservation, there are minimal relational causes. Jesus does not focus on how people cause other people to do things. There are several implied people-centered causes. One could conjecture how people influence human decision making, but it is not really in the text.

Matthew 6:19-20 is really about our internal relationship to material things and to God. The text is not about people's relationship to one another. So, the speaker can highlight the personification of relationships of people with their material possessions.

Relationships are replaced by elevating the value of the material world. There are new relationships that have replaced valuing people. However, this is only implied in the text and cannot be preached with that much force because the issue in the text is treasure, not people.

Human forces abound, however, when reading the Bible. They are almost always present or implied. People are constantly influencing other people. From a preaching perspective, the expositor needs to demonstrate *relationship* in sermons, the human forces that drive people to bring about change in others.

For example, in Proverbs 1:10-19, Solomon draws a parallel corollary between the call of wisdom and the call of the sinner. Human influence drives decision making which in turn drives a certain set of life-consequences. Wisdom cries aloud and promises rewards to those that follow her. Sinners also put out the call for mischief. The result in the case of the latter is death.

While this example is crystal clear, often relational cause requires that the preacher analogize with modern examples. In Proverbs, the sinners entice then collectively gather to take down the innocent. What does this look like in modern day culture?

"Come on. Let's go hang out. Joe knows this guy who's a sitting duck. He's loaded. We're going to see if we can't take him down and steal his wallet! Why don't you come with us?"

Relational causality is everywhere in the Bible. Eve convinced Adam to taste the fruit. Job's friends tried to get him to curse God. Andrew found Peter. Ananias influenced Paul. Abraham rescued Lot.

The reality is that most of us fail to recognize how others influence our decision making. Before a person decides, it is not uncommon to think, "What would Sue do?" "Would my father approve of this decision?" "She told me to do it. If I don't, what will she say?"

Most of us are not just driven by goals or even by God, we are motivated, for better or for worse, by others. It is important for the preacher to demonstrate from the text how biblical models parallel similar influences from those of our peers, our family, and our friends.

Consider this text from Acts 8, where Philip influences Simon the Sorcerer in Samaria. Verse 13 says that "he continued with Philip and wondered." It might be easy to simply pass over this verse, but the reality is that the verbs contain relational components of causality. What follows in Simon's conduct is a result of being with Philip and experiencing the Spirit's power. The preacher can go on to explain the influence of relational proximity to holy people of God and how it gives rise to our sin.

In the end, a full-orbed application process involves a comprehensive scope of consideration, from relationships to emotion to fixed objects. Among the many possible connections that a speaker might make for listeners, the Holy Spirit gives real life to some. Those comparisons are precious and need to be spoken with authority, and as those applications fall on the ear of the listener, there emerges a supernatural connection of people with their God.

Questions for Engagement

1. How might raw exegesis be different from capturing thought units that can be used for illustration?
2. In developing illustrations, what components of the process aid in meaning-transfer to the listener?
3. In what ways are textual ideas like a web?
4. What is textual movement, and what kinds of movement are possible within a text?
5. What does it mean that there are causal factors within a text?
6. How might the idea of derivation be used as an illustrative concept and method?
7. How is illustrating a process different from illustrating movement?
8. What does it mean to illustrate speed, delay, rhythm, or repetition in action?
9. How is illustrating moral human behavior different from illustrating emotion in a text?
10. How is the concept of state more fundamental than issues of movement?
11. What does it mean to analogize an emotion?
12. What are some of the components of causality in relationships?

10   Preaching in the *hEAR*-and-Now

Jesus' preaching was *unlike* our own. He often moved freely from Natural Revelation and human experience to spiritual truth. He used creation extensively. He was also very concerned about sin and communicating clearly to the sinner. He was concerned about human suffering, justice, and spiritual alienation. He figuratively addressed causes and solutions through verbal analogy to common people, scenarios, and things. He did it right then and right there. This was the circumstantial nature of immediacy.

Our Lord referenced sparrows, rebellious sons, pearls, talents, coins, lights, baskets, buildings, and a myriad of other items from the concrete world to teach people. But why did He do it?

Matthew tells us that Jesus used parables to divide His audiences.

This is why I speak to them in parables, because seeing they do not see, and hearing they do not hear, nor do they understand. Indeed, in their case the prophecy of Isaiah is fulfilled that says: "You will indeed hear but never understand, and you will indeed see but never perceive." For this people's heart has grown dull, and with their ears they can barely hear, and their eyes they have closed, lest they should see with their eyes and hear with their ears and understand with their heart and turn, and I would heal them. (Matt. 13:13-15)

Parables reveal and conceal. To the unbeliever, they speak conviction and not healing. Many scholars don't like the export of this passage because of its implications about election, hard-heartedness, or Jesus' refusal to heal. However, there is a very important practical lesson about the Savior's philosophy of illustration that cannot be overlooked: the strategic use of Natural Revelation convicts men of sin. This was also Paul's belief.

In Romans chapter 1, Paul tells us that "wrath of God is revealed from heaven against all ungodliness and unrighteousness of men" by means of general revelation (Rom. 1:18). He even goes on to say that "the invisible things of him from the creation of the world are clearly seen, being understood by the things that are made, even his eternal power and Godhead; so that they are without excuse" (Rom. 1:20).

Natural revelation is convicting. It is not saving. That is the clear teaching of Jesus and Paul. It is the way God laid out the fallen universe.

The idea that nature teaches men about sin is kind of negative. I wish I could establish another foundation, but I cannot. The preacher has an implicit obligation to divide the audience on the topic of sin. This is the negative side of what should follow, that is redemptive messaging.

Jesus' explanation to the disciples in Matthew 13 is not what we are looking for when we turn to the Master for His preaching philosophy. We think we will drive people away. In one sense, we might, but in another sense, the crowd is drawn to a speaker who speaks truthfully to the common details of life and reinforces messages that the audience has already heard.

Reminding People What They Already Know

It is pleasing to be reminded about things we have already learned but forgotten. We like it when the audience muses, "That's right. I've seen this before."

Unfortunately for the sinner, he or she follows that thought up with the, uh-oh feeling. "I am an unholy person standing before a holy and glorious God."

By the time the audience arrives in the presence of the speaker, God has already preached on particular sins in a thousand different ways to every individual hearer in the audience. The messages have gone out into all the earth. The heavens are declaring it. There is no speech or language where their voice is not heard (Ps. 19:1). The people already have experienced God's sermon.

The psalmist tells us in Psalm 19:6 that nothing is hidden from its heat. The glory of God is shining in all its convictional brightness. Nothing escapes His preaching, either His General Revelation or His Natural Revelation.

So, if God has already preached a thousand sermons, my job as a preacher when communicating to lost people is to remind them of what God has *already* taught them. That is one of the jobs of illustration.

The Physical Universe as a Chorus of Conviction

The rules of the universe, the natural law, are, in and of themselves, a collective law written on the hearts of humanity as a means by which God can break through. He preaches. They listen. Or that is what we hope they do.

Paul said in Romans 2:15 that the moral law was already written on their hearts. In other words, God has internalized His expectations and reinforces them through visual sermons, consistently heralding the same message of sin and separation.

The physical universe is a chorus of conviction, proclaiming an invitation to repent from sin. The majesty of creation is like heat, burning the messages of God as continual law.

Those messages are not easy to accept. Jesus said that hardened people have ears, but "they can barely hear'" (Matt. 13:13). They don't want to be converted or healed (Matt. 13:15).

The idea of using Natural Revelation as the basis for evangelical illustration is a controversial one. It should not be. It does not take the place of exposition. It is only a bridge. That's how Jesus used it. "He did not speak to them without a parable, but privately to his own disciples he explained everything" (Mark 4:34).

This verse teaches us that exposition, it seems, came after engagement. Jesus took interested people aside and explained spiritual truth to them in detail.

In other words, Natural Revelation raises issues that only the specific revelation in the Bible can answer. Natural Revelation saves no one. Jesus saves.

Take for example the star of the Magi. The star did not communicate saving grace. It did not even preach sermons about the blood. It only brought the wise men to Jerusalem, where they made further inquiry. It led the wise men to the feet of Jesus to worship. While many saw the star, only a few recognized its implications.

Natural Revelation bridges the culture gap. Basically, it shows God's universal anger at sin and points people in the right direction, making them look for answers for the foundational problem of separation from God.

Jesus' Bridging-Process

So, to overview the process, it looks like this: Jesus used things in the world to bridge to the crowds. He in essence repeated the messages people had already heard from God in the common activities of life. From there, He reaped the harvest of those who were willing to acknowledge their need for a Savior. He then taught them in detail in private.

This methodology is simple and repeatable. It involves using stories, images, and illustrations to connect to people who may have never laid eyes on a Bible and are alienated from print in general.

As a preacher, namely someone who speaks to lost people, the preacher can establish common ground by reminding listeners of the messages they have already heard. Ultimately, disciples are those who hear the message and are converted.

To contrast this approach with what we usually do, let's talk about the venue. I don't want to use a Sunday morning preaching engagement. That would be too easy. We have all been in church services where the preacher drones on and bores people with the exciting word of God. People are sleeping, looking at their watches, and are as far from the scriptures as is humanly possible.

To illustrate the distance between an educated preacher and a somewhat ignorant audience, I want to relate a story that happened to me in an airport, of all places. In this case, I was the ignorant 'audience.' It was in this brief 2-minute conversation that I realized there is a colossal disconnect of seminary-trained ministers and the common person.

Pay Dirt

In 1998, I was coming back from the Amazon, traveling through Miami International Airport. A United States Customs agent asked me for my passport. I handed it to him.

To understand how this marked me, you must consider that I was a fresh missionary in the Amazon who had just left my young wife for a week of meetings. I was troubled, having left my three little children in a house, where just a few months before, there was a shooting across the street, where a young boy of 10 years old was shot in the leg when a thief broke into the house without knowing he was home. He shot the little boy. We were, at the time of this story, living across the street from that house in Cayenne, French Guiana.

I was discouraged and rattled. I missed my wife and kids.

So, picking up the passport, this customs agent looked at me and paused for a very long time. He asked me what I was doing in French Guiana. I told him I was a missionary.

He then asked, "What kingdom is the wicked kingdom?"

"I am sorry. I don't understand," I said.

His voice elevated, and in all seriousness, he asked, "*What kingdom is the wicked kingdom?*"

I thought to myself, what's this guy after? Does he mean Colombian drug lords, Middle East terrorists, Jim Jones-type cult enclaves, or countries that harbor illegal immigrants?

I stammered, and very nervously said again, "Please excuse me, but I'm confused about what you are wanting."

"What seminary did you go to?" he asked.

"Dallas Seminary," I replied.

He paused for a very long time and said, "The Northern Kingdom was the wicked kingdom." He was not laughing and continued, "Didn't they teach you anything at Dallas [Seminary]?"

He again paused and looked at me, stamped my passport with an entry pass, and said, "I went to XYZ Seminary. You can go. Have a good day."

I was very upset as I walked away. I did not know how this little conversation would shake me. I did not know I had hit pay dirt.

Obviously, he was a graduate student in theology. He did not care that my heart was broken, having left my wife and three small children in a foreign capital knowing only a handful of people. He did not ask me about my call, my passion, my hopes for sharing Christ with lost people.

He asked me about a generalized fact that had no bearing on anything. It was contextually pointless. He overlooked my broken heart and only contributed to making me feel isolated.

As I walked away, I also thought, "Why of course! It was the Northern Kingdom." Naturally, I say to myself now, "What an idiotic thought that was."

This small story is a microcosm of the Sunday drama we call a church service, with its somewhat silent dialog. The dialogical nature of the preacher/congregation exchange can reinforce the ignorance of hurting people.

They come with pain, with passion, and with incredible ability. They are bursting with excitement to tell their story along with their hurts and dreams. The disconnected preacher in turn delivers information, decontextualized and rarified. He does not connect to them in their situation or pain.

This, of course, is not the situation with every preacher, but it brings us to what is traditionally known as the conduit metaphor. The preacher assumes his job is to transfer his/her full mind into the empty reservoir of the poor listener because, after all, the audience needs the information.

Rather than the Christian speaker looking at the hearer as a vast wealth of human experience and as a prior recipient of the General Revelation of a living God, He sees the hearer as an empty vessel.

Several years back I was sitting in a Sunday School class of a very fine Christian man who was teaching about a dozen people. His delivery connection was not nearly as sterling as his character. He droned on for almost an hour. I, as well as the others, could not wait to escape the hour. It was information overload.

Think about the weekly church scenario. Early on Sunday mornings, before people even venture out the door, they are sitting at home wounded, but they manage to take off their pajamas and robes and turn off their TVs to come out to listen to the preacher paint a picture of a better life. Instead, they are sometimes shown their ignorance rather than their knowledge.

Yes, I do mean knowledge. Every listener is a wealth of experience, an expert on millions of details, about which I know nothing, or almost nothing. God has already been at work.

The heavens are declaring the glory of God and the firmament is showing His handiwork. There is no language where their voice is not heard (Ps. 19). God is preaching, preaching, preaching. He is pleading and pleading. He gives invitation after invitation.

When a person enters the church sanctuary or into the presence of a believer, countless experiences have marked that individual. If I open my mouth, I need to join God in a conversation He is already having.

If I have the idea that Christian enculturation begins with me, I have sacrificed one of the greatest tools God has given me, the experiential past of the listener. What they have already lived is undeniable.

The power of Natural Revelation to reinforce the specific revelation of scripture is unimaginable. Most preachers don't use it. Most Christians don't use it.

As a governmental authority, this nameless Custom Agent noted above could have used his position in ten seconds to bring peace to my heart. What if he had said something like this, as he grabbed his border entry date-stamp: "God bless you for your sacrifice and following the Lord Jesus. I'll be praying for you as you go, that God would protect your family while you're in the States. I have seen many faithful people who separate from their families and do great work. Don't be afraid. God is going with you. I have seen it before."

He could have reached down into his occupational reservoir and said something that would have resonated with my need. Instead, he chose to litmus test my ability to correlate a piece of historical information from the Old Testament to a completely foreign setting. The Northern Kingdom had nothing to do with anything, at that moment.

Where are we in our preaching? Even the best exegetical preaching walks the potential tightrope of becoming information transfer or advice-giving. However, we must leverage the experience of the common person, that wealth of spiritual experience right there in the pew.

Sure, contextual analysis is a part of the preacher's study. Sure, Greek and Hebrew are absolutely necessary if we are to rightly divide the word of truth. But where is the heart for people, and how do we engage the common person with the wonderment, passion, and optimism of word of God?

We first must show them how much they already know, how much God has already taught them. Even if it pertains to sin, mistakes, and a thousand bad decisions, we still need to honor them by reminding them that during their rough and tumble road, it was God breaking through, or at least trying to.

Beyond Information-Transfer

Information inspires very few. In fact, the Bible says that it puffs people up. For the preacher to deny the sermonic discourse of Natural Revelation is to abandon one of the most helpful tools God has given us. We need to embrace and not abandon our observation of the world.

Western education, including Christian discipleship methods with all their rarified data-accumulation, can generate alienation between Christians and lost people. For ministers, this is an especially great danger. Paul said in 1 Corinthians 8:1 that love is, in some respects, the remedy for a puffed up, graduate education.

Naturally, evangelicalism litmus-tests future ministers with their ability to do semantic studies of word-range. However necessary this may be, if we cannot love people by the way we speak, what good does our exegetical sermonizing do?

Preaching the word of God works better if the heart of the speaker is not pharisaic. Exposition done poorly with word arguments and unnecessary questions can cause conflict (1 Tim. 6:4).

God's design for illustrative bridging, while also being conflictual, is highly intentional in that regard. Jesus knew His parabolic delivery would be divisive. However, He was looking for people whose hearts God had touched, people who were good observers and good listeners. He was intentionally separating out those whose hearts were right.

In our practice, the question is whether we reinforce our educated, prideful ethnocentrism or whether we foundationally leave our knowledge in the background, in the undercurrent of our preaching. Hopefully we do not wear it on our sleeve for all to see. Jesus certainly didn't.

He used the common elements of life to illustrate spiritual realities. The culture gap between the preacher and the kingdom immigrant going through the customs gate, the one seeking entry into the local church, is large.

There is nothing sinful about making an analogy to common experience, and even more so, there is a necessity and a call to which we must respond. It is also quite natural.

If I use Natural Revelation to remind someone about his or her sin, I am not preaching something foreign. I am preaching what God already has taught them. They will even agree with me.

Some might say that people are not observant. They do not see the messaging God has placed in the universe. With all boldness, I would say this is not true. It would be easy to argue that they have both seen it and suppressed it (Rom. 1:18).

If Christians are to reach the unbelieving generation before us, that ever distant and biblically illiterate Gen Z, we must recognize that God has already preached a thousand sermons. It is our job to repeat them for those that have ears. That's why we need to preach in the *hEAR*-and-now.

In the cross-cultural matrix of parabolic bridge-building, Jesus traversed communication barriers with images, comparisons, parables, and stories that reinforced the audience's own observational truths about God.

A parable is a simple image, comparison, or story used to express spiritual wisdom. It is a brief narrative with a simple plot and 'flat' characters. He did not use complex plots as we use in performance-based storytelling, the theater, or what we have come to enjoy with the advent of television. He used simple plots with uncomplicated characters. Most parables can be told in about 15 seconds, while the longest ones extend to only two to three minutes.

Parables are not intricate or knotty and don't require the kind of elaborate twists and turns of Hollywood storytelling. Essentially they are a polarizing medium, showing people on which side of the fence they are standing.

Questions for Engagement

1. How does Jesus' preaching reflect a hEAR-and-Now method?
2. What are parables and what are they not?
3. What power lies in Natural Revelation and how does that relate to preaching?
4. What is the role of an audience's prior knowledge in preaching?
5. What was Jesus' philosophy of engagement?
6. What does the story of "Pay Dirt" teach us about an improper use of Bible knowledge?
7. How is application different from information transfer?
8. What are some of the qualities of educated, prideful, ethnocentrism in our methods of communicating the Bible to people?

11 Preaching in the Here-and-Now

Many teachers of scripture scour the Internet for illustrations to supplement their delivery. However, there is a fatal flaw in this practice: the immediate context of the biblical passage is often not correlative to the content of the illustration.

People choose movie stars and pop singers to model behavior, but the audience says, "That's great, but I am not famous." It is not uncommon to find material in magazines or in blogs, but the reality is that contextually, the application is only partially related to the audience.

To formulate a good illustration, there needs to be sensitivity to the immediate context. We must preach in the here-and-now, otherwise we leave the door open to audience denial.

Organic development strikes the listener as genuine application. The auditor knows that the speaker understands the context. Naturally, many illustrations found in books or on the radio might work, but the typical church member wants to hear something that emerges from something or someone nearby.

There are several contingent questions we ought to be asking when we prepare sermons. They are questions about the context and setting.

Who is in the room? What are they thinking? What happened this week locally, nationally, and globally? How can I speak relevantly to my audience?

Every communication context has a myriad or a matrix of overlaying factors. We are in a physical context, but there is additionally a group of cultural contexts that are unseen and altogether real. There are verbal and linguistic factors that one adds to the visual and gestural manners of the speaker. These elements are only scratching the surface to the host of environmental elements present when someone speaks.

A Perception Apprenticeship

How does a speaker synthesize contextual elements to be relevant? This is a tall order and, in fact, an impossible one.

What really needs to happen before someone creates a means to communicate spiritual truth through application is that the speaker first identifies how spiritual truth needs to be communicated contextually and locally.

To identify the contextual elements and triggers that are often suitable for creating illustrative engagement, it is helpful to recognize environmental ingredients that are present during sermonic delivery–people, needs, distractions, etc. As previously stated, contexts are complicated and varied. Just take age for example. How one communicates with an 80-year-old person living on Social Security is different from a sixth-grader being bullied in gym class.

There are so many image-generating factors that the contingencies are endless. The posture of any speaker should be one of supreme sensitivity of the observable, contextual phenomena that are obvious. The auditors generally interpret a great number of local elements exactly as a speaker does.

It is critical that the person delivering the message attempts to interpret audience variables and develop or alter presentation based on what the Spirit is teaching about the contextual variables. The same interpretive responsibility would fall on several people in those contexts where there are multiple speakers or a teamed approach to leading worship.

Contextual engagement, correspondence, application, and imaging-method in illustration represent an entry into an evolving delivery that is modified by circumstantial realities, whether we want to accept that fact or not. There is a necessary cultural or spontaneous accommodation that involves the speaker's response to specific or combined elements of seen or unseen factors.

This is not the alteration of truth or situationism. It is applying the Bible to a particular audience in a particular way so that people can understand the glory and reality of the scriptures.

When we study contextual phenomena with love for people, we realize that the objective truth, the eternal perfections of God, and our theological structures can be communicated with a new range of language.

It is important to find amid the mass of contextual elements, those that are important to God, have teaching value to the audience, and possess a universal quality. We should capture a textual idea and associate the truth to the relevant components in the context, ones we identify through prayerful observation.

The evolution of a textual truth from the scriptures is clothed in an image or story that captures the message of the word of God. There is an engagement that results from combining the textual idea, the contextual variables, the purpose of the speaker, and an encapsulating figure.

The context of a communication setting is not the objective; the connection of God with listeners is the goal. However, when the speaker knows the audience, situational factors give rise to a suitable way to communicate. The knowledge of the audience and cultures present can alter communication style or negate intention.

Ultimately, the speaker, after preparing a textually accurate understanding of a biblical passage, goes through a delivery adjustment. A sermon prepared in advance is only hypothetical in the pastor's study and is ultimately modified. Eventually there is the inevitable immediacy of delivery, where, if the speaker has properly anticipated the contextual variables, can reach the hearts of people.

The idea that we 'prepare' sermons is somewhat of a contradiction. Sermons are delivered in controlled attention witness settings. What we do in advance is usually just outlining because a sermon is oral.

Beyond the textual manipulation process of manuscript, there needs to be an anticipation of the reception frameworks of the audience. How will they receive what I am saying? If I come at this with love, how will my tone change so I can reach the frustrated couple, the distracted teen, the sleepy retiree, etc.?

The immediacy of the aural, or sonorized, contextual delivery brings a flexibility of utterance that does not exist when we preach sermons in our heads, wherever we happen to be when we are engineering them. Once we are behind the lectern, we are in the world of vocalized discourse, with all its ambiguities.

While it is never too late to roll back the clock to reconstruct, for in fact, we do construct our sermon when it comes out of our mouths, it is better to consider contextual factors in advance. That is why we need to consider the following listening-factors when we construct an application.

Poke Them in the Eye and Drag Them by the Ears

People come into church with amazing resistance and skepticism. Even our finest church members are some of our most reluctant people because they are discriminating. They likely sit in church and run the sermon, along with every other element of the service, through their filters.

Our monological, one-way delivery system in western churches is not reflective of Jesus' method of dialog and contextualized application. Additionally, and probably more unfortunate, is that our current pulpit-centered system is one that does not permit questioning. The preacher delivers a sermon with an implicit, 'don't-question-me' medium.

We reap what we sow, however. The preacher may have to deal with silent stares if the sermon was not prepared with relevant application. The people might appear like they are under anesthesia.

The speaker, however, should overcome audience resistance by helping the people visualize the truth by concretizing abstraction. To do this, here are some suggestions.

First, poke the listener in the eye. What I mean is that you can show them the truth with something they already know and have experienced.

Second, drag them by their ears. If you say something they have heard before or that resonates with their past, you will trigger their interest.

It may sound strange to you, but you must intrude into their consciousness by means of the spoken word and resurrect things from their dead past that they have buried but still know to be true. When you do, you will bring to the surface joy and smiles or perhaps even an emotional sigh.

Triggering tension, smells, cries, or unmet expectations is part of life, things most people experience every day. When we unfold a story, right at that moment, feelings are at their height, and a touch from God might bring healing.

Vivid perceptions illustrating the Bible are not just emotional hooks, they are doors to the human spirit whereby God can arouse consciousness and call people to holiness. Profound convictions are usually held with feelings and emotion.

Some might argue that they want to address the mind and reason, and we ought to engage people with cognition. However, all thoughts are tied to emotion. The deeper the conviction, the stronger the value system and its associated feelings.

When people live in separation from God, with a sort of disequilibrium, they do that with pain, regret, and an unsettled spiritual life. We should not be surprised that when we anticipate the immediate and contextual sensitivities of an audience, we will raise in them a reaction that could involve resistance or emotion.

We are passionate beings and bring our senses with us to the listening endeavor. We endure our suffering and suppress or cultivate our memories. We should not avoid these elements of the communication exchange but celebrate them in the speaking/listening context.

Shared Environmental Factors

Environmental factors can be very powerful when we are voicing illustration or application. For example, if there has been a lot of snow recently, using an illustration that involves the weather will bring resonance with the listeners. The same can be said for rain, heat, food, sickness, and a host of other societal experiences that might be shared.

Shared experience is relational in a strange sense. In the same way that we develop connections between individuals in the human arena, we have shared connections with the material world.

Some of the most powerful applications revolve around what we commonly experience. We discuss, argue, and overcome common things. We all visit doctors, suffer a hard work schedule, endure loss, and run from conflict.

This shared pool of experience is a living stream that we can use to connect the scriptures to the life of the listeners. It is from this stream we can create a figured bridge. The current phenomena that exist in a community or a geographical area create commonality and an emotional climate that is by its nature participatory.

The speaker should seriously consider the immediate contexts around which a group of individuals live. By not doing this, the speaker not only loses one of the most fruitful means of reaching people, but might even insult the listeners.

For example, if there is a remarkable event, like a shooting or a fire, it is impending on the speaker to reference it. "We know that the Smith family experienced a tragic loss this week…." Not to mention it when everyone is looking for clarifying rationale is almost disrespectful. The audience is saying implicitly, "Help me make sense of this."

Audience Expectation

Communication venues bring with them a host of implicit expectations. Most of these are unseen. They are norms, either institutional norms or cultural ones.

We might expect the sermon to last about 30 minutes, for there to be 3 hymns or 6 worship songs, and someone to give announcements about the coming week. Typically, we might plan our worship in conjunction with the message and plan message-content around a shared theme. However, there are other things that are critical in message preparation.

Some people come to a teaching service expecting miracles. Do we prepare messages to answer the thirst for God's intervention, or are we constructing an application void of listener expectation?

People need healing. Our applications might address God's healing power. The same could be said of wisdom, intervention, prophetic direction, or simply to feel the Holy Spirit's presence amid a host of pressures.

People have every right to expect divine intervention, so it is my responsibility to anticipate how the text I am preaching relates directly to this need for the supernatural presence of God. This is not just in an altar-call following the message. It is in the message itself. I must have a message that is infused with the comfort, deliverance, touching hand of God, or whatever precise application the scriptures are exporting.

This oralized application-decision is a sermonic content issue for the speaker. It is not simply an audience attitude or something *they* hold. If I am a good shepherd, I will recognize the power in what God is about to do through His word and my preaching of it. This demands the construction of an illustration that works in the immediate circumstances.

It is not always possible to know humanly what God is doing in the audience, either before or during the preaching. However, the Holy Spirit is our Teacher, and we ought to ask God what message components need to be articulated to reach the people who will come. We then adopt the tone and stance to communicate that with love.

However, we may not know many of the expectations of an audience in advance. For example, preaching a lectionary calendar or preaching during a seasonal holiday, there are common themes with which everyone comes into the sanctuary. It may be impending on us to illustrate accordingly or, at a minimum, leverage the seasonal expectation for empowered delivery. However, if I am asked to speak at a church to which I have never been, knowing the expectations might be considerably more difficult.

Expectations of Order

It may seem odd to read about expectations of order in a book on illustration, but when we move to imaged delivery or narrative story, some people's expectations about textual explanation are violated. However, illustrations are a precise way of explaining. In fact, those illustrations explain more than we realize.

Imaged delivery and narrative-supports for preaching require that the leader take control of the expectations of order. Figures of speech have concrete correlation to reality, and wielding those figures requires a certain authority and intention by the speaker.

When the speaker uses a speech figure, s/he temporarily abandons linearity of thought. Ordered delivery yields its place to associative analogy.

Logic is not lost, however. Some people believe that speech figures are subject to a myriad of interpretations. However, imaged delivery has rules by which it functions. There needs to be highly disciplined, ordered control of the story. Emotional export needs to be walled in by a careful choice of words and delivery frameworks.

Stories and images are subject to the same interpretive spectrums as declarative statements. If I said, "God is love" (1 John 4:8), this statement needs a similar explanation to the phrase, "The Lord is my Rock" (Ps. 18:2). The first is discursive. The second is metaphorical. One is not clearer than the other. In fact, in some ways, the metaphor is more concrete than the abstraction.

When a speaker wages spiritual war with illustration, s/he challenges the experience of the audience or uses the very experience of the audience as a weapon against the bad thinking of the listener. It transfers responsibility of the message outcome to the audience.

The figurative delivery has a way of appearing like disorder because it diverts from the traditional ways of explaining discursively, but it brings concrete order out of abstracted chaos by reflection, conscious-raising, and listener experience. The listener has a past reality that forces an orderly response to the speaker's message.

Sensory Issues in the Immediate

Because a written sermon does not possess eye contact, inflection, volume, and pitch, we must recognize that verbal aspects of speaking reinforce or undermine our communication. If I am screaming a sermon about love, there will be some difficult mixed messages to overcome. Similarly, if I am unsure about a message concerning boldness, there is an inherent contradiction.

The sensory component in the context is also not something that we can overlook. What appears to be a whole different area of communication–the visual, auditory, olfactory, tactile, and kinesthetic parts of life–is integral to being relevant. If I avoid what I am seeing, smelling, or hearing, my illustration will be less relevant than it could be.

For example, what might you think if you heard this in a sermon? "This text of scripture teaches us about risk. Last week I was in the Tops grocery store and saw Harvey Gristmeyer talking to the Muslim produce man by the oranges. Later when I talked to Harvey, he told me he was sharing Christ with him and prayed for his wife who was sick."

Immediacy and contextual application are strengthened by what we see, hear, smell, and touch. If we can show people what is experiential in the present, the power infuses what we have to say with a certain authority.

In some ethnic churches, this immediacy is supplemented by call-and-response, music, chant, cadence, inflection, intensification, and climax. These qualities are typically less evident in Anglo churches. However, again, these are matters of congregational expectations in the immediate.

Holding objects or bringing in visual aids are instantaneously received, although they still must correlate with textual correspondence if they are to be effective. Nevertheless, the physical presence of items is accompanied by a sort of common experience because everyone in the room sees and hears the speaker's visualization.

Proxemics

Relative distance between participants in a communicative exchange, both physically and ideologically, is studied in the domain of proxemics. Typically, we associate the study of proxemics as a measurement of distance between audience and speaker. It is much more than this, however.

Love is the great discerner of intent. I avoid those I don't like. I get away from them, literally and physically. I draw close to those I love. Yet ideologically, we can associate the same parallels. When I care about someone, I come near their thought process and meet them in a way they can understand.

Beyond the spatial nature of a room or the arrangement of the chairs, I must ask if I 'draw near' to the thinking of others. That is in fact what Jesus did for us. He became a man and took on flesh. If I deeply care about the people to whom I am communicating, I embrace forms, language, and topics that can be decoded by those with whom I am speaking.

Matching What I Say with How I Say It

As was already noted, how the speaker says something communicates its own message. The oral side of preaching is often seen in preaching books as a matter of delivery expertise and training. I don't look at it that way. I have seen the most faltering and weak second-language learners break the hearts of hearers. It is by the power of the Holy Spirit that we control our voices.

The typical components of immediacy, volume, pitch, tone (timbre), rhythm, register, pause, space, separation, repetition, range, intensity, inflection, pace, tension, intention, schematization, emotion, reception, and energy are all, like word selection, a matter of the Holy Spirit's leadership.

I know that some who read this will mock this idea because many of these things are instinctual and almost autonomic. Yet, love for people and the contextual circumstances must control our voices when we preach. These oral components might flow naturally without intentional thought, but that is not ideal. The Holy Spirit should have control over every aspect of delivery.

In the same way I prepare outlines, words, phrases, and illustrations, I can also anticipate the spirit with which I must talk and associate sound with meaning in the articulation of words. What I mean by this is that love for people controls my choice of tone. If my motives are pure and godly, my volume will work in step with my content and not force a meaning contradiction during my delivery by my insensitivity to contextual variables.

Adjusting to the Context

One aspect of contextual application and delivery is the importance of cultural phenomena. These can be unexpected or culturally rhythmic, for example. If something has happened days, hours, or minutes before the teaching time, the speaker has a ready-made platform to communicate something, if it fits the textual message.

Because events are often locally defined, there are local archetypes present in the geography. Some examples might be the movie statue of Rocky in Philadelphia, hurricanes in New Orleans, a snowman in Quebec City, or a 'Hollywood' sign in Los Angeles. These are shared things in the consciousness of an audience that will work as platforms for message illustration.

Worldview archetypes or local phenomena are cultural framing devices that can be used to communicate. They may also have to be dismantled if they possess theology that is unbiblical. American culture advances pioneering individualism. This is not good if I am preaching 1 Corinthians 12 and the power of the body of Christ. My illustrations might have to challenge parts of the culture that are not always helpful. On the other hand, if I were asking for volunteers to do a mission trip to a closed access nation like Malaysia, I might appeal to the very quality that in another sermon I dismantle.

All spoken discourse is impromptu or extemporaneous in some way, even if the message is written out. There is a spontaneous generation of material that comes out at the moment of delivery. The speaker needs to be aware of the fact that spontaneously generated stories unfolding in the drama of the moment might not support the overall message from the text. It is possible to even undermine our own process of exposition by our spontaneity.

Carefully thought-out delivery usually helps control one's use of symbols and the existing conceptual frameworks. I can better confront ideological problems in the local context by using illustrations that are generated from the context itself, or at a minimum, are precisely applicable to the immediate audience.

A Genre of Application

In the same way that television shows might be divided into forms like westerns, soaps, news, or primetime dramas, we can classify illustration with similar titles. An image might work where a story will not. A hymn could be more appropriate than a country song. A proverb might illustrate something better than quoting a movie plot.

There are genres of application, and they all do not sound the same. Illustrative applications can take multiple forms. Some are narrative, some images, some comparisons, and some parables. When we consider application arrangement, there is an appropriateness to the illustration form that often goes unaddressed.

Illustration form should match the immediate context and not violate appropriate norms. For example, a shocking ending might be tame to a teenager but offensive to an elderly person. Age might indeed dictate delivery. Conversely, a farm metaphor could be tame in a farming community but vulgar in a city setting among middle aged families with small children.

Contextual factors should control discourse, and often the communal meaning clearly understood by everyone needs to be the overarching litmus test rather than a single person we pick out from the audience.

The assumptions and generalizations by which we function when constructing applications will, to some degree, determine whether we strike to the heart of the listener. The audience's ability to accept what we say in a speaking setting could be contingent on the collective experiential culture, something unseen but very real.

A speaker's ability and desire to concretize abstraction, measure societal feelings, perceptions, and other local factors could mean the difference between meaning-transfer or befuddlement. These are typically not taught in preaching classes, but they can seriously influence the approach to application.

If I properly understand the audience, it can help me know if I should use a healing image, a story about restoration, a prophetic confrontation, or an encouragement of some kind. These choices are only partially based on the meaning coming from the text I am preaching because I can illustrate the opposite and demonstrate by the negative why the textual idea is so important. For example, if I am preaching why we should have faith from Jesus' instruction in Matthew 19:26 about all things being possible, I could tell a story about someone who had no faith.

Knowing my audience helps me understand what they can receive or tolerate. Youth, for example, might be able to understand reverse story-telling or frequent shifts in point of view, but an adult could be confused. How I carefully pray through my illustration formulation comes because of love and care for the people to whom I am speaking and ultimately molding my delivery to the textual idea and then to the immediate context.

Questions for Engagement

1. What does it mean that all preaching is circumstantial to the immediate context?
2. In what ways might the communicator of the Bible make application relevant to the immediate context?
3. How is Bible application different from situationism and relativism, and how are localization and contextualization different from truth-altering?
4. How does immediacy and localized-application help overcome the realities of audience resistance? How might it anger listeners as well?
5. What are shared environmental factors?
6. What kind of expectations do listeners have when they hear people preach or talk about the Bible?
7. Why should Bible application usually follow audience expectations of order?
8. What does it mean that there are sensory issues in the immediate?
9. What is proxemics and how might this discipline teach us about Bible application?
10. What is the connection, or congruence, between the content of our message and *how* we say it?
11. When is it healthy to point to contextual phenomena and when is it not appropriate?

12 'Preaching' is a Missionary Term

Once upon a time some unsuspecting Jewish servants were sent out as a lynch mob to round up Jesus.[5] They had difficulty fulfilling their task, because in their words, "No one ever spoke like this man" (John 7:46).

Spoken word delivered in the power of the Spirit by the Master of metaphor Himself left the mobsters verbally captured. Their concluding words echo Christian consensus about Jesus and represent the communicative pinnacle to which most preachers of the gospel desire to rise, the point where one can say that the audience is awestruck and entranced by the message and God's use of the messenger.

The church leader searches for the door through which he might find approaches to preaching that are so captivating that his message rivets the listener's attention with its simplicity and wonder. Preachers want what Jesus had, namely, that "the common people heard him gladly" (Mark 12:37).

However, this simple attraction and engagement is difficult to find today. For this reason, I believe, is that most sermonic paradigms have not begun with oral assumptions about the nature of words, with the fluid and metaphoric nature of language, and the simplicity or uneducated audiences, but with text-based and text-centered orientations that are essentially framed in high levels of literacy and the reading/writing habits of preachers.

Preaching as Circumstantial Delivery

As was already stated, preaching is a relational action. It is a meeting of people with their God, a relationship in perpetual construction, a communicative exchange always in the present, always delivered, never prepared. It is founded upon communicative expectations and exchange between speaker and hearer. The preacher seizes an audience in a particular place at a particular moment, and the two experience an "encounter" in the immediate, definable here as a circumstantial embrace. The speaker anticipates an emotional meeting ahead of time by forecasting the listeners' cognitive, affective, and behavioral reactions (e.g., decision, consent, disagreement) to a given idea.

Contrast this with other forms of preaching engagement. Many preachers preach 'how-to' sermons: How to Save Your Marriage; Five Principles of Living from the Sermon on the Mount; God's Plan for Salvation. In one sense, these methods are engaging and even sequential, but they are 'how-to' and not forcibly 'now-to'.

When a preacher delivers a sermon on "Getting Your Relationship with God Right," there is an implicit tone of advice-giving. The preacher takes a stance or a tone where he is above his listeners. It also does not guarantee that the teaching experience will help the listener meet God or experience Him personally. It may be a grocery list of advice given from the stance of condescension.

By contrast, circumstantial delivery demands accessing the context. True engagement demands that the preacher recognize listener autonomy and the local context. Audiences are active during the listening process and practice prediction, deciphering, anticipation, interpretation, clarification, disagreement, rhetorical questioning, etc. So, while there may be advanced preparation for engagement by a speaker who wants to foster an encounter, the reality is that preaching is ultimately vulnerable to listener response. It is for this reason we must redefine 'preaching.'

The consequences of this idea of preaching encounter are several. First, sermon preparation changes significantly. The speaker is obligated not only to prepare his communicative idea, but also to prepare thinking to verbally take hold of people. Second, engagement changes delivery mechanics. The speaker recognizes that her delivery is not primarily concerned with communicating an idea but addresses ideological and emotional capture. It does this by taking advantage of auditors' listening habits. Third, the speaker's expectations are altered. S/he no longer hopes that the people will just understand the concept, but that God will use the message to build a relationship in the immediate. Engagement asks, "Are we meeting together—God, the listener, and I?"

In seeing preaching as a liaison rather than a monologue or a dialog, engagement introduces the aspect of relationship and emotion. The speaker seeks more than ideological or dialogical connection. He wants personal involvement with the listener. Consequently, the preacher alters her method and content to produce this rapport.

By highlighting emotional exchange, the focus shifts from an informationally oriented delivery to a relational one, from an explanation to an invitation, from a textual clarification to a hermeneutical encounter.

In this model, preaching is a missionary endeavor. It is not information exchange.

This reality also changes the way preaching should be taught. Pedagogy must be constructed around relationship. Historically, teaching preaching has often revolved around the organization of material. By contrast, engagement revolves around constructing encounters. Moreover, the ideological sense of the text, something traditionally viewed as paramount in expositional method, eventually gives way to the emotive export and practical relevance of biblical material. Information yields to motivation and obedience.

An engagement model recognizes that relational exchange is subject to communication factors that are not strictly based on the speaker or his words. Connection is largely a byproduct of certain listener-centered dynamics, namely: the correspondence of spoken words with listener experience, the association of ideas with the material world, the coping of the listener with ideological or emotional tension, the listener's anticipation of the resolution of plot, and the desire for disclosure.

When a preacher accepts the idea that communication is always circumstantial, the nature of the sermonic task changes. The sermon is no longer a bundle of prepared ideas shared with listeners but includes a series of verbal invitations to experience Christ and His word. The speaker then believes that the fundamental element in the delivery context is an audience that desires encounter. Consequently, the need for engagement starts to shape the sermon itself.

A preaching model that takes advantage of emerging, circumstantial material requires: first, a strong anticipation of listener expectations; second, speaker freedom to recreate the sermon at the moment of delivery; and third, skills to interpret and adapt to what is happening in all the different contexts within the setting. Preaching is no longer simply about the transmission of textual meaning; it is textual meaning communicated to people who are breathing right now and wondering about the roast in the oven. "Preaching the word" now involves using a scriptural idea to improve relationship with God by overcoming the environmental factors and distractions. The task of the preacher evolves into orchestrating a missionary connection, an engagement.

Preachers who see the sermon as circumstantial engagement view their task from the vantage point of the auditor and construct a message that has relational cadence. This means that speaking is framed not only to facilitate listener decoding, but also to position the listener to respond to interpersonal clues.

The preacher adopts a delivery mindset that involves interpreting a text or idea *to* someone, not simply *for* someone. A preacher who communicates *to* someone treats the listener like an individual who needs to meet God in the midst of whatever informational exchange takes place. The value is in the meeting, the engagement.

Reconceiving the Preaching Engagement

Preaching has historically been viewed as a stepped process of preparation-delivery-reception. Our theological vernacular unwittingly betrays the modern concept of the sermon. In the English-speaking West, sermons are prepared by means of textual analysis, summary, and a written outline. Preachers then deliver the product already prepared. Lastly, that delivered product is heard or received by a relatively passive listener.

I would like to redefine the "sermon," or "preaching" more exactly, as an inventive, creative process of speech delivered with precise verbal engagement in a delivery context that must cross cultures to reach the listener who does not know Jesus in a personal way. Engagement demands speaker sensitivity to both contextual variables and audience needs, particularly whether or not the person knows the Savior. This is missions. The speaker is not delivering a sermon, but engaging people in the immediate about a relationship with God.

It is my contention that all sermons are constructed the moment they are delivered, regardless of whether they are prepared in advance. This is because sermons are oral, not written. They are spoken by a preacher and heard by people.

Creating a sermon is an oral exercise, and any type of preparation, whether written or memorized, is only preparatory for delivery when the sermon is constructed (spoken). How we perceive sermon construction, that is the *model* of sermon development, directly affects how we construct illustration.

Traditionally, preaching is conceived and executed as a step-by-step exercise and not as a process model where there is constant revision to delivery ideas, all the way up to the completed spoken delivery. Because of the preacher's conditioning with respect to the model of sermon preparation, s/he arrives with a prepared outline or text and basically delivers what was conceived in advance with little change based on the immediate circumstances. S/he views the task as one of idea preparation-delivery. It should be, however, preparation-observation-revision-engagement-revision-engagement. This idea will directly influence how illustrations are constructed.

Often, a preacher's ability and openness in preparing for engagement or for reading the contextual setting at the very moment of delivery is minimal. From the moment a speaker decides s/he will deliver a sermon until the time s/he opens his/her mouth, s/he makes choices. Most often, these choices are about what s/he wants to say and how s/he wants to say it. Unfortunately, s/he is not trained to ask questions about engagement: What do I need to say or do so that these people cannot escape an encounter with God? Will the audience be able to decode this message and still pay attention? What environmental realities can I integrate into the message to make it more living and present?

Conservative evangelical preachers often conceive of preaching preparation as the management of sermonic material beforehand. However, engagement involves more than message management. It is an interactive process. It is not simply speaking. It is first assessing, synthesizing, and embracing the hearing community.

The type of theologizing required as a base for engagement springs from a proper view of the local context. In missiology, this idea is called contextualization. Contextualization is known by a myriad of other names: cultural adaptation, incarnating, localization, indigenization, inculturation, ethnotheologizing, etc.

Ultimately, to properly put an idea into an experiential or relational form that people can understand requires localization. The verbal utterance, whether figured or discursive, must obtain its shape from the pool of local signifiers. If I am not using speech that is common to the hearer, there will be loss of meaning.

In a similar way, the interpretation of the message by listeners is defined by the community's sense of language and how they might interpret words from within their cultural setting. This decoding is as complex as the tapestry of auditors. Everyone has their own age, gender, socioeconomic, and occupational filters.

Contrastingly, abstraction militates against engagement. A rarified idea communicated without local detail does not hit home, literally. The skill of abstraction seems to be standard in preaching settings. We have exported this western idea of communication around the world, and I have seen partially literate men in suits teaching illiterate church folk with theological categories without a shred of concretizing metaphor or story.

The ability to make an abstraction live is mastered by very few. The talent to take an objective idea and transform it into practical, life-changing delivery is even more rare.

The principle-to-example bridge, where people extrapolate concrete applications from propositions, is not traversed by many.

Usually, advanced stages of literacy increase a capacity for abstraction because thinking skills are refined and modified by a print-orientation. Printed literature changes the way people think.

People who are more accustomed to objectifying truth in a reading process have an easier time following a sermon sequenced by propositions. The reality is that the preacher is often among the most literate and adept at theological abstraction within the four walls of the church. Most hearers, by contrast, function out of experiences, images, and relationships.

The average person lives in a concrete world, one that only occasionally moves into the abstract. Consequently, the delivery philosophy of the educated preacher can create enormous distance between him/herself and the congregation because of a tendency to neglect the simplicity of the common person. Abstract principle tends to translate into a transcendent theology, when in fact most listeners want to meet God in the immanence of the moment.

The wise preacher who desires to engage people, intentionally works against a tendency to use only abstraction. A consistent immersion in print media can deform one's perception of those who have to listen to the message. Consequently, the speaker must regularly remind her/himself that messages become more relevant when they are tied to the physical world and the circumstantial environment.

Descriptive Problems with 'Preaching' as We Know It

Definitions of preaching should be descriptive of the act of engagement, not explanatory statements about the premeditated structuring or verbal arrangement of the words as seen in an inscribed, text form. Text-based definitions of the sermon proceed from certain views of literacy and fail to adequately recognize that preaching is encounter, exchange, and oral delivery.

Preaching is not written words, but it is spoken sound to people. It contains intonation, intention, hesitation, emotive subtlety, volume, pitch, accentuation, slurring, sequencing, and a host of other non-written elements.

Yet despite these realities, literacy controls how many people traditionally define preaching. The societal memory of the history of Christian preaching as a text-based methodology makes it difficult to describe preaching any other way. Churchgoing people assume that delivering a sermon is explaining meanings discovered through textual/exegetical method.

As I previously stated, I assume that preaching is the delivery of a message based on the biblical text. I also assume that literacy has destroyed the unique relational aspects of purer orality in the immediate.

The ever-present historical memory of text-oriented Christianity imposes an extraordinary influence on preaching form. Since theologians have employed text-based deductive methods for two thousand years, preaching definitions are sometimes unconsciously linked to certain forms of organizationally defined delivery, namely, a thirty-minute discourse with several points.

To take this idea even further, the vocabulary that defines preaching has evolved around word arrangement and structures of logic. Sermons are often defined as being inductive, deductive, narrative, expository, or doctrinal.

It is entirely possible to invent other preaching categories that are not based in sermonic structure itself but in circumstantial factors. I could see asking questions like this: Is the preaching verbally interactive preaching, networked/multi-speaker preaching, contextually nuanced preaching, figured-participatory preaching, audience-ignored preaching, or listener-response-generated preaching?

Grammatically speaking, the word "preach" is a verb, denoting an oral action. Preaching should not be defined by the logical arrangement the words display when they are written down before or after the fact. Jesus often spoke without propositions, and the nature of His preaching was not always discursive. His narrative artistry is often a figurative and illustrative model of oral, sermonic discourse usually in a narrative form.

Redefining 'Preaching'

Although I have consented to use the term 'preaching' in its vernacular sense of a man who delivers 30 minutes of instruction to saved people, this is clearly not the biblical definition. Biblical preaching is connecting Christ to unbelieving audiences.

Beyond this, it attempts an experiential capture of ideas through the ear and addresses immediate need in the *hEAR*-and-now. Biblically speaking, it is certainly not usually exegesis or prepared delivery. This habit is a teaching habit, but it does not fit the biblical use of the Greek words for preaching used in the New Testament,

Preaching in the New Testament seems to attempt a connection of people with their God. It is certainly not a how-to endeavor. It is much more a task of showing hearers how the living God connects with their immediate need. This is a very different 'how-to' paradigm.

In contrasting local church methods in America with the typical preaching model of the New Testament, we seem to teach communicators how to instruct believers. Often lost people present in our congregations are not part of our equation. Beyond this, we preach without localization. In other words, we often fail to connect to the immediate context of the hearers, that is, where they live from day to day.

Despite this method, we are quite biblical in our approach to discipleship. Jesus said in Matthew 28 to make disciples of all ethnic groups by teaching them to observe all things that He commanded. What is done on Sunday morning is the disciple-making process. It is not really preaching, however; at least technically.

'

Preaching' is a Missionary Word

In the New Testament, the word 'preaching' is almost never used to describe discipleship oratory within the four walls of a building. It is missionary proclamation to lost people. The audience is generally a group of people who have not been introduced to the Savior.

The ramifications of this idea are immense. What preachers do every Sunday is not biblical preaching, unless of course their audiences are composed of people who do not know Jesus. They may be doing sound biblical teaching, but according to the biblical witness, it is not really 'preaching.'

What seminaries call 'Preaching 101,' where professors do expositional training in Theology Departments, is vital; however, it does not align with the center of the meaning of the term 'preaching' as we read the word in the New Testament. Evangelical preaching today does not reflect Jesus' proclamation model. Jesus would not have studied in a Theology Department (where most preaching training takes place) to prepare for His ministry. He would have refused to do that. It would have been against His theological convictions.

Having said this, were we to change our approach to engaging our world, preaching departments would have to be under the Missions faculties in the academy. The results would be dynamic. Our proclamation model would approximate that of John the Baptist, Jesus, Stephen, or Paul. The audience would be the uninitiated. There would be far more mass conversions, and the electricity would once again flow into gospel meetings.

Mind you, this idea is not a commentary on our exegetical method, a model indisputable and vital to church life. However, it is an indictment on our use of the term 'preaching' for what we do on Sunday mornings.

A very elementary study of New Testament words translated into English as 'preaching' (*kērussō, kērugma, euaggelizō, diaggellō, prokērussō, laleō, kataggellō, dialegomai, logos, akoē, plēroō*) shows there to be an audience very much *unlike* our own. We will detail this out in the appendix. When the apostles and biblical figures preached, they witnessed. They were not doing book studies and exposition to a group of individuals who already knew our Lord.

Within the evangelical church, many young men want to be 'preacher boys.' For them, this means teaching God's people each Sunday using expository method. Unfortunately for them, they need to be properly directed. If God has called them to preach, they ought to be missionaries, whether it be here in America in the local church or overseas doing pioneering.

Imagine what Christianity would look like if preaching was viewed the biblical way, as a missionary engagement endeavor. We could positively alter our growth plateau in one generation. We would also be training *all* our people to do preaching in the world and not just training them to listen to the professional 'preacher' within the confines of a church building.

Additionally, there would be such a need to learn to apply the scriptures, people would be thirsty for ways to make the word of God relevant with images and stories. This, however, is not the case.

By some strange twist of fate, we have come to use the term evangelism almost exclusively to describe witnessing to lost people, and we have reserved the term 'preaching' to describe what ministers do on Sundays. This is highly unfortunate. It was not the way of our Lord. He came preaching (Matt. 4:17).

Jesus' message is still the same; He tells His church to "preach the gospel to every creature" (Mark 16:15). 'Preaching' was and remains a missionary term.

Questions for Engagement

1. How might our communication of the Bible to lost people be more captivating?
2. How is circumstantial delivery on the one hand a missionary endeavor and on the other hand different from 'how-to' sermons?
3. What is the practical side of circumstantial engagement?
4. In what way is all Bible teaching prepared at the very moment of speaking?
5. What are some of the problems with the definition of the term 'preaching' as we know it?
6. How does our definition of the term 'preaching' affect the preaching *form*?
7. What does the New Testament usage of words teach us about 1st century 'preaching'?

13   The Parable and the Cultural Divide

Not only was Jesus a missionary preacher, someone who practiced engagement with the unlikely person on the street, but he also had an accompanying style to fit his method. He preached in parables.

When someone says the word 'parable,' a smile comes to the face of the listeners. Parables are short, fun, and give a twist to life, or so we think.

Parables are darker than most people know and come out of the wisdom literature of Jewish tradition. Parables are the aphoristic descendants of the proverbs, and in the Greek translation of the Old Testament, the Hebrew word 'proverb' is usually translated by the Greek word for 'parable.'

The Polarizing Effect

One purpose of the New Testament parable is to help people navigate through spiritual choices. It places listeners into categories and polarizes both people and their options.

This polarizing effect is not entertainment, nor is it gentle. "Two men went up to the temple to pray. One prayed like this, the other like this. Which one do you resemble?"

In studying parables and parable form and delivery for much of my adult life, I have found that the essential nature of parables can be summed up into one verb: polarizing. Parables separate.

This simple fact can be almost universally attributed to all of Jesus' parables, even the image parables. There is always an implicit creation of experiential categories in Jesus' teaching.

When a listener hears a parable, the identification quality of the drawing-in almost inevitably leads to a conclusion of comparison: "Am I like this?"

Often, parables create negative and positive examples. At times, as in the case of the Parable of the Talents, there is a 'good, better, best' aspect. However, this multi-graded aspect to the conclusion is very rare. Even in the Parable of the Sower, while there are four types of soils, there is only one suitable soil-listener.

The implication is that most people fail to produce fruit. Some fail because of their love for riches or their shallow theology. Jesus did not coddle the crowd. In a sense, 3/4s of the audience failed to receive the seed. Only one type of soil produced fruit.

Here's a simple little parable one of my students made up about himself to illustrate Genesis 3:10. The guilting-power correlates closely with the text he wished to illustrate. It is one of several that I will share throughout the remainder of this book.

Cultural Distance

So, if Jesus polarized His audiences, how are we to understand the crowd dynamic? People loved to follow Him. Why would they follow a man that was divisive, someone who

And he said, "I heard the sound of you in the garden, and I was afraid, because I was naked, and I hid myself."
Genesis 3:10

Tovone was a student at Bible School. He loved his classes and enjoyed studying. One day he stepped out of the dormitory, but when he spotted his professor, he ran back into the dorm because he had not completed the application workbook exercises for the week. He hid himself.

Tovone Onowenerhi

at times hurt their feelings? He was someone who might even have been accused of inflaming people with separatism. He definitely was someone who showed them how far they were from the truth.

In addition to these realities, there is the question of how He did it. Most preachers would like to know.

How did He overcome cultural distance and drive a knife down the middle, both at the same time? How did He positively bridge the gap between common ignorance and spiritual realities, and simultaneously manage to bifurcate the sheep from the goats?

Of fundamental importance is how He overcame communication difficulties. The actual results of what happens to the crowd when parables are used seem to be contained in the answer to this first question of overcoming cultural distance.

Every preaching venue is fraught with cultural distance. There are age differences, ethnic distinctions, economic gaps, gender divisions, political sides, and endless variations of every type known to the most skilled anthropologist. When someone is done naming them, just wait a few days and there will be new differences we don't yet know about.

Globalization has made homogeneity a thing of the past, and meaning transfer is even more of a struggle for the communicator than it used to be. Multiculturalism is everywhere, and wherever we turn, it's hard to find an audience where people look or speak the same.

Even if we have an apparent unified collection of people, say all middle-aged men, the differences among them could be remarkable. Some might be divorced, some poor, some uneducated, some Hispanic, some white, some Black, some unemployed, and on, and on, and on.

Is there a solution to this reality? Is there a way across the vast expanse and endless variety of hearers? Is there a way to speak universally to everyone? The answer lies with Jesus.

There is a certain paradoxical reality in Jesus' preaching that many do not want to accept. The medium is almost universal and appeals across age, gender, and socio-economic borders. However, the result is not gentle.

Parables bridge people to spiritual truth through common life experience. People travel, eat, save money, raise difficult children, put furniture in their house, work, etc. When a story develops, it draws the listener in through the common ground of his or her own experience.

Unfortunately, the past is fraught with pain and mistakes. People know this. Consequently, when we as speakers create illustrations, they issue a call that goes out to the ear, which precisely and intentionally resonates with the audience's experience. There is also considerable pain there. Ultimately, the collective exchange returns to sin and its results, but hopefully the speaker offers a solution.

This sin problem is universal. It is verified by common experience and nature itself. The internal law that God has written on human hearts confirms categorically that man is without excuse (Rom. 1:20).

This universal plight is one of the greatest platforms for inviting people to meet the Savior. Hearers already know their immense quandary. They simply need to be reminded about it. Not simply to be reminded about the burden under which they have lived for the duration of their lives, but they need to be pointed to the solutions right in front of them.

The practice of finding common ground narrows the cultural distance between the speaker and listener considerably. It also provides substance to the illustrative process.

Many preachers loath the illustration-invention part of sermonic development and view it as a Grand Canyon, like an analogy-chasm, which is nearly impossible to span. However, this is very far from the truth. There are thousands and even an unlimited quantity of life details that are useful for illuminating the Word of God. The trick is in finding the ones that work.

When the illustrator finds the analogy that fits the meaning of the text and is also within the experience of the listener, the speaker has struck gold. He has found the truth of God reinforced by human experience. It is reminiscent of Job 28 where Job himself analogizes from creation about the wisdom seeker who strikes it rich in the gold mine of the Fear of the Lord.

Jesus was a Cross-Cultural Communicator

The idea that preaching is a cross-cultural endeavor should be obvious. It should also be obvious that God's culture is one of holiness and glory, while ours is one of sin and alienation. However, for the sake of laying a proper foundation for a new preaching paradigm, let's just rehearse again the contextual makeup of the sermonic exchange.

The preacher is usually a highly educated person. S/he is brought into the church from somewhere else through a job-search process. S/he is screened by a team to establish theology and credentials.

Studying 10 hours each week on a sermon and digging into the contextual elements of the New Testament background, hopefully that seeker can communicate a culturally relevant message. S/he translates the 1st century culture into a modern one, which is largely foreign to the blue-collar, work-a-day audience. Finally, the preacher attempts to make those ideas relevant to common, sleep-deprived folk who are preeminently distracted by a one-year-old who was up all night with teething pain.

The Sunday morning cultural distances are enormous. The preacher is a schooled historian, managing first century Levantine details. His marriage is probably stable, unlike his people. Her children are likely not sowing wild oats, keeping her up at night.

To demonstrate the cultural enormity even more, just think about how many communication problems you have with your spouse, provided you are married. Even if you are not, take your closest friend or colleague for this example. Is there communicative distance?

In the field of communication, this speaking/hearing/interpretation process is called by many names. It involves translation theory, reception theory, filtering, and a host of other complex elements, known by an equal number of complex labels.

When someone communicates, he or she encodes. The listener decodes. There is constant encoding and decoding going on in all communication.

To pretend that someone must be of another ethnicity in order for there to be cross-cultural communication is ridiculous. Every communication encounter is, in a sense, cross-cultural, and there is a meaning-mountain to climb. It is just a question of altitude.

Can you inspire your own wife? Can you motivate your child to clean his or her room? Can you convince your friend to come over and leave his family to watch a ballgame? This process of connection is the challenge of engagement.

The preacher's task is immense. If we fail to motivate and communicate with those within our closest circle, how can we expect to inspire the multi-ethnic audiences and age divided tapestry of a globalized society?

I would ask this critical question: How can the preacher reach the iPhone-owning teen with an unlimited data plan while at the same time capturing the attention of the 70-year-old widow-woman who can't make ends meet because she no longer gets her husband's pension or adequate health-care?

The answer is in the life of Jesus. He demonstrated a method of reaching everyone, especially the common person. After all, the common folk heard Him gladly (Mark 12:37).

Jesus and Paul would probably be grieved if we interviewed them about 20th century pastoral search committees and pulpit protocol. The Savior and the apostle would likely berate us for our lack of power as well as our fetish for oratory or showmanship. Frankly, our values and actions don't reflect New Testament behavior, particularly 'workplace' training for church leaders.

Yet, here is the picture that I have of Jesus. It provides me with the model of illustration I detail in the rest of the book.

Jesus and His Communication Practice

Behold the God-man, descended from the presence of the Father. He tells the story of a far-off land and value system of a coming kingdom. He ushers people up to spiritual realms they have not experienced before. He heals them of their sicknesses. He takes them on journey after journey, giving them image after image.

He knows that holiness is foreign to the sinful listeners, but also knows that the sinner has heard the Father's common grace and General Revelation a thousand times before by personal experience. Jesus knows that those who believe Him will become culturally distanced from their own families.

He creates alien subjects in an occupied land currently subject to some extent, at least, to an evil dictator called the Devil. He tells of heaven, the place from which He came and enraptures people with stories of how this current world teaches us about the one to come.

He brings the King of a far-off land, close to home. He prophesies that as the messenger of God, He will die delivering this message.

He's rejected by His own because they know He is not like them. He does not resemble the Jew of Nazareth and does not have the accent of those from Jerusalem.

Strangely, He is accepted by the lowly Galileans, Samaritans, centurions, lepers, demonized, and health-strapped individuals from all sectors of the socio-economic ladder.

He reminds them that the King is coming, while simultaneously maintaining relational vulnerability. He calls people to a commitment and to a foreign way of life, to follow a God who they thought they knew. He gives them a positive message in a suffering world.

He functions above the politically conflictual game board of polytheistic Rome but does not cave to the religious traditions of legalistic Judaism.

In all this, His way of the heart, His way of relationship, His way of love and light is about as culturally distant as holiness is from sin.

As a messenger, He is the model of cross-cultural communication, living in a real world, with a real God, showing that the apparent physical one is really the virtual, parallel universe to His eternal kingdom.

In all this, He does not hesitate to use that fallen world for illustrative purposes. He repeatedly draws from the common pool of human experience to show people that they have already heard the call of God in their lives.

Show Me Your Transcript

In contrast to Jesus, who was the God-Come-To-Earth communicator, we look for church leaders who are quite a bit more sophisticated. When most of us go looking for a pastor, that pastoral search team does not ask, "Can you accommodate the simple people of our church just as Jesus contextualized to the simple people of Galilee?" Instead, we ask, "Show me your transcript."

The risk for churches in formulating pulpit committees should be pretty evident: they are not trained to probe for connection skills of candidates. For effectiveness, those committees might try to employ teaching assessment methods that examine potential candidates' abilities in crossing common barriers of communication. The reason for this is critical.

Most homiletics course sequences that trained potential pastors should have specialized in Jesus' methods, but they did not. While schooling students in language-attentiveness and faithfulness to the text, extensive training in spoken engagement often gets lost. When preachers leave seminary, their preaching boat is now floating on a vast sea of congregational experience.

While exegetical skill is a first-order practice and foundational to biblical understanding, it is only the first step in a sermonic process. Were a preacher to spend extensive preparation time in exegesis, it would be like pouring the cement foundation for a 3000 square foot house without putting up the walls and roof.

Because schools stop short in their ministerial training, the results are not Jesus-like. Teachers of preaching must specialize in exegesis, but it is critical to dwell on effective speech delivery and audience reception. This is the love component.

Many professionally trained preachers expect their congregants to live in the cement basement of a homiletical house without walls and roof because of a sermonic failure to make the Word of God resemble the beauty and glory that even the unbeliever knows to be there.

We must create a new vision, almost a self-imposed one, where our supreme goal as communicators of the word of God is to replicate the connection vibrance of Jesus Himself. After all, He said we would do greater things than He did (Jn. 14:12).

Questions for Engagement

1. How do parables help people navigate spiritual choices?
2. What does it mean that there is 'cultural distance' between speaker and listener?
3. How might past realities of sinful experiences among audience members work to help the preacher bring listeners into a healthy connection with God?
4. What are some of the social realities that create cultural distance between speaker and listener in our modern contexts?
5. How did Jesus model cross-cultural communication as the living Word of God?

Part Three: The Nine Bridges of Bible Application

14   Illustrating Relationships

As we begin to take a closer look at each of the illustration bridges, I will begin each of the next nine chapters with a text and use it as a springboard to illustrate the core components of what I want to say in the chapter. You, the reader, should closely read these examples and try to determine what is happening in the passage.

Attempt to focus your observation skills on the core idea highlighted in the chapter title. In this first passage, attempt to find relational observations and implications. What relationships connections between people do you see, and what are some of the implications of those observations? After you do this, I will then unpack the example with observations of my own.

> ### Acts 13:1-3
>
> Now there were in the church at Antioch prophets and teachers, Barnabas, Simeon who was called Niger, Lucius of Cyrene, Manaen a lifelong friend of Herod the tetrarch, and Saul. While they were worshiping the Lord and fasting, the Holy Spirit said, "Set apart for me Barnabas and Saul for the work to which I have called them." Then after fasting and praying they laid their hands on them and sent them off.

In illustrating what is going on in this passage, we must focus on the fact that the Holy Spirit speaks, and it changes all the relationships. God commands a relationship change.

The prayer group gets broken up in a good way. The five men were seeking the face of God, but the relational changes were disruptive. There was unity in the group, but that good unity resulted in a send-off of two members. Imagine the church's adjustment when they lost two leaders.

When there is leadership loss, the church experiences a recoil. What does recoil look like today in church? What can the church learn from these leaders at Antioch? What parallels can we find in our contemporary culture?

In music, if a band loses two members, people wonder if they will stay together. If a volleyball player suffers an injury, the cost is great because there are just not that many players. If a college athlete becomes ineligible because of academic course failures, how does that affect the team, the fans, ticket sales, or filling stadium seats?

Relationships are fundamental to the biblical text, and they become a fruitful field of application because people know intimately what it means to live that human connection or the loss of relationship. Consequently, we need to consider what kinds of relationships exist in any given biblical text and how we can properly encourage people to live a biblical lifestyle by drawing constructive connections from the pages of scripture to life.

Biblical application and illustration are often about relationships, both with God and men. The question for the teacher of the Bible is how can we build connections through our delivery?

God loves people. Do we? Not only do we need to be in His presence, but the focus of biblical passages often addresses how we engage others. This encounter is often the meat of scriptural instruction.

In teaching the Bible, we examine what God is doing, particularly noting relational calling or change in response to the work of God. This involves illustrating how people get along, how they respond to Divine directives, or how collectively they are involved in spiritual work.

Relationships are directional and have basic qualities about them. The biblical text reveals the reciprocal nature of relationships and how we need to develop or dissolve them. It also encourages movement *toward* or *away* from people.

We might say that human interaction can fall under two main categories. It is either under construction or being dissolved/disrupted. Within these two poles of constructive improvement or disruptive breakdown, there are any number of feelings and behaviors that are communicated to us when we read the text.

Consider this passage and how it might be illustrated or applied. Think about whether you are looking at this verse from God's, Saul's, Barnabas', or the prayer-group's perspective. We might even ask what this looks like from the vantage point of the whole church at Antioch?

Types of Relational Realities or Relational Change

Without making this too complex, when applying the Bible, it is important to point out relational realities or change. If there is change, it typically falls within one of three types of alteration.

1. Construction and improvement/healing
2. Faithful maintenance
3. Disruption or avoidance

Are relationships moving in a positive direction or simply being maintained? On the negative side, sometimes relationships need to be cut off or severed.

Most often, relationships should be steady, something we maintain in a faithful way. However, there are moments when the speaker needs to remind the listeners to construct something that does not exist, improve an existing relationship, or discontinue/avoid a bad relationship.

Let's look at the behavioral application sequence within the context of a verse of scripture. Whenever we talk about behavioral change, we must address adoption, continuance, discontinuance, or deterrence, like illustrating moral change, an idea we will discuss later. Consider this verse. How might we apply the previous principles in a clarifying way to the hearer?

> I commend to you our sister Phoebe, a servant of the church at Cenchreae, that you may welcome her in the Lord in a way worthy of the saints and help her in whatever she may need from you, for she has been a patron of many and of myself as well (Rom. 16:1-2).

The passage is really one of relationship construction. Phoebe was perhaps unknown to the church in Rome. They were being asked to go overboard to assist her. How do we construct a new relationship from scratch? In applying this, the text implies that she was faithful and a remarkable servant on a broad scale. Assistance here needs to be answered in kind, despite not having any real obligation to this unknown woman.

Ultimately, the application is that faithful Christians should be helped in extraordinary ways. There is some kind of material involvement that is expected from the Roman church toward her, either in her spiritual work or to take care of her physical needs. This expectation needs to happen without any prior sense of obligation.

Here's another example. In the following verse, the expositional preacher who wants to determine the application involving how to define, improve, or discontinue a relationship must unravel the relational movement implicit in the words.

> ...but Jesus said to him, "Judas, would you betray the Son of Man with a kiss?" Luke 22:48.

Looking at the relational movement in this verse, we can see that Judas is leveraging his intimacy to identify Jesus in the darkness of the night to the soldiers by the cultural kiss of friendship. However, he turns Jesus over to those that hate Him. Judas does this for money. He destroys the relationship with a kiss of hypocrisy motivated by a bribe.

Application of this passage might look something like this. When we are in Christian ministry, regardless of whether we are vocational, full time, or volunteer workers, there will occasionally be people who will betray us in the most cruel and vicious ways. They kiss us on one cheek and then stab us in the back. Surprisingly, even we ourselves sometimes betray the Savior for personal advancement and sell out, so to speak, for personal gain. Haven't we all chosen the road of financial improvement over identification with Christ and its accompanying persecution?

Relational illustrations are typically overt and explicit, but sometimes they are implicit and not clear. Here is a text which is obvious: "Alexander the coppersmith did me great harm; the Lord will repay him according to his deeds. Beware of him yourself, for he strongly opposed our message" (2 Tim. 4:14-15). It is not hard to find an application from this. At a minimum, we can say that God desires us to stay away from people who are spiritually harmful. We might go so far as to say that we should avoid people who criticize the preacher.

When a passage is implicit, however, the expositor must dig for the meaning. Romans 16:7 says this in the King James version: "Salute Andronicus and Junia, my kinsmen, and my fellow prisoners, who are of note among the apostles." Were Andronicus and Junia actually apostles, as in some translations? Or were they 'among' the apostles? Some translations bring this into English as a phrase that implies that they were well known 'to' the apostles. "Greet Andronicus and Junia, my kinsmen and my fellow prisoners. They are well known to the apostles…" (ESV). The relationships in the text change. If they were well known 'as' apostles, then a woman was an apostle. There are serious church polity implications with this translation.

To apply this passage, one must nail down the grammar and explain the relationships that come out of that grammar. It makes an enormous difference whether the text is saying that a woman was an apostle or if she was known to the apostles. The inferences for Egalitarianism and Complementarianism are enormous.

Relational Direction

As stated above, relationships have movement. They are either improving, maintaining, or breaking up. We can encourage or discourage any of these three approaches, but before we find illustrations, we must determine *relational direction*.

Relational direction is a physical or metaphorical movement. It can be people moving in the right direction as concerns their relationships or in an improper direction.

Faithful relationships need to be maintained, even strengthened. "And Jonathan made David swear again by his love for him, for he loved him as he loved his own soul" (1 Sam. 20:17). When we are illustrating verses like this, we find parallels where good friends continue to establish remarkably strong ties, even though the relationship is healthy. To do this, we might show how a couple in a strong marriage recommits to one another in the face of a cancer battle by one spouse.

In a discontinuance scenario, the Bible illustrates the dangers of spiritually unhealthy connections. Take this verse describing Solomon's spiritual stability within his home: "For when Solomon was old his wives turned away his heart after other gods, and his heart was not wholly true to the LORD his God, as was the heart of David his father" (1 Kings 11:4). The export is clear; marriage can destroy a vibrant, healthy spiritual life.

To illustrate this further, I could, when the context is right, recount people in my past, who as single people, enjoyed a wonderful spiritual communion with God. Upon marrying a marginal Christian or one moving away from God, the marriage did not improve the person's piety, but crushed whatever intimacy they once had with the Savior.

Relational Health

Understanding how to illustrate relationships and direction in human interaction is about understanding health. We want people to be relationally healthy.

One way to identify the relational focus of an illustration is to isolate not just the health or inadvisability of a relationship, but beyond this, we locate the precise malfunction or clear reason for relational health. In 1 Kings 11:8-16, King Rehoboam is faced with creating an identity for his new monarchy. He has a public relations issue of how he should market himself and his cabinet. Unfortunately, he gathered around himself bad counselors, who gave him such bad advice that it contributed to the demise of his kingdom. There are several components here that deserve a closer look.

In illustrating this story when teaching the Bible, the illustrative crux of the directional movement should be for radical discontinuance. Stop getting advice from bad counselors. There are other specifics here that lend themselves to amazing illustrations.

He had the *ability to choose* his entourage. He had the *authority to choose* his friends, and he chose poorly. Beyond the authority of friend selection, he also had the

---

Relational Improvement

But Jesus said, "Someone touched me, for I perceive that power has gone out from me."
Luke 8:46

This story tells us that the moment a woman touched Jesus' garment, He turned around and recognized that someone touched Him. He pretended not to know who touched Him. This is very similar to when my father recounted to me that he could always tell which child was touching him by the feeling of their hand. Imagine a father saying, "Who is touching me? I don't know who you are?" In the same way a father is able to tell which child is touching him, Jesus recognizes His child when they reach for Him. He is our father and He addresses us as His children. We all have our own way to reach out to God in our distress. He knows who we are. He reassures us of our relationship to Him: "Daughter, your faith has made you whole."

Noah Flach

ability to discount their counsel. He did not do this either. On top of this, *he did not take time* for spiritual reflection. *Childhood bonds were also stronger* than the preferred choice to take a difficult stand for grace and love against his peers. He *refused to make the unpopular* move to side with the older generation.

This type of careful analysis must be done to create parallel illustration or application. In rehearsing how you can illustrate this, it would be good to rehearse historically in the preacher's experience if there was a time when the speaker him/herself had the ability or authority to discount bad counsel or peer-to-peer advice for an unpopular siding with gray heads.

The universal abstraction is quite simple: Don't listen to bad advice from young peers who have no experience. We can all find illustrations from the past when we went on the recommendation of someone who counseled us to take our car to the wrong mechanic or eat at the wrong restaurant. However, a biblical illustration for this story is much more significant; it involves appointing a cabinet that produces a bad foundation for the destruction of an entire kingdom.

So, to picture this for an audience, we must move beyond the universal to the details of the story. There are issues of ability, age, authority, complicity, and even nepotism of sorts.

Following someone's advice is exactly that: following. In other words, this relational model is clearly directional. In this story, Rehoboam yields and does not discontinue the relationship. The illustrator must make this crystal clear.

Parallel to this implied counsel to discontinue listening to people who function by threat and oppression, we are taught through negative conduct, that is, the choice to not heed the advice of the elderly. We *should* build relationships with older men and women, especially when they speak grace and love in a formal advice-giving mode.

In summary, relational movement and choices are critical in illustration because we constantly mix with all kinds of people from day to day. Audiences need to be solidly counseled on how to draw near or exit from people around them.

Relationship illustrations should be drawn out in clear, undeniable detail. When we make sermonic applications to high schoolers in the locker room, people that just got their first jobs, teenagers on dates, or students in the band, suddenly we are in the realm of life-changing choices that need to be driven home with clear narrative force. There is less room for generalization and ambiguity. Someone's career may literally be riding on the clarity or ambiguity of our story.

In any biblical text, there are a host of visible relational factors and existing personal connections. It may involve talking, arguing, discussing, convincing, or a host of positive interactions. Relationships might imply respect or disrespect, learning or power. All human connections within the scriptures become models for some kind of instruction.

Relational Continuance

The Lord is my shepherd; there is nothing I lack.
He leads me along the right paths for His name's sake.
Psalms 23:1, 3

Have you ever been in the car with someone, and you were headed to a particular destination using a GPS system? Did the GPS System ever lead you to a destination that you were not planning to go to or did the driver ever veer off the path that was set by the GPS System? I know that this has been true in my life in multiple instances where I did not want to go the route that was pre-planned by the GPS either due to feelings or personal preference. It is helpful to know that you and I have a Shepherd of our souls that has perfect intention and that never takes a wrong route. He is never lost or confused about where He should go or lead the sheep of His pasture. Therefore, you and I can know that we will have everything we need because we have a Good Shepherd who cares for our souls.

Daniel Halek

Questions for Engagement

1. What does it mean that relationships are directional, and how does this idea help us in Bible application?
2. What does it mean that relationships are undergoing constructive improvement or disruptive breakdown?
3. If the ideas of constructing, improving, or discontinuing relationships are three helpful categories, how might you use them in your application process?

15 Illustrating Through Parallel Emotion

For this chapter's illustration, consider and list out the emotions you perceive in this passage, then read down the ensuing discussion. Try to encapsulate the feelings in different components of the audience, regardless of the fact if they are initiated and uninitiated, saved and lost, young and old. How might differing individuals in different parts of the listenership feel about these verses?

> **Romans 3:23-24**
>
> **For all have sinned and fall short of the glory of God, and are justified by his grace as a gift, through the redemption that is in Christ Jesus.**

Illustrating the emotive force of an idea is often more productive toward God's aim of making someone Christlike than the logical or argumentative value of the text or simply appealing to the mind. This may be hard to accept in a scientific culture, but an evaluation of the scriptural content, the audience, and the objectives of the speaker will determine the suitability of communicating emotion to change hearts.

Texts have emotions. Not only does the reader feel things, but often those emotions are explicitly stated in the text. "Even with me the LORD was angry on your account and said, 'You also shall not go in there'" (Deut. 1:37). In this passage, the authority in Moses' life was God, and He was hot with wrath.

Frequently the text plainly communicates feelings and emotion. Consider the context of the following verse. "So that the people could not distinguish the sound of the joyful shout from the sound of the people's weeping, for the people shouted with a great shout, and the sound was heard far away" (Ezra 3:13). Old men who had seen and known Solomon's Temple 70 years earlier had a strong reaction upon the laying down of foundation stones for the Second Temple, the one constructed under the leadership of Nehemiah. People could not tell if the tears were tears of sorrow or joy.

This text is about remembering the past. So, in finding illustrations for reliving an old spiritual experience, the association of joy and elation is an easy parallel to correlate for us or for others.

For example, if/when we return to the place where we experienced Christ for the first time, or the place where we constructed a spiritual legacy, the natural emotion is joy, but weeping might be right below the surface. The application from the text to contemporary life is clear.

Sometimes geography is sacred and carries with it memories or innate emotions. For some it is the place where they won a sports championship, where mom or dad were in an accident, where they played as a child, or the house in which they lived growing up. Emotions are attached to everything. The preacher must make note of this.

We move from emotions in the text to parallel emotions in the lives of the listeners. We do this by capturing the feelings associated with some part of the text.

In 1 Samuel 13, Saul is confronted with 30,000 chariots and additional ground forces. The obvious message is fear and scrabbling in the face of insurmountable odds. The Bible illustrator can associate the feelings of fear with any number of current circumstances that might serve as solid illustrative parallels: a cancer diagnosis, the prospect of enrolling a child in a school with a bad reputation where s/he will be surrounded by lost peers, food insecurity for the homeless person, bills on every side for an unemployed father, etc.

Often, a passage may not say that the people were joyful or fearful, but the implications are clear. Consider this verse: "Therefore my people go into exile for lack of knowledge; their honored men go hungry, and their multitude is parched with thirst" (Is. 5:13). The Bible teacher must address willful ignorance and bad choices that result from

---

Emotion: Fear

There is no fear in love, but perfect love casts out fear. For fear has to do with punishment, and whoever fears has not been perfected in love.
1 John 4:18

A young girl stole some money that her father had left on the kitchen counter. After a couple of days passed, her father noticed some of his change was gone and asked his daughter if she had seen it. The little girl lied and said she was not sure. The girl was too terrified to confess her failure to her father and she hid. Though she was afraid of her father, she began to consider his love for her and her love for her father. She came out of hiding, ran to her father, and confessed. With love, her father responded, "I know you stole it." Hugging her, he said, "Thank you for your honesty. Don't do it again." The fear was gone, and the girl felt free.

Taryn Pfeifer

---

becoming a refugee. There are clear shortages as a result of exile. The verse is filled with emotion, especially considering the context. "They have lyre and harp, tambourine and flute and wine at their feasts, but they do not regard the deeds of the LORD, or see the work of his hands" (Is. 5:12).

Dealing with More than One Emotion

In the text-box passage at the beginning of this chapter, there is a complex of feelings, even opposite emotions in the same verses. How are we to address this?

In preaching about justification by grace through faith, one might have to treat both judgment and optimism. Read Romans 3:23-24 again. "For all have sinned and fall short of the glory of God, and are justified by his grace as a gift, through the redemption that is in Christ Jesus." There are both disappointment and restoration in the same verse.

How are we to preach this? We must consider the emotions as they progress from a textual standpoint. Sin and its consequences bring dread, that is, falling short of God's glory with its implicit expectations.

An unbeliever or someone not yet justified will sense God's disappointment and wrath. We create illustrations and applications appropriate to that part of the verse. Yet, there is more.

In New Covenant living, there is imputed righteousness by faith. It is gifted holiness by Jesus' redemption. The exported feelings involve undeserved forgiveness, relational repair, and being a recipient of an unlikely gift.

The preacher can move from these ideas of disappointment and forgiveness to find correlative application and illustration. The reader should attentively look over the list of emotions below to identify what else is implicit in these verses—shame, pain, surprise, satisfaction, relief, etc.

It may sound strange, but nearly all thoughts carry some emotion. When a Bible text simply describes an event or an image, there will likely be feelings attached to the language that will be conveyed to both the speaker and the listener. Even phrases that are totally objective descriptions do export feelings to the senses. If the Bible says, "...and before the throne there was as it were a sea of glass, like crystal," there is a sense that the text is communicating calm tranquility and immense beauty (Rev. 4:6)

Most passages export more than one emotion. As you consider illustrating and applying biblical passages, it is key to note two aspects of this discipline: 1) core emotion/feeling; 2) blended emotions in the same passage.

Passages with blended emotions have more than one feeling at play in the biblical text. There might be joy and sorrow mixed, as in the Ezra passage above. Observers did not know if people were laughing or weeping because of the joy of rebuilding. Many, it seemed, were crying because of the disappointment that the new building didn't look like the old one.

Here are a few more examples to help understand this concept of identifying multiple emotions. Earlier, we addressed the hemophiliac woman of Mark 5:28 in terms of relationship. Here, let's examine complex emotion. There can be anticipation and fear in the same verse. "For she said, 'If I touch even his garments, I will be made well.'" She was afraid to be noticed because she was ceremonially unclean because of her bleeding, but at the same time, she was convinced and hopeful that if she touched the Master, she would be healed.

With any kind of verbal movement, there is typically some kind of emotion attached to that, especially if there is bodily involvement. Our minds associate action with emotion. That action or motion will imply exhilaration, discouragement, or some other kind of feeling.

In trying to catalog emotions for replication, for that is indeed what we should be doing when we communicate the Bible, there are some helpful categories for preaching and for teaching purposes. While categories overlap and are never clean, it might be helpful to consider four major categories into which one might look for emotional application of biblical passages:

1.   Positive Emotions
2.   Negative Emotions
3.   Shocking Emotions
4.   Passionate Emotions

> **Emotions of Love**
>
> See what kind of love the Father has given to us, that we should be called children of God; and so we are. The reason why the world does not know us is that it did not know him.
> 1 John 3:1
>
> Once there was a group of girls who lived in an orphanage. These four girls longed for a father, and one day a man came and adopted them all. The man was not famous, and not many knew him. However, he loved them and called the girls his own. This is just what God our Father has done to us. We orphans had nothing to offer in return adoption love, but He called us His children. We may never be famous because of Him or known by the world, but the love we receive from Him is enough.
>
> Abigail Mescavage

Unfortunately, it is generally impossible to catalog emotion. Yet, many researchers have tried to do this. For me, it is helpful to begin with these major categories and move to the types of subgroupings listed below. It needs to be stated that many of these oversimplifications do not work, but they are helpful nonetheless because they assist the preacher to get a handle on the precise emotive export of a biblical passage.

To show the potential error in trying to even attempt this, let's begin with a fear passage: "The fear of the LORD is the beginning of knowledge" (Prov. 1:7). Fear in this passage is good. It is a positive emotion. Yet generally, many types of fear are bad. In fact, "God has not given us the spirit of fear" (2 Tim. 1:7).

Despite this conundrum of over-differentiating emotions and how to structure them, we must begin somewhere in attempting to learn how to apply biblical passages that export feelings. Below are some broad categories from which we can work. They are adapted from the 25 human emotions isolated by Allen Cowen in his excellent article on emotional range.[6]

In attempting to quantify them for simplicity in this discipline, I have separated out the categories of positive and negative emotions from emotions of shock and passion. This differentiation is a highly subjective quantifying of something nearly impossible to label, but I find these categories helpful for what we are trying to accomplish.

Positive emotion	*Shock*
Surprise	Surprise
Excitement	Awe
Amusement	Satisfaction
Admiration	Relief
Adoration	Entrancement
	Appreciation of beauty

Negative emotion	*Passion*
Sadness	Elation
Shame	Craving
Anxiety	Boredom
Horror	Calmness
Pain	Empathy
Confusion	Anger
Fear	Pride
	Awkwardness

Moving from recognizing emotion in a text to illustrating it or applying it to yourself or to a group of listeners is a process involving several simple steps. Once you have isolated the emotion that exists in the biblical passage and its setting, you must find a corollary emotion or set of emotions in a parallel situation accessible to contemporary hearers.

Finding a parallel situation in our contemporary culture involves not simply marking the emotion, but how that emotion is displayed or lived out in modern contexts. Here are a few examples: "The LORD was very angry with your fathers. Therefore, say to them, "Thus declares the LORD of hosts: Return to me, says the LORD of hosts, and I will return to you, says the LORD of hosts" (Zech. 1:2).

In plotting out the emotions in this passage, there is both anger and restoration in the same verse, but the end of the passage is positive healing. The connection point may be in the invitation to return with its promised redemption. God the Creator/Owner/Superior is angry with His creation, but He calls for a return to relationship.

Where in our culture do we have a picture of this kind of anger and promise? If there is a spouse who cheats on a marriage vow, the other spouse who has been wronged can call for a return and restoration of the relationship. Sometimes someone might quit a job, but the boss chooses to give him or her another chance by restoring the job. A child might get mad at a parent and leave the house, but the loving parent calls the child back home.

Naturally, emotional parallels need detailing, but the cycle of anger-to-restoration is clear. It is just a matter of isolating the emotional consequences of anger—disappointment, shame, and pride—and correlating them to similar emotions. In this case the issue is relational disappointment.

Some Technical Aspects of Finding the Emotions Being Generated by the Subject

The ability to isolate the feelings being generated by the subject is largely based on the preacher's intuitive power to identify expressive factors. Sometimes those emotions are captured in the vocabulary or in the overall narrative tensions of the text-section.

While some people view emotionally based appeals as potentially dangerous, there is great value in addressing listeners as emotional beings. Sermons that fail to address the emotional side of audiences fail to respect both the text and the innate desires of people who are often looking for a speaker to organize their feelings in a godly way.

The analytical process detailed in these chapters does not in itself guarantee speaker/listener rapport but involves finding the emotional qualities of the textual idea and creating the groundwork for effective engagement. As speakers, we must properly separate out suitable feelings generated by the text and then assemble applicable supplemental material that will clarify, inspire, or captivate the emotional side of listeners.

Identifying the emotions being generated by the textual subject is often the most volatile aspect of the inventive process. Once the emotional aspect of the idea is located and clarified with respect to the precise illustrative crux, the speaker is ready to look for analogous correspondence in the common terrains of life.

If a speaker is not doing explanation of an idea or demonstrating something when preaching from the Bible, that person is probably trying to move the listener. Moving the listener is a type of persuasion, and when our principal objective involves convincing someone of something, we are both in the domains of cognition (thinking) and affectation (feeling).

Many communicators focus on argumentation as only a cognitive task, attempting to convince people by logic and sequential thought. However, persuasion is also an emotionally tied matrix of thoughts, feelings, and history.

Words stimulate memory, pictures, images, and feelings. The emotive aspects of speech are clearly referenceable and easily comprehensible to even the simplest person, even if s/he is not aware of it.

In trying to create a way to capture a process to teach speakers about this very important component of language and teaching in the church, a student might ask the following questions while preparing sermons or biblical teachings: How do we want to make people feel, and is that objective clearly spelled out in the biblical material? What figures produce such feelings, and what analogies will engender the sentiments that are appropriate to the communicative subject and context that I am arguing? Once we know this, we can generate illustrations according to their *emotive purpose*. Finding appropriate figures of speech to advance an argument is a skill that involves differentiating the following: 1) the speaker's main idea; 2) the corresponding associative feelings; 3) the motive of the speaker. The preacher must first identify whether her *subject* is an emotive one or an informational one. If she finds an emotive quality in the subject, then she can find a suitable figure or story that communicates that feeling.

Since in the realm of illustration, words sometimes take on non-traditional meanings, emotive sense is constructed around parallel relationships or concepts that tie the textual meaning to the feelings in a story or outcome. This means that in the mind of the speaker and listener there must be parallel emotive correspondence, not just within the language but in the results communicated by the employed figure. To move someone toward sadness, toward elation, toward pity, or toward anger, one chooses images that evoke similar emotions.

Very often in expositional preaching, we think that the meaning is in the power of explanation. However, emotional context brings with it a force of its own that contributes to the overall force of God's message.

The traditional classical dualism of moving/persuading undergoes meltdown in the fusion of some figures, especially metaphor, as well as in a carefully constructed story where there might be explicit affective export. Moving becomes persuading and persuading becomes moving. Emotions and logic are mixed.

As the preacher preaches and uses images or stories, there is a complex of emotions and conglomeration of thoughts and feelings. At the moment of delivery, it might be hard to differentiate between logical and emotional purpose. This was certainly the case with Jesus. He was often thoroughly argumentative, while at the same time highly deliberate about emotional impact and force. He functioned in the realm of a fusion of purposes.

For the sake of simplicity, speakers generally have a particular purpose in their argumentation; they are generally either trying to correct/build thinking (cognition) or move/motivate people emotionally toward a precise aim. I personally believe it is impossible to separate these, but it is valuable to know if you as a speaker are trying to convince people with concrete language with which they associate feelings as opposed to more abstract thinking that involves categories and analysis.

If we are trying to capture attention, we are working at the level of primary process and the emotional connection that is possible with the audience. I want my audience not only to track my thinking but also feel what I am saying.

Understanding the Range of Emotive Image

Within the emotive aspects of language, speakers have a vast array of symbols present in the culture. They can and should be used carefully and appropriately to captivate listeners and build connection credibility.

It is important that the connections are pure, holy, and biblical. Those choices need to be made with proper motive and in the power of the Spirit. When speakers use metaphors, those images tend to change attitudinal disposition toward the subject and toward the speaker. Those feelings can be positive, negative, or forceful in many ways.

To illustrate the ideas we have been addressing, one might picture an emotive parallel like this. In an emotionally charged text, sometimes feelings of detestability exist in the biblical passage: "Like a dog that returns to his vomit is a fool who repeats his folly" (Prov. 26:11). This is quite different from the feeling of brave compassion when Jesus touched the leper in Matthew 8:3.

Delight

For the Lord will not forsake his people, for his great name's sake, because it has pleased the Lord to make you a people for himself.
1 Samuel 12:22

The manager of a soccer team is leading his team. His name is at stake. Whenever the team loses, the media attributes the defeat to the manager and his lack of actions and tactics. Whenever the team wins, the players often get the glory. Even the players sometimes fail to thank the manager for his efforts, his coaching, and his slowness of anger when they fail. Nevertheless, the manager won't forget his team. They are his. He loves the players very much and believes in them. He is with them on the cold and rainy training days as well as on the sunny home games. The manager is pleased with his soccer team and all the players that are in it. Even though they mistreat his name when they stop following his strategy and lose games, the manager still recovers and keeps sending them support and backing them up in the media. He wants success to show the unbelieving people how great of a leader he is by managing his team to a winning season.

Raphael Alum

The detestability of a dog eating his own vomit generates a repugnancy that has incredible rhetorical force, almost too much force. Similar abhorrent emotions are present with words like maggots, blood, pus, etc. To be syntactically congruent in this passage, the feeling must be placed in a complete idea that is submitted to the textual meaning, namely, that an individual repeats grotesque consequence because he chooses to relive his error. "The beggar intentionally, painfully picked at his open sore day after day to prolong healing simply so he could generate pity in those passing by who might donate money."

Even the thought of preaching emotive congruence in this passage would be abandoned by most preachers in typical western church settings. The speaker would likely opt for euphemistic figures. However, in cultures where sights and realities such as this are common, affective similarities might be entirely appropriate and communicate well.

A figure generates feelings and interpretations that are based on the experience of the listener. This makes the listeners' pasts the basis for accepting the truth claim. In addition, the individual listener's own feelings and her previously validated experience encourage her toward a new behavior or thought.

Consider the following verses: "For they themselves report concerning us the kind of reception we had among you, and how you turned to God from idols to serve the living and true God, and to wait for his Son from heaven, whom he raised from the dead, Jesus who delivers us from the wrath to come" (1 Thessalonians 1:9-10).The process of identifying and generating emotive parallels might be graphically represented like this.

Propositional Idea	Core Feelings or Emotions	Parallel Experience with the Similar Emotion
God is a forgiving and living Father.	Justifiable fear of accountability	Fear of debt collection by an authority like a bank God as a debt collector
	Joy of grace Love as motivator	Joy of forgiven debt by friend Love for a child when he does his best but fails an exam
Jesus will return in anger.	Anger	Angry boss dissatisfied with the quality of work
	Revenge	Vengeful king after an insurrection

All propositional ideas possess distinct innate feelings or emotions. The speaker should identify the emotive center and search for similar images or scenarios that express similar sensations. In hearing them spoken in the form of a verbal picture of some kind, the listener can associate familiar feelings with the new idea the speaker is proposing.

Figures that appeal to the affective side of human nature strike the imagination and help us clarify thinking. In the employment of images, logical exactitude is not the chief feature, and the obscuring of the subject can be a negative result in some cases. In other words, speakers can use emotional language or stories and the audience gets lost in the process. They might leave the communication setting remembering the figure and not the speaker's purpose in using the figure. This is because figures form a bond with the listener's past. Resurrecting these feelings might obscure the core ideas of the speaker.

Also, sometimes the listener is not able to make the implied connections. It is for this reason that the speaker must create precise clarity when connecting emotive force to a text. It is helpful that when the important, biblical subject might be lost in the emotive force of the illustration, the expository speaker returns with surgical precision to the main idea or the homiletical subpoint. If not, the purpose of the story or image becomes an end in itself, divorced from the word of God.

The speaker must understand her role, and the speaker's motivation becomes a significant factor in the effectiveness of the illustration. When using figures, the speaker appeals to the experience of the listener and experience is tied to the emotions. The resulting consequence for a listener in the audience might be catastrophic and completely alienate a person from the textual idea.

Feelings can actually take over the rhetorical context, both in the mouth of the speaker and in the ear of the listener. Ultimately, the use of emotionally charged figures must be made with care because they have significant power to influence listeners, both in positive and in negative ways.

I have found that working with students on this highly subjective endeavor requires that the exegete first isolate the feelings engendered by the communicative subject. This is done through careful analysis. Differing educational levels and capacities for analyzing a textual idea create the spectrum of results but not always. Sometimes people have innate abilities to locate emotion in textual ideas.

When a person learns how to break down verse units, assess communicative concepts, and prepare the ideas for image development, the emotionally charged material flows in abundance. Ultimately, the development of a reflex for finding the emotive side of the illustrative crux of a passage becomes instinctual and highly accurate, bringing with it exciting language for precise exposition.

If the speaker captures the emotive force of a biblical passage, that speaker learns not only to preach the meaning of the text but also the sentiment being communicated by God. When this happens, there is a union between thought and feeling that resonates with the listener. The person hearing the discourse intuitively knows that the way the speaker is preaching the text is congruent with the sense of the text itself.

Questions for Engagement

1. In what ways do texts have emotions?
2. How does a speaker connect to listeners by communicating parallel emotions?
3. If there is more than one emotion embedded in a biblical text, how can the speaker determine a priority for communication?
4. For an illustrator, what is an 'emotive purpose'?
5. Once we have found an emotion in the text, how might we find an associative feeling that might strike a chord with the listener?
6. How is the idea of capturing the attention of the audience different from using the embedded emotions in a text to bring people into an encounter with a living God?
7. If you find a core emotion in the text, how do you locate a parallel experience or similar emotion in our modern context?

16 Illustrating Movement in a Text

One of the most important skills of illustration and application is examining movement and illustrating its importance. Almost any sentence has movement, either direct or implied. Consequently, the illustrator who applies the word of God must ask, "What is happening in the text, and to what response is the listener called?" Both are movements.

Physical and ideological movement can be complex, so before we look at some extensive passages in detail, let's analyze a simple passage of just a couple of verses. Examine this text and try to identify what is happening by way of movement.

Genesis 17:17-18

Then Abraham fell on his face and laughed and said to himself, "Shall a child be born to a man who is a hundred years old? Shall Sarah, who is ninety years old, bear a child?" And Abraham said to God, "Oh that Ishmael might live before you!"

We might be quick to equate movement with verbs and wrongly ask, "What is happening with the verbs?" However, movement is much more complicated than that. Yes, there is the obvious movement of falling, laughing, and questioning, but look a little deeper.

Movement in application not only addresses what is happening physically but also involves implications. In this passage, Abraham literally falls to the ground and laughs. The act is as important as the implied meaning–unbelief. He falls to the dust.

Looking beyond the physical, the reader can move to the next level and ask implication questions. The speaker might grapple like this: "What should the listener *do* about the sarcastic mocking of God?" In other words, there are implicit questions that involve ramifications.

When considering a biblical text, the listener is compelled to change direction, and that change involves alteration of thinking, feeling, and of action. Movement is everywhere implicit and could go in many different directions. The speaker must determine which way the application moves.

If Abraham prays in Genesis 17:18, "Oh that Ishmael might live before you!" the implicit export is that we don't follow the bad example of godly people when they pray for things that are not part of God's plan. The movement is a discontinuance of sinful action. The movement of Abraham is to pray, but the text is clear that we are not to replicate bad behavior.

Application might involve encouraging people to do the opposite of what is explicit in the text. If Judas betrays Jesus, the preacher moves the audience to consider how not to replicate the behavior. Consequently, we are not just preaching the text but might have to address what the text implies, that is, how we should think, feel, or act.

Similarly, movement can be a matter of degree. Applying the Great Commandment to love the Lord with all one's heart, soul, mind, and strength is not typically an all or nothing proposition. Most Christians are somewhere on the continuum of obedience. We intensify our passion which is typically not as hot as it should be. The illustrator must address the *degree* of love and its outcomes. This is definitely a question of movement.

Daring Movement

But immediately Jesus spoke to them, saying, "Take heart; it is I. Do not be afraid." And Peter answered him, "Lord, if it is you, command me to come to you on the water."
Matthew 14:27-28

In this passage, Peter speaks up and asks Jesus to call him out to do something impossible—to walk with Him on the water. Have you ever been in this position; God is doing something miraculous, and you want to join in? This is kind of like a young girl who has no experience with power tools seeing a carpenter and asking if she can help. So the craftsman takes her hand in his and puts his hand over her hand on the skill saw. Or, maybe as a kid you sat in your parents' lap and 'drove' the car. You had no clue how to drive, but it was amazing!

Sapphira Waymire

Audience Familiarity and Types of Movement

Movement is of several types, and for illustration invention, the one who applies a scripture to the modern context should nail down exactly what kind of movement the text is stating or implying.

Typically, movement is very identifiable when someone is preaching. We live in a world of movement, and things change, transition, and advance from one state to another, but audience engagement will also never take place if the isolated textual idea being preached is beyond the grasp of the auditor in some way. It is helpful if the idea is placed in concrete terms and recognizable to a listener.

Illustrating movement in the text has several key components that might involve change in function, cause, effect, power, sequence, quality, sense-appeal, and human-like action.

Texts use verbs and those verbs state or imply movement unless they are stative verbs. Stative verbs involve sense, internal musings, being and posture (i.e. hearing, thinking, being, and standing). This is not what we are trying to illustrate when we speak of movement.

Illustrating action requires identifying component parts of movement in more detail. Here are some questions to ask to accurately quantify the nature of the movement that one finds in the text.

1. Who is doing the action?
2. What power is s/he/it acting under?
3. What or who is acted upon?
4. What is the effect of the action?
5. What is the function of the action, or what is it doing?
6. What is the 'position' of the action?
7. What is the directional movement?
8. What is the speed, timing, or rate of the action?
9. What is the sequence of the actions?
10. Does the action trigger the senses?

Once the reader understands some of these factors from the text, it is possible to draw analogies to current circumstances and images that can serve as the basis for biblical application. The person seeking to connect listeners to the textual material first must isolate what aspects of the movement are important for illustration. For example, consider this passage from Jonah.

Jonah 1:1-3

Now the word of the Lord came to Jonah the son of Amittai, saying, "Arise, go to Nineveh, that great city, and call out against it, for their evil has come up before me." But Jonah rose to flee to Tarshish from the presence of the Lord. He went down to Joppa and found a ship going to Tarshish. So he paid the fare and went down into it, to go with them to Tarshish, away from the presence of the Lord.

Based on the above questions, here is how we can analyze these verses when we assess action in the text. I am outlining this here to demonstrate the fruitful nature of asking questions that involve movement.

16   Illustrating Movement in a Text

1. Who is doing the action? Who should be doing the action?
    a. God's word comes to Jonah.
    b. The one receiving the word must go according to the word.
    c. Jonah gets up and flees, so the receiver of God's word flees.
2. Under whose authority/power is s/he/it acting?
    a. Jonah receives the call under God's authority.
    b. Jonah goes to Tarshish under his own authority.
3. What/who is acted upon?
    a. The prophet is acted upon by God Himself.
    b. God Himself allows Himself to be implicated when the evil 'comes up before' Him.
    c. The word came to Jonah. The prophet was passive.
4. What is the effect of the action?
    a. Creation rages and the sea is not calm.
    b. The crew of the ship threw him overboard at his command and in desperation.
5. What is the function of the action?
    a. The function of Jonah's action is to get away from God.
    b. Jonah wants to possess his future destiny.
6. What is the 'position' of the action?
    a. The position of the action is that it takes place 'before Him.'
    b. In a strange twist of irony, the text employs the terms 'arise/up' and 'down/away' in contrast.
7. What is the directional movement?
    a. When Jonah flees, he flees from the presence of the Lord. He is moving away from God.
    b. He went *down* to Joppa and found a ship going in the opposite direction of his calling.
8. What is the speed, timing, or rate of the action?
    a. In this brief passage, the speed is not as important as the sequence.
    b. We are not told in the text how fast this happens, but it seems that the disobedience is immediate.
9. What is the sequence of the action?
    a. The sequence of action is: receive, rise, go down, pay the fare, and go.
    b. There is an expected sequence (receive, rise, go), but Jonah violates the expected sequence.
10. Does the action trigger the senses?
    a. What might the smell of the sea air *feel* like when you are called to the desert?
    b. The open water at the port *looks* freeing, but it holds danger.
    c. There might be the *sound* of loading ships, the sound of the sea wind.
    d. He can probably *taste* the salty air and think it is probably better than desert.
    e. There is the *tactile* component of sea ropes, decking, and planks.

In attempting a sermonic application or illustration of this passage, it is easy to draw analogies to this textual paragraph and correlate component parts to modern circumstances. When we are called, do we run in the opposite direction? We are acted upon by God. Our lives are played out before Him. We are in His presence, and this is something from which we cannot flee. Sequentially, the order is set by God, but we want to go to the Spanish Riviera, that is, Tarshish.

In the preaching delivery where we might be trying to illustrate this passage, we can correlate **directional movement** in solicitation, in decision-making, in execution, and several other ways. The realities and the choices in the text are common, even thousands of years later.

Humans are still prone to go in the opposite direction, to rise up at the wrong time, to settle the raging seas of life in the wrong way, and to create convoluted plans to avoid the inevitable call of God.

Conversely, it is not difficult to find a story where a person makes the correct choice, that is, to run toward the presence of God. For example, in Exodus 24 Moses was called up into the mountain; that is exactly where he went.

Exodus 24:12-18

The Lord said to Moses, *"Come up to me* on the mountain and *wait there*, that I may *give you the tablets* of stone, with the law and the commandment, which I have written for their instruction." So *Moses rose with his assistant Joshua,* and *Moses went up* into the mountain of God. And he said to the elders, "Wait here for us until we return to you. And behold, Aaron and Hur are with you. *Whoever has a dispute, let him go to them."* Then *Moses went up* on the mountain, and *the cloud covered* the mountain. The glory of the Lord dwelt on Mount Sinai, and *the cloud covered* it six days. And on the seventh day *he called to Moses* out of the midst of the cloud. Now the appearance of the glory of the Lord was like a devouring fire on the top of the mountain in the sight of the people of Israel. Moses <u>entered</u> the cloud and *went up* on the mountain. And Moses was on the mountain forty days and forty nights.

Movement is critical in making analogies with modern circumstances. For example, Elijah calls down fire from heaven under God's authority. How and when is it appropriate for church leaders to bring judgment down on people? Downward motion can be good or bad. Judgment comes down, but so do angels. Fire comes down to consume, but so does manna.

When correlating the movement of an ancient text, the analogy of the modern story must be appropriate to the meaning of the original narrative. Pharaoh's magicians can 'throw down' their staffs under governmental authority, but their snakes can expect to be swallowed up. In the modern world, the government lays down the law, but can the Christian swallow up the consequences with righteousness? The implication is clear; we may need to confront governmental leadership.

When Stephen told his listeners that they are like the pagan Israelites who resisted the Holy Spirit and persecuted the prophets, he found himself being stoned. The results may be similar if we say that our congregants are like children that fail to listen to their mother when she says, "Don't touch the hot stove."

For practice, examine Exodus 24:12-18 below and apply the questions concerning movement. Once you have done that, find parallel corollaries that you might relate to an audience to apply this passage.

There is so much movement going on in this passage that it is almost too much to cover. To simplify things, we might give a summary along with a way to illustrate this.

It is very apparent that Moses is going up the mountain for a meeting with God. This image of going up the mountain of God has been in the Judeo-Christian tradition for thousands of years. However, there are a few things that are often overlooked.

1.   Moses does not go alone.
2.   Moses went up to receive something, namely the tablets with God's words on them.
3.   The cloud covers the mountain, and Moses went into it.
4.   To the people, it looked like Moses went into a devouring fire.

Illustrating Speed, Timing, and Rate

The question of speed, timing, and rate is very important in illustration. Almost any command can be delayed or done infrequently. This can make for easy illustration.

When Paul says, "Husbands, love your wives" (Eph. 5:25), an audience member can say to himself: "I do that." However, the question is how often?

Frequency can be illustrated as an important value. Is a sin often or infrequent or never? Is the command obeyed regularly or sporadically? Is there consistent obedience or intermittent obedience?

This issue of when to, when not to, or how often are critical when teaching the scriptures. For example, because the speaker refuses to say 'when' it is important to disciple the nations (Matt. 28:19-20) or to "go into all the world" (Mark 16:15), the absence of timing lets the listener off the hook in a sense. However, if the speaker asks people *this week* to share Christ, the people have a goal that is precise.

It is easy to gloss over perpetual issues and make them theoretical. When Solomon says not to, "desire her beauty in your heart," this is a constant and enduring call for most men (Prov. 6:25). It is not an occasional command open to sporadic obedience.

Power as Authoritative Movement

Movement often involves authority, so how we illustrate movement frequently possesses power implications. These can be because a person is operating under a power or exerting personal power.

While it is quite clear that Moses and Joshua are doing the action in the previous text just mentioned, it is less apparent that he acts under the power of invitation from God. Positionally, he is in the place of an invitee, not a seeker. This is not a pilgrimage up Mount Sinai.

To illustrate this, the teacher of the Bible should look for where in modern culture we might find parallels. A child can be called up to the teacher's desk for 40 seconds not 40 days, although it might seem like that.

It might be important to ponder where in our culture someone could be invited by an authority out of the leadership of a community to commune with that authority to take back standards for broad implementation in that group from which the person came? One might look at the military for a parallel. A captain gets called out of his company to go on a two-month deployment so s/he can return and implement special training. Even this, however, lacks correspondence because Moses was over a nation.

Would a world leader ever announce that he is absenting himself from his people for two months? Probably not. It might be hard to find a suitable parallel in terms of numbers. Yet, there are many parallels that work in this paradigm of being summoned. The owner calls up the CEO. The President calls up the general. The leader calls up the subordinate. The principal calls someone to the office. The board calls up the chairman.

Contemplating Exactitude in Subject Analysis

Before creating an appropriate figure to engage a listener, it must be entirely clear what one wants to illustrate. Clarity and suitability of thought about the figure arrive via attention to the precise meaning of words and concepts needing to be put in image or story form. In the end, one isolates the exact notion needing to be illustrated. This progression varies in difficulty based on the complexity of words as well as the subtlety of the idea to be pictured. Refinement of the crux of the illustration involves working through four basic questions (see the table below).

In an analysis of the biblical subject, the rhetorical techniques of defining and dividing precede subject expansion. Locating the figured potential of words comes before techniques for narrative extension, that is, story and narrative illustration. This is an idea that will be treated extensively in a later chapter, but for now it is important to say that textual examination is the basis for storied extension. Examining figured potential involves a search for image qualities inherent in words and ideas already in the text itself.

In my personal experience, not only as a preacher but also as a teacher of illustration, I have found that locating the subject for illustration is far more difficult than inventing the subsequent image or story. It is for this reason that skill in subject analysis is of extreme importance in the whole process. It becomes the basis of correct figurative development.

Exactitude in subject analysis is a relative art and only the speaker her/himself will know when s/he is satisfied with the fine-tuning of his illustrative theme. The quality of a person's judgment is very important in this respect because after the figure is put out to the audience, the listener becomes the final judge of the appropriateness of the speaker's figure choices.

Accurate nuance in topic is one of the first and critical steps in establishing communicative correspondence with an audience. If the precise notion being illustrated is not identified with exactitude, an analogous idea in image or story form will not be congruent to the subject, but rather be an idea analogous to a deformation of the intended subject. The reality to which the figure corresponds will not be the reality the speaker wants to communicate. The result is a puzzled listener who struggles to make a connection between the figure and the truth it is supposed to represent.

What I have discovered by experience is that students' innate capacity for constructing the illustration is often remarkable, but what s/he needs is a door into subject analysis. Movement qualities such as cause and effect are located in the verbs or in entire contexts. Ultimately, analogies can be invented to correspond with any one of several syntactical elements: word, word-compound, phrase, sentence/proposition, or parallel verbal idea.

Some of us create parallels instinctually, but for others, we must apply a method of substitution to help us. It is possible to find suitable analogy through substitution of elements in a simple sentence. Each major grammatical element is replaced by a corresponding part of speech.

For example, we can approach a text like this from Isaiah 4:12: "He marked off the heavens with a span." One might create an image by substitution: "The Great Architect grabbed His compass and circled the universe on His tablet." If I wanted to lengthen this, I could then make it a narrative by supplying extensive detail, tension, and a time element. The correspondence would evolve from lexical substitution to a narrative representation.

To do this, one starts by identifying the essence of the nouns. It is possible to look closer at the fixed qualities of the nouns to find associating elements. This will seem confusing and complicated at first, but after a few examples, the value in pinning down movement and state reveal just how profitable this effort can be.

Trans-Formation and Nominal Change

When analyzing a noun for biblical illustration, we are primarily concerned about fixed things. However, sometimes those fixed objects morph or change. In this way, illustration of objects and nouns can be illustrated with movement.

Examine this illustration. Paul states that when we build on the foundation of Christ, it can be that our works have the worth of "gold, silver, precious stones, wood, hay, straw" (1 Cor. 3:12). God's fire will test the quality. In illustrating movement in form, we can talk about our works improving in quality to become things that are precious and enduring. We might have straw-works of kindness-for-boss-approval at our job, or wood-works of helping the destitute for selfish public recognition. Why not transform our stubble-works to some silver and gold, self-sacrifice without reward and donations to missions when no one is looking?

Things in space might change in unusual ways when they are illustrated, particularly as it relates to geography. Words or solid forms might be fixed in the text, but the implication of the text is that people are called to look differently at things than simply as they appear. We can illustrate people moving in positive or negative ways by how they *adjoin in space* or where they should be in space. In the first Psalm, the one who meditates on God's law is planted BY the rivers of waters. The ungodly STAND in the company of sinners. Their proximity has results. With whom are you standing?

If people are in the company of sinners, they need to move to the place of meditation. They have no business fraternizing with ungodly influences. The movement is implied, at least for those who should be meditating on the word of God night and day.

Precisely Identifying Verbal Action, Movement, or Transformation

Creating figures of movement requires that we precisely identify verbal action. When we classify verbs by their actions, events by their causes and effects, people or things by their functions, we must address in some way the type of action. A detailed breakdown is listed in this table below.[7] After looking at the table, look at how the biblical verses that follow yield illustrative material.

This table details different ways to identify the movement of a subject to construct an appropriate figure. It describes a way of looking at words in terms of their action in the broadest possible terms. Here we are primarily concerned with movement. In a later chapter we will address illustrating the form of a 'thing.'

Movement	Precise Description	Observation Method	Negation
Is it action?	What something does (its function)	Look for similar functions.	The opposite action
	How it gets there (its cause)	Look for similar ways to move.	How it could not get there
	What it does to things or to others (its effect)	Look for similar effects.	What it does not do to others
Is there some other kind of implied movement?	What power it operates under	Look for similar power operations–its possessor.	What it does not operate under
	Its time sequence	Look for similar sequences.	Interrupted sequence or stopped sequence
	Its human quality	Look for human parallels.	Human imperfections
	Its sense appeal	Look for similar sense stimulants.	Without sound, smell, etc.
	Its human-like action	Look for human actions that are similar.	Non-human like action

When taking biblical passages and expanding them for illustration and application, one takes the precise state or movement in the biblical text and reduces it to a generalization so that it is possible to find parallels that are closer to an audience's experiences. Consider this text in just a general way, before we get into the specifics:

> Again, the kingdom of heaven is like a merchant in search of fine pearls, who, on finding one pearl of great value, went and sold all that he had and bought it (Matt. 13:45-46).

The nominal components (nouns) or the 'state' of things are the merchant and his pearls. The movement, by contrast, is that the merchant is searching, finding, selling, and buying. This is a progressive sequence, typically not difficult to replicate in an illustration.

When we add the 'state' or thing-ness to the movement/action, the illustrative export becomes clearer. The preacher can then ask, "In life today, where do we see someone searching, finding, selling, and buying--collectables, antiques, jewelry, etc.?" If we want to illustrate this for an age demographic—teenagers, senior women, middle-aged men—we simply find the corollaries that fit the demographic, where a businessman targets certain commodities and audiences—cell phones, diamonds, tools.

The subject—merchants--can be correlated to a contemporary setting by finding concrete corollary nouns. We might say 'business owners' in American English. They are addressing supply chains, vendors, or consumers. The businessman dealing in clothing, sold all he had to purchase a designer label manufacturer. In a spiritual sense, we can use human resolve or passion for something as a model for extraordinary sacrifice.

Here is an example from my early childhood that illustrates this. My home pastor, Frank Vurture, was recruited by the New York Yankees in the 1930s, during the Lou Gehrig era. He was on a train to Binghamton, New York to play for the Binghamton Triplets farm team when he saw a billboard that said, "What shall it profit a man if he gains the whole world and loses his own soul." When he arrived at the station, he got off the train, went back to Long Island, and received Christ as his Savior. He gave up his personal dream and became an evangelist, ultimately sending 500 people into the ministry during 40 years of pastoral work. He never took a salary. He saw the Pearl of Great Price, and as a result, he purchased a total investment in God's business.

Within an evaluation of movement, things can transform. That is, their 'form' will be altered, and the movement expresses itself in an alteration of state. In a later chapter, we will address state. It is one of the most critical ideas in all of illustration, but it is among the hardest to comprehend. All physical objects are in a state. Movement is only a series of clips or a sequence of things that experience an alteration of the state.

Understanding this, consider how 'forms' experience 'trans-form-ation.' " Then I saw a new heaven and a new earth, for the first heaven and the first earth had passed away, and the sea was no more" (Rev 21:1).

In John's description, the earth is in the process of renewal. Its form changes. Illustrating this is not difficult. The preacher might ask, "Where in my experience have I seen someone create something, destroy it, and then recreate it?" An artist who paints over his whole canvas and then recreates the painting, might work. When a father helps his children build an elaborate sandcastle close to the waves can commit to rebuilding the entirety away from the sea and waves. This is obviously not what God is doing because his re-creation is eternal. This would need to be stated and might serve as a negative illustration of durability.

People, churches, and situations can be described in static terms, but they are fluid. Examine how God describes Himself: "His heart is hard as a stone, hard as the lower millstone." (Job 41:24). We might consider this a static form, but this is not the end of the story. Even the ensuing verse demonstrates how form evolves to movement and rationale. "When he raises himself up, the mighty are afraid; at the crashing they are beside themselves" (Job 41:25). God will not be manipulated or moved, like a father who has clear resolve before a child who does not have a clear picture of the circumstances.

Illustrating 'Function' as Movement

There are verses that state or imply *function*. People and objects may have *ways they work* in a passage. Those exported results demonstrate function, either good or bad, desirable or undesirable, profitable or unprofitable. Consider these verses.

What do you mean by repeating this proverb concerning the land of Israel, 'The fathers have eaten sour grapes, and the children's teeth are set on edge'? As I live, declares the Lord GOD, this proverb shall no more be used by you in Israel. (Ez. 18:2-3)

The grapes are bad deeds that affect children. Kids suffer because of parental mistakes. The grapes function as a metaphor of discipline or bad consequences. Why should I suffer from my parents' sins or from the decisions they made that adversely affected me? The sour grapes cause bad things to happen. If we stop making bad choices, our children will not have to suffer.

Beyond this, the passage also states that the proverb itself had a function, that is to remind Israel of ancestral sin or even as an excuse of the younger generation to rid themselves of guilt by blaming their parents for their then current condition.

Functionally, it is good for the Bible illustrator to show people how the passage encourages us to conceptualize reality or not conceptualize reality. We demonstrate how function drives a point home and encourages change. Do we really like the taste of sour grapes? Stop eating them. Why should you have generational suffering because of poor parental choices?

If the meaning of the verse is that children blame their parents for the grief that they have to harvest from the grapes they imbibe, we are commanded to "no longer" use it that way. We are told to no longer rehearse proverbs that blame others for our sin.

The movement in the text is stated, that is, don't blame your parents. But other more extensive ramifications of movement are implied. So, the person applying this passage can preach against the function of sayings as catchwords of verbal blame.

The Importance of Cause and Effect

Preaching this type of textual movement, that is, implicit ramifications for an audience to a textual idea, is very close to illuminating **cause and effect** in preaching. There is almost always the idea of cause and effect in any given passage of scripture. The illustrator asks, "What preceded this verse or statement, and what follows logically or literally from it?" Here's an example:

When Elijah throws his mantle over Elisha in 1 Kings 19:19, there are antecedents and consequents. There are nearly always both of these.

The figurative ordination of Elisha follows Elijah's isolation and depression in the cave at Horeb. That is the prior context. God asks Elijah twice, "What are you doing here Elijah?" (1 Kings 19:9, 13). After God answers his questions about ministry loneliness, He shows the old prophet his ministry partner, Elisha. This is the reason why Elijah anoints Elisha as a prophet to take his place. God told him to. That is the antecedent to the prior causal impetus. The effect of the anointing is burning his past life as an agriculturalist. He lights up the yoke with which he is plowing and offers the oxen as a sacrifice.

The export is clear. We don't ordain someone in a ministry transition without a word from God, and when we obey Him, we can fully expect total investment by a God-ordained successor. Another cause/effect correlation that hinges on this act of anointing is the movement from retreat to return-to-ministry.

In the Esther story, we are told that the king could not sleep (6:1). While in itself the effect of something, namely the thought that he missed something in his leadership past, he uses the reciting of the chronicle records to promote Mordecai, the successive consequent. God can wake us to past neglect and use us to advance His kingdom.

Causes can be **singular or multiple**, but effects are almost always diverse and extensive. This is what makes applying the principles of effect/movement so fruitful to the preacher.

When Paul was forbidden by the Holy Spirit to go to Asia and Bithynia on the second missionary journey, a night vision of a Macedonian appeared to him, resulting in a missions effort to Europe by Paul's team. The effects are vast: churches were planted in Philippi, Thessalonica, Berea, Athens, and Corinth. The extent of the lives touched by this move are remarkable, and space does not permit elaboration. Yet, the implications of the vision result in movement. The vision involved invitation, but the effect or response explodes with movement. Application almost always involves movement.

Causes can be illustrated as being **justified or unjustified**. Then they can be shown to have pure motives or faulty ones. For example, if I am preaching the text of Romans 13:1ff about being submitted to the higher powers, it might be appropriate to talk about speeding in my car or not declaring income on my taxes. How does a man justify disobedience to law?

Sometimes textual components are best defined by **function** and not by cause and effect. For example, you could talk about the cause and effect of being a deacon in 1 Timothy 2:8, but it is much more suitable to discuss the function of an office. Function is a more complex discussion of how something works. This inevitably involves movement, or in the case of a deacon, what the office-holder does.

People or things might have a cause, but often they are defined by behaviors. These behaviors have movement, and that movement is clearly defined by stated parameters. A deacon is reverent, not double-tongued, and not drunk or greedy. These show that he functions with integrity. His sobriety or his verbal integrity is not an effect of being a deacon. Character is part of his function. By ordaining someone to the office of deacon, that person does not become someone of integrity. Integrity is not causal.

In analyzing a text to illustrate function, we search for parallel functions in our experience or the material world. To show that a deacon cannot be greedy, we might show that in a corporate organization where human resources hires a manager, that manager cannot simultaneously work for a competitor or force sales goals to get her own bonus. Her motives are personal, not corporate.

Movement by Sequence

Everything that takes place over time has sequence. In other words, unless something is static, like a noun, there is a temporal quality that involves a timeframe. Things that move across time can be sequentialized, that is, broken down into clips, episodes, or some kind of framing.

Before we get into how that helps in illustration, let me explain the idea of framing or dividing movement into clips. Making action episodic helps in several ways. It helps to understand the biblical or Divine progression, and in narrative terms, descent or ascent, from bad to good or from good to bad.

In Luke 23:13-25, Pilot addresses the chief priests, rulers, and people about the innocence of Jesus. He offers to exonerate the Savior and presents the people with a choice, Jesus or Barabbas. The people of course reject the offer and insist on Jesus' crucifixion.

When we look at the text in terms of sequence, there is the following set of clips, so to speak: proposed innocence, offering of release, rejection of the offer, and a capital sentence of condemnation to appease the crowd. Each component can find parallel in an illustration.

In the same way that Jesus' was presented to the crowd and ultimately condemned, there are many parallels that can be drawn from human experience, especially when Pilot says, "I have found no fault in this man" (23:14). On the playground, a nice boy or girl could be the object of bullying by a jealous aggressor because the nice and gentle child is well liked and popular. In the event of a conflict between an innocent student and a notoriously sinister classmate, if all the students stand around and accuse the innocent child of wrongdoing, the principal might do an investigation and believe the gentle child was innocent. Yet, he may be forced to suspend the innocent child because of the chorus of false accusations which 'prove' his guilt.

Sometimes a successful contractor who does excellent work could be wrongly accused of wrongdoing and attacked by a competitor simply because clients want to litigate for spite and put the man out of business. The man is not guilty, rather a victim of injustice, but the judge finds him guilty anyway because of an abundance of falsified evidence.

Actions, even small ones, are sequential. They generally have a beginning, middle, and end. That evolution over time, however brief, involves either an ascent or descent or both. Consider this verse. "And when they had kindled a fire in the middle of the courtyard and sat down together, Peter sat down among them" (Luke 22:55).

The sequence progresses like this: random people were cold, built a fire, and Peter just wanted to keep warm and go unnoticed. Many people in the Christian world want to be 'warm but unnoticed.' The crucifixion of Christ takes place all around us, but we want to be 'warm' with lost people, while simultaneously hiding our anonymity for personal reasons.

Some stories have a clearly stepped order. In Galatians 2:11-13, Peter comes to

Antioch and eats openly with everyone. When the Jerusalem Jews come, he pulls away and no longer eats with the Gentiles. Paul gives him a sharp rebuke for his hypocrisy.

The steps move from fraternity to hypocrisy to rebuke. Here is a similar progression. A teenager has good friends who all play in a band together. He is willing to be seen with them, if a certain different group of jock friends is not around. When the jock friends show up, Billy no longer wants to be seen with his band friends because they are not as cool.

Identifying movement by sequence helps the illustrator find analogous correspondence in parallel scenarios. However, it requires breaking down the series of events into smaller episodes.

Transformational Movement in Dispositional Quality

Sometimes people change their attitudes. This is very common, but how does one illustrate that?

If you look at the chart above, there are many other factors around which one can build an application, depending on the quality of the movement in the text.

If the scripture passage has a sense appeal, the pastor might consider focusing on that. Joseph, in responding to his brothers, spoke 'harshly' to them (Gen. 44:15). We can all relate to harsh words, but it is quite difficult to measure if those words were intended to test the character of the listeners or punish them with cruelty. These are two different things, and the illustrator would want to differentiate them; in a way, it would be to teach the audience about the sense factors evident in the text. Why would someone speak harshly to others? Is it to test them or to punish them?

Something similar might be done with Moses' final song in Deuteronomy 32:2, when he says, "May my teaching drop as the rain, my speech distill as the dew, like gentle rain upon the tender grass, and like showers upon the herb." The sense is the gentle, refreshing words of the divinely inspired word and His messenger. Are our words falling with renewal on the hearers?

When there is a change in the disposition of one person toward another or one group toward another in the Bible, the illustrator might want to note this. It could be explicit as in Genesis 31:2, "And Jacob saw that Laban did not regard him with favor as before." When we are no longer viewed in a positive light, we can expect human difficulties, while at the same time anticipate the faithfulness of God.

The quality of a disposition might clearly change, as in 1 Samuel 19:9: "Then a harmful spirit from the LORD came upon Saul, as he sat in his house with his spear in his hand. And David was playing the lyre." However, the dispositional result in behavior is vengeance. "And Saul sought to pin David to the wall with the spear, but he eluded Saul, so that he struck the spear into the wall. And David fled and escaped that night" (1 Sam. 19:10).

Saul was consumed with the spirit of revenge, and the text progresses from spiritual harm to physical harm. This might be at the heart of the illustrator. Saul moves from internal intention to external harm. A preacher might correlate like this: Fertilizer nitrates in farms around the Susquehanna River don't pollute the Chesapeake Bay for months, not until the run-off fills the tributaries. The worm crawls into the apple, but you don't know it is rotten until the spoilage reaches the outside skin or you cut it open with a paring knife.

Questions for Engagement

1. What is the difference between direct or implied movement within a text?
2. How are change and movement similar or dissimilar when it comes to illustrating a text?
3. How are the concepts of speed, timing, and rate useful in illustrating human responsibility?
4. What are some ways that movement and authority are connected in texts?
5. How are fixed objects and nouns related to movement and verbs in a text?
6. What does it mean that textual movements have an implied 'function'?
7. What are some types of causes and effects when analyzing movement in a text?
8. How might the Bible illustrator use sequence to help a listener make a life-change?
9. What does it mean to break down event sequences into episodes?

17 Illustrating Moral Human Behavior

Acts 6:1

And in those days, when the number of the disciples was multiplied, there arose a murmuring of the Grecians against the Hebrews, because their widows were neglected in the daily ministration.

Before we get into analyzing this passage as a simple model, consider these approaches to behavior. When one thinks about applying or illustrating the Bible, one immediately thinks about action, obedience, or compliance. Upon careful examination, however, there are many ways to approach this idea of behavior.

Moral human behavior is all over the Bible, and one must contemplate whether the text is advocating **adoption, discontinuance, continuance, or deterrence** of any particular action. These four categories have been used for centuries in teaching argumentation.

In looking at the above passage, what are the behaviors of the participants? Should the behaviors be adopted, discontinued, continued, or deterred?

For those that preach, we are typically calling the audience to one of these components. We need to ask what the Bible is saying we should do or not do. Should we start, stop, continue, or avoid? Let's look at these four basic responses from a moral perspective.

Typically, adoption has a very positive feeling. It has newness, challenge, and transformation. However, it might not always be easy. For example, Jesus tells us this in John 15:12: "This is my commandment, that you love one another as I have loved you." If we are not doing that, then we need to *adopt* the behavior. This is a tall order.

Beyond this, it becomes much more difficult to address in the corporate setting of a congregation, especially if the text implies that the church must change its culture to please God. In this passage cited at the beginning of the chapter, the disciples had to make a modification of how they treated the widows in a culture that did not have either a Social Security system or health care.

If someone attempts to address this issue in a collective setting, like a church structure, the issue will likely be *adoption.* Should the church create a systematic widow ministry?

If the local church already has a widow program, the preacher's application might have to be one of *continuance*, either with or without change. The church must ask if there is some kind of modification to the current practice. The speaker applies the text to create proper management, modification, or even intensification. All are types of continuance.

Sometimes texts have either explicit or implicit issues of **discontinuance**. The reader is asked to *stop doing something*. Consider this passage: "The night is far spent, the day is at hand: let us therefore cast off the works of darkness and let us put on the armor of light" (Rom. 13:12).

Casting off the works of darkness is a matter of discontinuance. The speaker must remind the listener that s/he is likely doing something that needs to stop. This can, of course, be a delicate matter. This idea of stopping behavior is everywhere in the scriptures.

In explaining narrative, the text might make something obvious. For example, when the disciples were arguing "who was the greatest" (Mark 9:34), it was not a good habit. The export is clear for the listener, but it must be stated. We should not jockey for position on the church board, in our home group, on committees, and in any of countless ways in the assembly of God. We have no business climbing the ecclesiastical ladder, using the neck of our brothers and sisters as the rung of a ladder to a higher position. If we are doing it, we need to discontinue this type of practice.

Moral Human Behavior: Discontinuance

Jesus said to them, "If you were blind, you would have no guilt; but now that you say, 'We see,' your guilt remains.
John 9:41

This verse can be likened to a corn maze. Imagine you are in a corn maze with your friends. Now imagine that you are leading the group the wrong way. If you admit defeat and confess that you don't know where you're going, you're not responsible, if your friends keep following you. But if you claim that you know the way out and continue to lead your friends astray, you're now responsible if they get more lost than they were before. In the same way, if you claim to be righteous and yet continue to willfully live in sin, you will be held accountable. Humble yourself and admit that you don't know everything and that there's still a need for God to teach you.

Amira Morales

However, in a contrasting way, we could illustrate the positive approach and the type of conduct that should be adopted. We can let someone take our place in the position of authority. We can clean tables on Wednesday night at the church dinner. We can delight when others are asked to speak or assume leadership.

Analogous Correspondence in Moral Behavior

Creating an application through some kind of parallel scenario or contemporary situation is a process that requires several stages of development in teaching or sermon preparation. Notice how the following sequence evolves. The listener must:

1.   Be given a reminder of bad behavior.
2.   See the need for dismantling lies behind which the audience might be hiding.
3.   Process through the steps necessary to stop doing something.
     i.   Possess cognitive resolve.
     ii. Decide for physical modifications of behavior.
4.   Live with the consequences.

In creating an application, one first identifies the moral behavior, whether it needs to be adopted, continued (managed, modified, or intensified), discontinued, or deterred. In considering the following text from Psalm 1, there are many ways to apply this identification process for the listener.

> Blessed is the man
>   who walks not in the counsel of the wicked,
> nor stands in the way of sinners,
>   nor sits in the seat of scoffers;

In this text, the progression of deterrence is sequentially more severe. If one walks with bad people, s/he will eventually stand and ultimately sit with the wicked. The posture of the Psalmist is observational; however, the implicit teaching is deterrence. He is trying to help people avoid the obvious negative consequences of fraternizing with wicked people. He is saying, "Please don't do this. Here are the dangers."

Creating applications to help people change moral behavior requires finding parallel scenarios in our current context that model parallel components to the text AND also reflect continuance, discontinuance, modification, or deterrence. Consider this story to illustrate the verse from Psalm 1 above.

> Tom was a young man who was placed into a school after moving into a district from out of town. He craved acceptance. One day, some of the boys in the hall invited him to walk to the next class. He immediately realized that they were talking with bad language about other girls in the class. Since there were a few minutes before the next bell, Tom was standing outside the classroom with the guys making inappropriate comments. Lunch came a few periods later. The same guys invited him to sit with them in the cafeteria. He grabbed his tray and sat

down. He went from walking, to standing, to sitting. He did make friends that day, but the Psalm tells us the cost.

Behavioral change is like coaching someone; the changes and results are hard, sometimes very hard. In the process of making behavioral change, the start of behavior change typically gets progressively harder. Consequently, the results of attempting discontinuance, for example, might be brutal. Therefore, the illustrator might consider addressing mental shifts before behavioral ones.

What goes on in the mind before someone makes the decision to "walk in the council of the wicked?" There is the prior, mental decision to walk, stand, and sit. So, the battle really begins in the mind before it ever begins in the feet. Consequently, it sometimes pays to illustrate the mind-battle before the behavioral one. Here is one solution from Psalm 1:2.

But his delight is in the law of the Lord,
And on his law he meditates day and night.

Deterrence from the 'walking—standing—sitting' downward-spiral is delighting in God and meditating on His word. So, how might the illustrator present a parallel solution to the potential problem? It happens by creating an illustration that deters the person from compromising first in his mind.

When Tom got up in the morning, he was to start at a new school in the district where his parents bought a house. He knew it was going to be a hard day, and as much as he wanted attention and to make friends, he decided to meditate in the scriptures and find delight in his relationship with God, regardless of what happened. He read a couple of chapters in his Bible, prayed, and then left for school. By the end of the second period, he was invited by some guys standing outside the classroom to join them. He walked over and heard their conversation. He immediately realized the speech was inappropriate. He told the guys, "I'll catch up with you later, I have to find my way to the next class." He walked away and had a deep sense of delight in God. He was alone, but he was clean inside.

Universals and Their Connection to Moral Behavior

Universals are principles, values, or thoughts that are shared across human experience. It does not matter where we are in the world or who we are with, regardless of the culture in which we find ourselves, people understand law, feeling, temptation, or a thousand other common notions and actions.

Many scholars of religion emphasize cultural relativism to show differences, but the reality is that we all live with common actions and sentiments. These are the universals that bind us as human beings.

When God spoke to Jacob and recounted the prophecy in Genesis 48:3, the patriarch was relating his submission to a family call that he wanted the children to clearly understand. The promises were universal to Jacob's children. The specific promises of Jacob's forecast cannot be universalized. The future of tribal inheritances was not something for the New Testament believer. However, within all the specifics there are many particulars that are applicable to us.

The passage was, among other things, one of promise: wait for the Messiah, Shiloh. Implicit in the chapter is the idea that the children of God need to return to the place of blessing and stay there. He is saying, "God has a place for you. It is real and concrete."

Universals and Moral Commands

What if the text expresses a moral command that obviously addresses human behavior? How does one preach this? Well, some of the answers to this question depend on the nature of the command and how that command can be expressed under the New Covenant.

For example, in Exodus 20:5 we are told not to make carved images and not to bow down to them. In the West where we do not usually carve idols, the universal might be that God does not want us to place our hope in anything but Him alone. Sacrificial offerings fall under the same purview. Sacrifice might have to do with giving, with worshiping together, with preparation, or with the state of the heart. It will also surely be a picture of Christ Himself. However, in India where idols are everywhere, it might be taken literally and without universalization.

Commands are typically more than simply behavioral standards: they address desire, intent, and core values. It is important for the preacher to express what constitutes New Covenant action and failure. Our job as New Testament believers is to live by kingdom principle and not by law.

In Judges 1:27ff and Judges 2, there are clear failures of the Israelites to drive out the inhabitants of the land. However, what is the teaching? At a minimum, it is a resolve to remain in God's plan, regardless of the obstacles.

Ultimately, the command has both a practical and a symbolic meaning. There are implied ramifications in actions, and those ramifications are universal. So, while the immediate contextual implication for Israel comes from the cultural, historical setting, the wider implication for us is implicit. That is the one that needs to be explained, illustrated, and applied.

The Illustrative Crux of Moral Ramifications

Engagement is heightened when listeners know that something serious is at stake. The benefit of moral precision in preaching is clear. Everyone struggles with the rightness or wrongness of thought and action. Listeners appreciate it when the speaker addresses the moral advantage or danger of certain choices.

Identifying the figured qualities of the subject and more specifically the skill of locating moral ramifications was something developed extensively during the medieval period when Christian preaching had a highly refined sense of ethical call. Preachers in that period used a method of invention that moved beyond the simple classical identification of subject to include this aspect of moral export and suitability. What does this look like at the practical level, however?

Each term of a scripture portion can be defined and expanded by definition and then developed by considering the effects of vices and virtues, that is, ethical suitability or bad and good qualities.[8] This is different from cause-and-effect invention, for example, in that a virtue/vice focus addresses ethical motives, usually by means of praise or denigration, good reinforcement or bad warnings. The moral value that one discovers can be used in preaching to correct or encourage.

This praise or denigration can be with respect to the person doing the action (the agent), the thing used to act (instrument), or the one acted upon. For example, in the story of the Magi in Matthew 2:1-12, rather than speaking generally about the men coming to see the young king, a speaker might take time to praise in detail the wise seeker, his sacrificial gift, or the worthy Jesus. The speaker can focus on one, two, or all three components.

To simplify these ideas, it is possible to encourage or discourage people by idealizing in a moral sense either the good or bad quality of words, phrases, or the entire proposition. In the same way that one might enumerate advantages of good deeds and virtues, one could accentuate the bad things or vices. If the speaker really wants to get specific, it is also possible to negate the non-grammatical elements--the emotive, the sensory, or the behavioral.

Besides contrasting good and bad, praise and blame, or virtue and vice, one might also create images of degree, that is, good, better, or best. Images like this do not show extremes but show degrees of good or bad. It is sometimes important to show people how a mixture of good and bad should be discouraged.

Most people live in the realm of moral indecision. If people can be presented with pictures of what is good, better, or best, namely, images or situations of degree, it will be easier to decide what one ought to do. The speaker can negate, if necessary, partial goodness as an illegitimate category and show people what the best choice is: "One might pray daily. One might pray hourly. But praying with an honest heart, that's praying effectively."

Questions for Engagement

1. What are the four ways to understand behavior according to classical literature?
2. Why and when might it be advantageous to illustrate the opposite behavior that the Bible commands?
3. What is a universal or a generalization?

18 Illustrating Desire

When teaching the Bible, there is a tremendous need to address desire or internal motivation or demotivation for change. In other words, people either do, or do not want to, alter behavior. After all, who wants in their flesh to deny himself and carry the cross. We have to have a handle on what it takes to teach others and address the human will. Consider the following passage, and catalog what desires are stated or implicit.

> **Exodus 3:2**
>
> **And the angel of the LORD appeared to him in a flame of fire out of the midst of a bush. He looked, and behold, the bush was burning, yet it was not consumed. And Moses said, "I will turn aside to see this great sight, why the bush is not burned."**

When looking at a passage like this, our inclination is to immediately recognize Moses' curiosity. However, that is not where the passage begins.

God's desire is that He be known. He wanted to reveal Himself. Do we give God the benefit of the doubt that He is appearing, speaking, and wanting to be in relationship with us?

For Moses' part, he sees the anomaly of a bush that does not burn up. He desires to turn aside. This is not a habit. It is not a passion. He is driven by curiosity, curious desire. Sometimes man needs to see what is unusual and that God is at work, even when motivated by the abnormal.

Moses needs to stop his employment, leave his sheep, and seek what God is trying to tell him. An 80-year-old man is never too old to seek the fire of God!

When dealing with people's desire, there is a complex of emotions and passions that are wrapped up in connecting with listeners verbally for change. They have inclinations and yearnings, but the question is whether the speaker can motivate them to assume preferences if they are hesitant to do right, or motivate them to shut down destructive habits and behaviors.

Our impulses often define us, and quite frankly, they are hard to change. However, if someone is shown the advisability of the eternal value in change, human impulse will inevitably move in the right direction.

Three Facets of Desire: Motive, Passion, Need

There are facets of desire that can be separated out for clarity of understanding. They are **motive**, **passion**, and **need**. When we consider these, we know how to approach application, whether the issue is intention, habit, or necessity.

Illustration involves surgical accuracy. Questioning someone's **motive** is not the same as reforming someone's habitual desire. Additionally, many types of desires are fundamental to human need and might be amoral, so it is not necessary to address them from an ethical perspective.

Desire for Denial

For whoever would save his life will lose it, but whoever loses his life for my sake will find it.
Matthew 16:25

A seed needs to be planted to start growing into a tree. It has to endure before it starts to bear fruit. Similarly, a disciple of Jesus must deny himself and sacrifice his own ideas in order to grow in his relationship to Jesus. When that disciple perseveres through various challenges, he can live in faith and bear fruit in his life.

Gene Badavath

Before someone acts, that person is motivated by desire. Consequently, it is a good place to start when considering how to illustrate a rationale of intention. Motive is quite different from a general understanding of the will. Motive speaks specifically to the 'why' of intention, what drives someone. Motive is the motor behind the will. Consider Matthew 16:25 in the textbox. The verse addresses motive, that is saving one's own life. We avoid losing our lives because it is our desire to stay alive and be self-centered. Motive addresses drive.

When a person preaches, a speaker can dissect motive to demonstrate rationale, demonstrating how intention speaks to a value system. People reveal their values by the choices they make. One way we know people is by what they wish for. It is the center of human life–where we want to eat, spend free time, or spend our cash.

Is someone's motive pure? Is it mixed with selfishness? Is a person driven to live for the benefit of others?

What drives your audience? You must ask this question. Do they genuinely desire to follow your advice or are you asking too much?

"Husbands, love your wives, and do not be harsh with them" (Col 3:19). If we analyze this verse based on motive, we might ask if men have pure motives to be tender?

How might I as a speaker empower men toward total investment of kindness toward their wives? How can I engineer illustration to address a refinement of motive?

> John was interested in relearning to love his wife with all his heart, even though he had long abandoned his tenderness toward her. He took up a 30-day challenge. He decided he would do one significant thing every day to show his wife love. The first day, he stopped on the way home from work and bought flowers. The second day, he decided to give her a back rub while watching TV and ask her questions about her personal interests. The third day, he picked up takeout, so she did not have to cook. He did this for 30 days and built new habits of love and tenderness. His wife immediately saw the difference in her husband and their marriage began to change for the better.

Motive is a highly complex matrix of impulses. Often, motive has no moral barometer. There is no moral violation between choosing Coke over Pepsi or the Buffalo Bills over the Cowboys. It is just a preference. So, when a preacher preaches, it is important not to make an issue out of someone's hankering. It may just be fun, or an itch, or a wish, or their fancy.

On the other hand, when that motive becomes a craving or competes to gain control of a person, the desire is out of control. While some longings are pure and genuine, aspirations need to be controlled and placed under kingdom sovereignty.

Motives speak to intention. Our hopes need to be God's hopes. Our hunger has to be God's hunger. We need to thirst for what God desires for us.

In addressing a pure desire for God and the motive that surrounds that, it is central to biblical literature and at the heart of the Christian life.

The ideas of motive and desire are implicit when we preach a change-ethic. We do not simply ask people to change; we also address their desire for change.

If I am preaching that Abraham left his country, his people, and his extended family as was commanded in Genesis 12, it is important to deal with motive and not raw obedience. We don't go on the mission field to obey the Great Commission. We sense God's heart to share Christ with the nations and to do something great through us before we go.

If Gideon set out a fleece to discern the will of God, it was to be certain in his life-changing call (Judg. 6:36ff). The motive was delayed obedience. His desire was for certitude.

The negative side of motivation within desire is insincerity or counterfeit intention. Motives can be false and insincere. Purity of motive might be possible to illustrate by addressing the opposite, that is, dishonest intention. If a speaker wants to address the danger of false motives from this passage in the Book of Judges, it is possible to show how some people use fleeces to delay obedience or to look for a way out of following the Lord in what is clearly something that needs to happen.

Another way to understand desire is to differentiate it from the concept of **passion**. Passion deals less with motive and more with habit and recurring preference. When we say someone is passionate, we are really making a judgment about consistent burning desire.

Desire: Passion

For all that is in the world—the desires of the flesh and the desires of the eyes and pride of life—is not from the Father but is from the world.
1 John 2:16

John was 18-years old. He had just seen an advertisement for the brand-new iPhone for $1500. He had just enough money and wanted to get it, even though he already had a phone. His Dad told him not to get it because it was a waste, and it would pass away one day. Johnny desired to have the phone but knew it would go against what his father wanted. However, he decided to obey. He used the money to get himself to Bible School. His father was right. He saved the money and used it for a good decision. This pleased his father.

Noah Flach

Additionally, passion is often accompanied by determination. Resolve as a motive is different from determination in the continuation of an action. Sometimes people need to be encouraged to fan the flames of habits already begun. Conversely, people might need to be discouraged from a passion that is inappropriate.

Ultimately, preachers should be concerned about an audience's drive. In other words, what do they love to do and keep on doing? Their personal preferences reveal their aspirations and future. So, while illustration addresses current habits in time, it also encompasses future outcomes.

For a teacher of the scripture to strike at the heart of the human will, it is possible to describe passion and recurring fancy. We all long for things, and typically our yearnings define us.

> You shall treat the stranger who sojourns with you as the native among you, and you shall love him as yourself, for you were strangers in the land of Egypt: I am the LORD your God. (Lev 19:34)

In this verse, it is obvious that we should love foreigners, but it is not always easy, especially since we are asked to love them in the same way that we love ourselves. In considering this verse for preaching, we might probe with questions that assess desire. When we see someone, is it our first inclination to say, "Look a foreigner. I should love that person just as I love myself. I wonder if I could help this person?"

Because desire often cuts to our personal priorities, we can preach to the natural tendency to avoid those not like ourselves. Conversely, we can ask why that is. Do we treat foreigners harshly, think they are here to steal our jobs, or racially-intermarry our children? What is our passion? Is it for them or for ourselves?

To reorient our audience toward a consuming love for internationals is quite a task, but it is at the very center of the church. To preach passion for international mission within the local context is a hard priority, and examining enthusiasm for internationals can be done by addressing passionate desire for those not like us.

An additional area that addresses desire is **need**. There are basic human needs that we desire, which are not negotiable. These needs have less to do with personal motive or passion and more to do with necessity. There is a certain ache that comes with day-to-day obligations and bondages.

However, not all necessities are cumbersome; they might simply be non-negotiable. In some cultures, basic needs are, in fact, both a cultural necessity and a passion because life is fragile.

> You yourselves know that these hands ministered to my necessities and to those who were with me. (Acts 20:34)

Many verses are not this obvious, but there is explicit desire here to do what must be done. He desired to work and make a living, not only for himself, but also for others.

Scholars have designed a hierarchy of needs; it is helpful at this point. There are basic human needs like air, water, food, and shelter. Paul is addressing basic human need in this verse. We should have a passion to supply for our own basic needs as well as for others.

When we move to how we prioritize need, the Bible speaks a lot to this, and its conclusions might surprise us. Jesus put Maslow's hierarchy of need on its head when He said, "It is written, 'Man shall not live by bread alone, but by every word that comes from the mouth of God'" (Mat 4:4). Our basic need is for God and His word. He examines our desires and measures them against a spiritual priority that He owns.

As a final thought on passion, the reader should consider that the issues of passion, motive, and need are all forward thinking. They address the future.

When a person is eager for something, be it bad or good, the temporal component is future oriented. It addresses what is about to happen. The next step could be out of reticence or out of enthusiasm. Either way, we are addressing the future.

This is a great leveraging point for the teacher of the Bible. Most people want improvement. Some see how to get there and only need a nudge. Others do not have a clue and need complete reorientation.

To address motives, passions, and needs in preaching is one of the best ways to bring congruence between God's will and our own muddied or stifled intentions. The reason why illustrating desire is so effective is that people want the best for themselves. As Paul stated in Ephesians, "For no one ever hated his own flesh, but nourishes and cherishes it, just as Christ does the church" (5:29). We should help people clarify what they cherish.

Questions for Engagement

1. How is desire different from emotion when illustrating the texts of the Bible?
2. What are three facets of desire, and how are they different?
3. What are some aspects of motive, and how is the idea of motive useful in Bible application?
4. How is passion different from desire?
5. What is the difference between need and necessity (basic human need)?

19 Illustrating Fixed Objects by Using Analogies

Often people that illustrate the Bible believe that the illustrator should primarily be concerned with action and story. However, one of the most important things the careful teacher of the scriptures should elucidate is nouns and things in a fixed state. Here are a few examples that show the importance of this reality.

Let's begin with a very familiar passage. Identify the nouns and fixed objects that are present in this passage from the Sermon on the Mount.

Matthew 7:24-27

Everyone then who hears these words of mine and does them will be like a wise man who built his house on the rock. And the rain fell, and the floods came, and the winds blew and beat on that house, but it did not fall, because it had been founded on the rock. And everyone who hears these words of mine and does not do them will be like a foolish man who built his house on the sand. And the rain fell, and the floods came, and the winds blew and beat against that house, and it fell, and great was the fall of it.

It is an easy passage to identify fixed objects—'house,' 'rock,' 'rain,' 'floods,' 'winds,' 'man,' 'sand,' etc. However, it is quite another matter to move from the literal to the figurative. Yet, that is the intention of Jesus.

After the expositor interprets the meaning of the nouns and finds approximations of their **symbolic** value ('house'= life; 'rain'=difficulties), the hard work of application begins. How far does one take the application?

Can 'floods' equate to health issues, the loss of a job, divorce, miscarriage, or some other common life occurrence? The most obvious direction to take the nouns is to identify their symbolic connotation. However, there are many other things going on with the fixed objects of this passage.

There is a **place in space**. The passage contrasts two houses. Is this you and your neighbor? You and the girl who shares a locker next to you? The man in the next cubicle? This is a spatial connotation.

There is an issue of **number** here as well: plurality. There are 'floods,' not just one. There are not only health issues, but school failure or a car breakdown. There are many floods, and people don't usually have to just deal with one problem at a time.

There is an issue of **degree**, that is, the question of severity. The rain is not a gentle, calming farm-rain. It is repeated torrential downpour, ready to take the house away in a mudslide.

These are just a few of the ways to look at fixed objects, and the implications are very important. Skill at identifying the significance of fixed components in a passage is critical.

What if the Lord's prayer said, "My Father, who art in heaven, hallowed be your name"? This would fit into a Western individualistic culture. Yet, the text says 'our Father' for a reason. Our prayers should be corporate. We need to be transparent.

What if Paul had written in this introduction to the Book of Romans that Jesus was "declared to be 'a' son of God with power" rather than "the Son of God with power"? We would be right back in dispute over Arian's view of the deity of Christ and the validity of Trinitarianism in the Council of Nicaea.

Objects and their form, symbolism, place in space, number and a host of other qualities are extremely important to the export of an application. Additionally, these simple observations are easy to make and teach people to be careful when reading the Bible. The preacher or teacher can change the number and elucidate the implications and make theological or moral application as appropriate. Here is a summary of how to analogize from essence or quality in fixed objects.

Essence or Quality	Observation Objective	Negation
Its form	Look for things with the same form, its container, or its contents.	Look for the opposite form.
Its place in space	Look for two objects that are close in space.	Look for objects removed from the specified one.
Its symbolism	Look for another thing that has symbolic meaning either positively or negatively.	Identify the opposite or competing symbols.
Its human qualities	Look for human qualities to which you can liken it.	Identify its non-human qualities.

Among the general domains in illustration, such as movement, emotion, moral behavior, abstraction, etc., there is this very obvious reality of nouns and pronouns, often overlooked. These 'things' can be concrete objects, or they can be non-material ideas.

Here are some examples of beginning the process of discerning a way to approach illustrating nouns and fixed objects. Determining what needs to be illustrated or applied involves differentiating the exact thing being illustrated. Many times, it is important to focus on, or differentiate, the **quality** or export of something in a fixed state. What is a 'pearl' in the pearl of great price? What is a 'house' in the Sermon on the Mount when the rains and floods came? Where is the 'seat of the scoffers' for a reader of Psalm 1? What is the symbolic meaning of the breastplate of the priest as he wears the jewels of the 12 tribes? Why are there 12 gates in Nehemiah's temple?

Isolating Syntactic Importance

When the Bible reader tries to interpret and then apply the meaning of the text, the question s/he is apt to raise involves the meaning of static nouns—their number, their definiteness, their degree, their place in space, etc. For example, when the Bible says that the soldiers placed a crown of thorns on Jesus' head, what does that object mean (Mark 15:17)? If it is a symbol of mockery, how do people 'crown' us that follow Him? If it is a symbol of the sacrifice of atonement, it is entirely different. It represents the cost of forgiveness and ultimately the love of God.

Once we isolate the component noun or thing that is in a fixed state, it is important to answer the following question: What is it about this thing, or the state of this thing, that must be communicated to an audience? What needs illustration? What has precise meaning for the audience to which I am talking? What is important about the object, its component parts, its use, or its relevance to the listener?

Let's return to Nehemiah's gates. What is contained in the idea of multiple gates? There is a lot of symbolism here. The first one is an invitation. In the place where God 'places His name,' the invitation is always open to come in; we have an eternally open door. Do our lives as Christians have twelve gates, or do we have a single gate with towers on each side, ready to shoot at the enemy? This idea is also picked up by John the Apostle in Revelation 21:10-13, when he says the Bride, the Lamb's wife, was the holy city Jerusalem, a square or cubical city bejeweled with twelve gates, eternally lit by the Lamb.

There is inherent export in fixed objects that facilitate analogy. This was the principle of the analogy of intrinsic attribution explained earlier. Jesus repeatedly employs this teaching method throughout His life, and it is all through the gospels.

Categorically Speaking

When we read the text, what might appear to be a simple noun or typical object has representative value in both syntactical meaning at the sentence level as well as spiritual export. Even the most mundane things can carry eternal weight when they are looked at in the light of scriptural implications and God's intention for us in teaching. This is why a jot-and-tittle-bibliology is critical. It helps us find value in the details.

Upon looking at the state, usage, and essence of nouns in particular, or what is called morphology by grammarians, one can classify things in helpful ways. Although these categories below are innate, they are not always easy to see or to extract.

Fixed Object: Incense

And when he had taken the scroll, the four living creatures and the twenty-four elders fell down before the Lamb, each holding a harp, and golden bowls full of incense, which are the prayers of the saints.
Revelation 5:8

Our prayers go to the Lord as if we have used mouthwash. God makes our breath a sweet aroma. Do you believe or know that your prayers are of the greatest value before the Lord? Do you believe that He delights in the sweetness of your prayers? Do you know that your prayers are important and directly before Him?

Irina Danyuk

Essence might be latent in **form, symbolism, possession, number, place or position in space/hierarchy/degree, or human qualities**. There are other aspects one might add to this list, but for now, we will work on these.

To illustrate, consider the following questions. They reflect different aspects of fixed things. How do we define the localization of idol meat and its implications (1 Cor. 8:10)? Why do we need two or three for Jesus to be in the midst (Matt. 18:20)? When James addresses a lack or absence of 'wisdom' in James 1:5, what is this 'thing' we call wisdom?

In trying to grasp the teaching value of a culturally entrenched concept like meat being offered to an idol, it is important to break down the reality of the implied export. There it is, the meat, presented by the first century Greek butcher to his god. The person walking by the market makes implicit, split-second decisions that are paradigmatic for illustration and application.

The issue of **'form'** of meat would have to be extrapolated by historical study and cannot be validated. The same could be said for its place in space. However, hierarchy is clearly an issue. By offering the meat to an idol, the merchant is sanctifying it to a god. It's an offering. The purchaser is entering into a religious offering. Although an idol is nothing according to Paul (1 Cor. 10:19), he still counsels people to avoid having fellowship with demons. Fraternizing with the demonic is ill advised because one might enter a satanic hierarchy of engagement. One can apply this text in multiple ways through the correlation of inappropriate human action via the mediation of seemingly innate objects that can defile or entangle the Christian. It might be an e-cigarette, a pyramid scheme, a beer, or an anti-depressant medication.

There may also be **symbolism** in meat offered to idols. Since that food was associated with a system of religion, there is intrinsic symbolic value that moves beyond just the meat, kind of like branding in the United States. For example, saying, "I'm gonna have a cold one" implies having an alcoholic drink. It might export symbolic meaning that could be inadvisable in some Christian settings.

Once we find the component of a text that needs to be applied broadly in a teaching setting, the student of the Bible needs to probe down on the reason for application. The text should reveal both the important crux as well as the way to explain or illustrate it.

Following the isolation of the component part, we look for corollary and analogy to show relevance to the audience. The elements of correspondence between the textual component and the real world should be natural and obvious. For example, in preaching Acts 5:6 where Luke says, "The young men rose and wrapped him up and carried him out and buried him," I could reference the symbolic meaning of young pole bearers.

One clear aspect in considering fixed objects is the reality of ownership or **possession**. When we consider action or movement, we often ask the 'who' question. In examining the state of nouns, we must ask this and several other types of questions: Who is acting? Should that person be acting? HOW are they acting? Should someone else be in possession? What is possessed? How tightly is it owned?

Take a close look at the following verse. "The next day a harmful spirit from God rushed upon Saul, and he raved within his house while David was playing the lyre, as he did day by day. Saul had his spear in his hand" (1 Sam. 18:10). There are several components of possession here. The harmful spirit is in Saul. David is in possession of a lyre to bring freedom in praise, and by contrast, Saul grasps the instrument of death to kill.

The preacher should ask, "Is someone you know afflicted by demonic forces? Who possesses whom? Doesn't God possess you, Christian? What is in your hands to drive the spirit away? This is naturally a figurative question. What do you possess, or what is in your hand that is God's means of deliverance for those around you? What is your instrument of praise, literal or figurative? Other people may be around us holding the spear of death to pin us to the wall, but we hold the instrument of praise. God is our shield."

Another example might be In Deuteronomy 7:6, where Moses tells the Israelites: "For you are a people holy to the LORD your God. The LORD your God has chosen you to be a people for his treasured possession, out of all the peoples who are on the face of the earth." The people are God's. He is their owner, and He treasures them. We are, in fact, God's treasure.

In moving to the '**number**' of the noun, we might not realize it, but there are critical aspects to singularity or plurality in terms of interpretation and application. Paul counsels us in 1 Cor. 10:32 to: "Give no offense to Jews or to Greeks or to the church of God" (1Co 10:32). He does not say 'churches of God.' He says THE church of God. By implication, it means all Christians. He is employing a synecdoche, using the whole (the church) for the parts (people in the church). In other words, we should not give offense to any person.

Imagine if we change any of the nouns in the following passages from singular to plural or plural to singular: "I have not come to call the righteous but sinners to repentance" (Luke 5:32); "And I, John, am the one who heard and saw these things" (Rev.

22:8); "Therefore lift your drooping hands and strengthen your weak knees" (Heb. 12:12); "Let your eyes be on the field that they are reaping" (Ruth 2:9). In this latter example, Boaz wanted Ruth to stay close and protected on his own land and to reap in his field. If our eyes are on the 'fields' where our destiny is not found, we will certainly reap something other than His blessing.

Place in space/hierarchy/degree

When applying biblical texts, sometimes there is an obvious illustration that can be made by isolating and referring to someone's **place in space**. In Joshua's early life, he did not leave the temple, but chose to abide in the presence of God (Exodus 33:11).

Here is the issue of proximity. It may be obvious, but are you abiding in the presence of God? When everyone leaves, do you stay and pray? When others pass on to life's mechanics, do you choose to remain in communion?

Beyond this, Joshua was a young man, and even with all his youthful pressures, hormones, desires, and family obligations, he chose proximity. His 'place in space' was close to the atoning blood and to the worship of the people of God.

One's place in space could correlate to remaining supportive to an ostracized, pregnant fiancée (Matt. 1:19), to sinful people who need the Savior (1 Cor. 5:10), or remaining with God's leader, willing to do battle (Judg. 7:3). Asking an audience their place in space is not difficult. That localization can be figurative and move people to acknowledge their proximity to God and God's people.

In a more **hierarchical** way, people place themselves in harm's way in a spiritual sense, when they submit to a damaging authority in life. The place in space is not physical, but positional. Naturally, submitting to men is part of everyday experience, but gentle reminders from the pulpit or during a Bible study, can help someone re-center and fall under healthy authority.

Sometimes encouraging people with human distance is quite necessary. Paul is quite matter of fact about Demas having abandoned him (2 Tim. 4:10). When the disciples returned to fishing and boating in John 21, their physical proximity to the very things from which the Savior called them away was a critical mistake. Of course, in the same passage, Peter leads the way; the others follow in kind. There is a ready-made application. The critical question is this: When is it proper to distance from a backslidden leader?

Like many things in life, position in space or one's place with respect to influence is a matter of **degree**. We can be close, but not close enough. We can be far, but not far enough. We can be safely distant in the worst sense of the term. We can bring others with us to the safe-but-disobedient locale in which we have taken refuge.

It is entirely possible to be moving closer, but at a speed that is dangerous, like walking away from an active shooter rather than running for cover. Illustrating proximity, speed, and hierarchy is often best illustrated by degrees of closeness or distance or even by pace.

In other words, there is a spectrum of danger, of love, of commitment, and of relationship. Distance is a very real concrete reality. People understand it readily. The farther you are away from the basketball hoop, the harder it is to make a basket. Distance can be bad. On the other hand, if the police shoot tear gas canisters, people run for cover. It is time to get away.

We can, as teachers of the scriptures, shoot the pepper spray gun to warn people that proximity is not a good idea. Similarly, we can give concrete illustrations to show why closeness is a good idea in certain contexts.

Human Qualities

One of the strongest ways to illustrate something is to make association to human characteristics. Is it time to be the ear, the mouthpiece, the feet, the hands?

Physical objects may have human form or may be given human form by biblical writers. The church is the body of Christ and has many members. This is the obvious illustration of Paul in 1 Corinthians 12:14-31. When this happens, illustration is logical because people readily associate with their humanity.

Fixed Objects with Human Qualities

As it is, there are many parts, yet one body.
1 Corinthians 12:20

The diverse General Motors assembly factory has a diversity of workers with multiple ethnicities and positions (mangers, supervisors, line electricians, technicians, cleaners, packers, etc.), but no matter how insignificant the job of a particular factory worker on the plant line may seem, the plant manager cannot say I don't need this staff member. All the workers come together to ensure the full functionality of that motor plant. Just as the manager cannot do the work of the cleaner or security guard, so the cleaner cannot do the work of the electrician or line supervisor. This is how we all are in the body of Christ. The pastor or leader of the church cannot do all the work, and no matter how small the job of the cleaner or the usher is in the church, the pastor cannot say, "I don't need him/her, because everyone is part of that body, and they all ensure optimum functionality of the body of Christ."

Danladi Dan-Ahmed.

The Bible teacher that uses Paul's allusion to the 'right hands of fellowship' (Gal. 2:9) might correlate this with reaching out to others. When Ezekiel rehearses God's words to the people to 'cast away the detestable things your eyes feast on," he is using human qualities to elucidate obsessive desire (Ez. 20:7). The illustrator can continue the metaphor in preaching by asking the congregation what their eyes are feasting on—four wheelers, that new boat, designer labels, or an illicit relationship.

Jesus does this in His parabolic images. In Matthew 6:22 He says, "The eye is the lamp of the body." We physically see things, and this helps us navigate. Spiritually healthy perception gives us spiritual navigation. The 'eye' becomes metaphorical for healthy, kingdom decision-making.

When Peter pronounces Saphira dead because of her collaborative lie with Ananias, Peter says to her: "the feet of those who have buried your husband are at the door, and they will carry you out" (Acts 5:9). Feet don't carry corpses; people do. It's another synecdoche, the part for the whole. What are our feet carrying? We better watch out or someone's feet will see the hypocritical offering we laid at the feet of the apostles and carry us out.

Texts and words that do not have innate human characteristics can be recast for the listener with human qualities. Were I preaching on Matthew 22:39," You shall love your neighbor as yourself," I might develop this by personifying love and asking people who they carried lately? Have you carried your friend who needs you? Have you carried that broken relative who just got a divorce?

Armies can have legs that personify going into spiritual battle. The congregational weakness can be Sampson's hair, cut by enemies of Christ. Eyes are perception. Ears are discernment. We can sniff out danger, sound the alarm with our mouths, or clothe ourselves in holiness.

The human body is almost an endless supply of illustrative material that can be associated with many verses in the scripture, even if they have no apparent human form. How we move from text to image is a question of several factors.

The noun or object possesses an innate form that may or may not have implicit movement. Associating a word or textual idea with a human quality is done by recognizing the inherent characteristics within the thing itself.

The human body has control (arms or mind), movement (legs), hearing (ears), speaking/rebuke/influence (mouth), and on and on we could go with parallels. It is up to the illustrator to see if the text lends itself to associating an idea with an imaged picture or with explanatory/discursive delivery.

Questions for Engagement

1. What is an analogy?
2. Why is the principle of comparison important in preaching?
3. What does it mean that an object has a fixed quality?
4. Of the four qualities of essence that are listed–form, place, symbolism, and human quality–which might be the hardest for you to illustrate? Why?
5. What does it mean that a noun has static importance or representative value?
6. In preaching, how does the idea of possession have value for sermonic illustration?
7. What are some scriptures where the number of the noun might be worth illustrating?
8. When is it important to illustrate place in space, hierarchy, or degree in a Bible passage?
9. Why does illustration through human quality have a certain resonance with the listener?

20 Illustrating Abstractions with Wings

Scriptural texts are filled with principles, ideas, and universals. How does one illustrate an abstraction? Consider this passage.

> **Colossians 1:15-16**
>
> **He is the image of the invisible God, the firstborn of all creation. For by him all things were created, in heaven and on earth, visible and invisible, whether thrones or dominions or rulers or authorities—all things were created through him and for him.**

There are many abstractions in this passage. An idea presented as an abstraction can, at times, be vague and obtuse. These images can also be subject to a vast array of interpretations.

Once the speaker has properly interpreted the abstraction, it is important to further narrow the gap of meaning when it comes to theoretical ideas. Beyond this, how can a preacher capture the essence of an idea and throw it into a picture without violating scriptural context?

It is sad to say, but many communicators in church are highly notional and conceptual. They talk about justification and atonement as if people in the audience know what they are talking about or are on the same page as the speaker.

We tend to universalize concepts naturally in everyday life. "That food was terrible," for example. However, what was wrong with it? Was it too spicy, too watery, too cold, or bland? Did it have a fly in it, or was it reheated, leftover, dry meatloaf?

It is second nature to abstract ideas and generalize, especially for those of us in the West. We talk about faithfulness, goodness, holiness, evil, and a host of other concepts. Yet often the audience is bewildered and lost, even bored. They say to themselves, "Can you put some flesh and blood on that, please?"

Without a clear idea of how to move from universals to specifics, the universal concept will fall on the ears of the listener as a distant speculation, not something that is real in one's everyday life. The abstraction is perhaps understood, but foggy.

In the above Colossians passage, there are some tricky lexical issues tied to the abstractions. What does the word 'firstborn' mean? What are 'thrones' and 'dominions'?

We know interpretively from Colossians 1:18, the passage that follows the one quoted above, that 'firstborn' is not a sequential term but a noun of preeminence because Jesus was not the 'first' one resurrected from the dead. There were ten or so people raised from the dead before him, Lazarus, the son of the widow from Nain, etc. The export of the idea of preeminence is also tied to who Jesus rules, that is, the 'thrones' and 'dominions.'

It is critical that the speaker make these terms understandable to the common person. The terms 'thrones' and 'dominions' are synecdochical, that is, they are representative of the individuals who hold power. Jesus is not the authority over a 'throne.' He is the 'firstborn,' the ruler, over demonic individuals and spiritual forces who attempt to exert authority on earth.

When doing application from a passage like this, it is critical to unpack the abstraction. It must be made concrete for the listener.

There are several ways to help an audience grab hold of common abstractions like attributes, perfections, theological categories, or generalizations. The way we can concretize abstraction and make it live for the listener is to nuance the abstraction with detail.

Nuancing an abstraction can be done in many ways, but there are a few clear and simple methods that we do in everyday life. These are skills you already know. Let me explain.

If my wife says to me, "I would like to get a new couch for the living room," my question would be, "What did you have in mind?"

I want details, cost, color, type, and size. I would ask her to nuance the concept of a couch with something that I can picture. "Do you want a printed fabric, leather, or a recliner?" In that same way, we must nuance ideas in church communication. We cast the abstraction into something tangible and tactile. We do this so the audience can see the result more clearly.

It is not enough to simply define abstractions for an audience. In fact, it usually makes things worse. If I said that holiness is the state of being holy, I have not added much to the mind of the listener. If I continue and explain that it is sanctity or devotedness or being religious, I have probably made matters worse.

Unfortunately, this is the way people teach theology, and the general public gets poisoned toward refining their knowledge of God. They assume that becoming theologically educated removes normal people from everyday life. Preaching also is seen as an irrelevant discipline, detached from

---

Abstraction to Concreteness

Is not my word like fire, declares the LORD, and like a hammer that breaks the rock in pieces?
Jeremiah 23:29

God's word produces life, just like the fire used to burn coal at the Tanner's Creek Generating Station in Lawrenceburg, and just like the hammer which cuts brick in Napoleon, Indiana. God's word produces energy and life. It breaks down hearts of stone and brick to be built back up on His authority. Living without it would be like trying to run the coal plant on water or cutting rock with a plastic fork or spoon.

Ben Bausback

the working man or woman who punches a timeclock.

So, how does a speaker clarify notions? How do we move from an idea to its concrete implications?

Nuancing the Abstraction

There are several simple ways to help make an idea clearer to people. We begin by nuancing the abstraction.

The first matter of nuancing abstraction is **proper definition**. We must have clarity of meaning. An idea can be improperly understood or defined. All else will fail if the concept is not a biblical one. Similarly, proper definition brings ideological power and practical accuracy in illustration.

If we clearly present a biblical idea and properly define it, we can move from there to where people live. The way this is done is through focusing on **quality, magnitude, and distortion**. Let me explain.

Preachers should make every effort to demonstrate the quality of abstraction. Quality demands adjectives and adjectives imply pictures.

If we were to take the abstraction of 'holiness,' how can a speaker make that more real for a listener? Once the preacher magnifies or defines the idea of holiness through exalted/deteriorated **quality,** enhanced/diminished magnitude, or clarified/distorted perfection, the speaker can then picture the nuance. For example, we might ask, 'What does distorted holiness look like?'

If I speak of a person who goes to church in slicked-out clothes, but that morning argued with his wife, the spiritual clothes are stained. He is not as holy as he looks. Similarly, a teen who is poorly dressed but stands with the bullied person, she is holy, at least as that instance of justice is concerned.

Nuancing an idea through qualitative description requires that the speaker shows how the abstraction 'looks' in the physical world. What does justice look like? What human action is required in sanctification?

To be clear, we might have a nuance like this. What would a person do to achieve atonement for sin? The Old Testament believer had to bring a hundred-pound lamb to the altar to have its throat slit. The blood would be spilled and sprinkled.

Detail solidifies concepts in the minds of the listener. Detailed description over time is even better. It **amplifies the magnitude.**

Nuancing is sometimes a question of magnitude or comprehensiveness. The abstraction can be diminished or made stronger with a detailed story. Rarified terms or ideas aid people's conceptual categories, but don't really give them solutions to real problems.

If "nothing will be impossible with God," what is 'nothing' (Luke 1:37)? Is it a human flying by flapping his arms? The 'nothing' is that answered prayer for rent money, for healing, or for divine intervention in the jungles of the Amazon for a missionary.

What is the Bible saying when we read, "But for me it is good to be near God" (Ps. 73:28)? What is good? What does it mean to be 'near' a Spirit? Does goodness mean belly-laughing or deep contentment that stops my stomach ulcers?

Amplifying the magnitude or diminishing the extent of a noun makes it concrete for the listener. A mother's 'love' is pictured by the 2:00 a.m. baby-feeding or the endless rocking of the baby with colic. Love is shown to be concrete by a common example.

Amplitude is a matter of **number.** For example, Daniel prayed three times a day with his windows open toward Jerusalem, the place of atonement, while under threat (Dan. 6:10). He still gave thanks anyway. While prayer is not a number and the real issue is not frequency, we can still illustrate magnitude with a number. If the prayer focus of a person is zero, we have a real problem.

Illustration by number is important. In John 21, six men returned to fishing in Galilee after being told to remain in Jerusalem. Where were the other 5 disciples? Were the disciples not unified about the vocational nature of ministry?

Number is very similar to the idea of **privation**. Is something conspicuously absent? When preaching, a preacher can simply ask if a habit, idea, theological concept, or quality exists or not.

The reality of privation naturally leads to blessing and good effects or terrible realities and bad effects. If an important thing is to have something present in one's life, to have privation is bad. If something terrible exists in my life when it should not, we need to seek it to be eliminated.

The opposite of privation is **excess**. Sometimes good things exist in excess even as do bad or sinful things. The preacher should take time to concretize the theoretical, but at that point, the question becomes the scope of a behavior. Do we have it in dearth or in excess?

Abstract concepts can be elucidated by the means of **distortion** or **negation**. People know when things are imperfect. If the scriptures say that we should rejoice and exult and give Him the glory, for the marriage of the Lamb has come, and His Bride has made herself ready," then we should know what it means to be 'ready' (Rev. 19:7).

Is the wedding gown of the church, the beautiful Bride, stained with gossip or men criticizing the pastor? What is readiness? Is it the missions-involvement of a focused church?

To show what this looks like in an extended illustration, I want to give you an illustration from a sermon of one of my students, Phillip Jones, an older, non-traditional student who was preaching on Hebrews 1:1: "Long ago, at many times and in many ways, God spoke to our fathers by the prophets, but in these last days he has spoken to us by his Son, whom he appointed the heir of all things, through whom also he created the world."

In his sermon, he reminded us that God is speaking, but asked if we were listening. He negated the idea of listening to God-talk and Jesus-talk. He did this by stating that hearing the voice of Jesus is like wearing noise-canceling headphones. He paralleled his ideas by saying that the microphones in the headset pick up the exact kind of sounds coming your way, and they measure the exact frequency. The headphones then begin to produce and emit the exact opposite frequency, this has the effect of colliding with the incoming soundwaves and effectively cancels them out, making it so that the incoming sounds never even reach your ears. The person wearing the headphones isn't affected and can continue listening to their source. In the same way, we need to hear Jesus' voice daily.

What this student did was to take the notion of listening to God's voice and focused on canceling competing voices. He preached the text by first negating the opposite.

Just to clarify one last nuance, abstractions are different from stative verbs. For example, the words 'satisfy' or 'feels,' are not abstractions. They are a type of verb that describes a state. These also need to be made concrete, although they are already within themselves vivid. Internal musings, being, and posture (i.e. hearing, thinking, being, and standing), do not describe action, but a strange sort of intrinsic activity

Clarifying Abstractions with Sense-Language

As preachers who are supremely interested in helping listeners relate to the Bible, we want to develop a means of constructing vivid figures by identifying the essence or quality of the scriptural components and then finding analogous images to which people can relate. This is done principally by appealing to **sense-language**. What does this look like?

An average speaker does not need a college degree on how to *identify* or *classify* figures to *create* them. Building images, stories, or speech figures is naturally done by a speaker who can picture an idea or its opposite. The speech just needs to be 'heard,' 'seen,' 'touched,' 'smelled,' or 'tasted.'

The base of figure-generative technique is a result of the student's observation and his interpretive power, not his imitation of written forms or scalping a good illustration off the Internet. The speaker needs to 'see' the component in an idea that can be cast in the language of the senses where people live every day.

It is one thing to say that kindness exists or does not exist in a person, something very easily done in preaching. "Are you kind?" However, correlating this reality of kindness illustrated in Ephesians 4:32 by talking about bruising on a child, verbally snapping at a boss, being short with your spouse, or rolling one's eyes in disbelief at the grocery cashier is quite another story.

What does following the Good Shepherd look like on the twenty-first floor of a corporate office in Manhattan or while repairing barbed wire on the prairie in the Sandhills of Nebraska during the winter? Show the listener what that crisis sounds like, feels like, or looks like.

If Paul says that he is not ashamed of the Gospel in Roman 1:18, what might that *sound* like? In preaching this text, can the speaker create a dialog of people in which the Christian speaks without shame before peers? What are the actual responses of the listeners? What do they sound like? Might someone respond positively to the bold witness?

An audience loves dialog. Can a speaker create a hypothetical dialog, something that one might hear in a real conversation?

Similarly, what did the love feasts of 1 Corinthians smell like just before they disrespectfully started eating without waiting and being disciplined enough to delay the start of the supper? What do the four horses of the apocalypse look like? What did the nets of James and John feel like while they were in the boat with their father, just before they dropped them to follow Jesus?

Almost everything in the scriptures can be heard, seen, smelled, tasted, or felt. We owe it to our listeners to make the scriptures live with words that appeal to the senses. It is very real and normal to everyday life.

Questions for Engagement

1.   What is an abstraction? How might that be different from a universal?
2.   What is wrong with preaching too many abstractions or universals?
3.   What are some ways of nuancing abstractions?
4.   How do details solidify concepts in the minds of the listener?
5.   Illustrating through the ideas of privation or excess is something we know well in the 20th century. How might this help us in applying the Bible in a specific way?
6.   How does sense-language help concretize abstractions?

21 Illustrating Through Text-Based Story Creation

When we move from text-to-story, typically the process begins with a singular thought. We must capture the illustrative point in the text that we are trying to expand before we create a basic plot. The theme should come before the detailing of story creation.

In story creation, typically there is a component of suspense or a plot movement that withholds the outcome. As the story is rolled out, people imagine in their minds how the setting and the characters are evolving. The audience processes along on the journey as each piece of the narrative is revealed.

Narratives are structural framing devices that are used by the preacher to create resonance with the audience, both an audience-text connection as well as a speaker-audience connection. There is a communal unfolding and scriptural engagement that is very real in biblical storytelling. Narrative frameworks give birth to ideas, beliefs, and solutions to life's questions. When the speaker properly communicates a biblical change idea, the listener sees the value of adoption and moves toward God in some sense, either cognitively or behaviorally.

Often the critical idea of a biblical text is the focal point of the homiletic endeavor and could benefit from expansion through a story or a short narrative image. The idea, word, or verse we are wanting to apply in a practical way does not have to be a narrative, but a story can help explain the truth.

For example, the man at Gate Beautiful in Acts 3 was sitting. It was a question of 'position of action,' or, of inaction. In raw terms, the man's position becomes the very basis of astonishment and contrast.

Later, we find the man walking and leaping. For the modern illustrator, the paradigmatic corollary would be to find someone frozen in a position for 40 years or more and who was also suddenly released from physical imprisonment—maybe sight from blindness, walking from a wheelchair, or to motherhood from infertility.

The illustrator needs to ask how the idea might be pictured in a parallel fashion. To illustrate how this works, consider the following example from the Pentateuch.

God asks Moses, "What is in your hand?" The Almighty tells him to throw it down. How might this be pictured using an image-divisioning technique and then put into a narrative?

It might be easy to develop a few core images and movements. We have the idea of a person's "hand" or a verb like "throw." What might a person have in his or her hand? A hammer, pencil, steering wheel, a baseball or piece of chalk? A carpenter could be asked to throw his hammer down and see what God will do with it.

As the speaker continues the search for a nuanced communicative concept, she might ask that question, "*Who?*" The answer is that it is Moses, not Joshua, not Aaron, and not God. It is a particular man at a particular time in his life. This is *timing*. It is at a particular location. For illustrative purposes, this is a question of *place*.

If someone looks at this *causally,* one will ask, "What were the good and bad effects?" It struck fear into Moses and also gave him confidence to obey God when the result might be death.

Illustration comes by finding analogous images and stories that illustrate the concept of *confidence in God in the face of death*, or the *unexpected encounter with God of a working man when he turns away from his place of employment*.

In identifying the subject exactly, the speaker is more apt to approach common ground with the audience. As the details of the communicative thought emerge, often the precision brings a universal appeal or a quality that a listener will find gratifying. A woman drops her chalk to see what a teacher can do in a school district to bring students to Christ. A business entrepreneur throws down his checkbook or credit card to see what that miraculous action might cause.

Unlike specific scenarios that provide concrete details to which the listener can immediately grasp, generalizations leave the listener wondering what the speaker's intentions are and what the exact meaning of the text looks like in real life. Detailed precision of subject builds clarity into the sermonic form and makes it easier to find sensorial properties that are recognizable to the listener.

Story as a Method of Resonance and Not Entertainment

Many pastors want to keep their people engaged, so they look for stories to reinforce their ideas and capture people's attention. However, what I am suggesting in this book is much more than this. It involves how to use the narrative form to remind people what they already know and have experienced, but maybe ignored or have forgotten.

Stories implicitly address fundamental realities in a culture. They express standards, convictions, habits, anomalies, and a host of other true-to-life scenarios. They challenge or affirm convictions which people already hold.

Stories can displace fiction or confront us in gentle ways. They help people realize the danger of bad living and false assumptions. They also provide a way forward for those that want to know what to do next.

We all hide behind our fortresses of lies, and stories worm their way into our consciousness and help us question the truth of our knowledge. We live with hopes, expectations, and the challenge of decision-making, and we proceed on a foundation of cultural assumptions that are not always good.

The assumptions by which we live can be described in stories. When those stories are recounted, it challenges our beliefs and the generalizations from which we make decisions.

The preacher delivers a story, and there is latent in the story a certain power. Just a glimpse at an audience during a story shows that there is resonance. When the speaker says, "Let me tell you a story…" or "Think of it this way. A woman once did such-and-such," the heads, groggy with sleep, suddenly perk up. The eyes open. The daydreaming stops.

The entertainment value of a story, however, is not the most important aspect of the medium. The underlayment on which the story is constructed constitutes the life-change challenge.

Story Basics

Before moving to story construction, readers should understand the nature of a story. What are the constituent parts? How do those parts work? How can I understand what makes the medium work? How is Jesus' method not a version of storytelling as we know it?

If we can suspend the last question until the next chapter, we will focus for the time being on breaking down the basic elements of a story, so it will be possible to construct them more easily. It will be much easier for the reader to envision using stories in sermons if s/he understands the components of what makes up a story.

Identification

Because I believe that story form should not be used by Bible teachers as an entertainment medium but as a change-agent, the first part of grasping narrative form is the idea of **identification**, something discussed earlier. However, within the nature of narrative form, the mechanics of preaching by comparison must be understood by the ear on which they fall.

Identification happens when the words of the speaker are decoded by the listener with some component of familiarity. Whatever is exemplified in the spoken word is equated by the listener to some correlative aspect of the listener's experience.

Identification between the speaker's words and the listener's experience is some form of analogous correlation. This identification by the speaker in advance of his or her idea to the listener's experience is based on the prior principles of analogous correspondence and the correctness of the intrinsic attribution.

When the speaker isolates a way to form an understanding bridge between the thoughts of the scriptural text and the common experience of the listener, there is an association that forms between the ideas being communicated to what the listener knows to be true in his or her life.

Below, we will discuss temporal identifiers in-depth, particularly, how the storyteller uses 'time' in the story. Temporal identifiers are foundational and form the clothesline on which the wardrobe is displayed to the world. However, before we do, let's talk about character because listeners assume temporality, and not character identification, is the premier go-to in story development. A listener is immediately attracted to the people, animals, or things in a story. It is the component that resonates the most. The temporal element is simply the ordering. It is an assumed element.

Character Identification

Character identification is critical in storytelling and is the most abused aspect of sermonic illustration. Preachers often use illustrations of movie stars, sports figures, or politicians. However, the listener can dismiss the illustration because the character is not totally identifiable. Sure, that person is recognizable, but s/he is not identifiable. Most audience members do not have a million dollars, fame, or name recognition. The listener can say, "That was a great story, but it does not relate to me because I am poor and insignificant."

Without identification or a close familiarity at the **socio-cultural** level, the story will create distance between the idea and the receiver. If I am speaking to middle-aged males, my story should be designed to grab hold of the experience of the 40-year-old, stressed, father who works 50 hours a week.

Identification should also be **environmental**. If my audience lives in urban Boston, telling a story of an indigenous tribe in Papua New Guinea will only work if the cultural components are transferable and the listener can decode with ease, either that or I give them orally the cultural decoding mechanisms to assure understanding.

Localization is a very powerful tool. I can say, "A woman got on a bus and sat down." It does not mean the same thing as if I said, "The lady got on the Dallas Area Rapid Transit Bus 434 at Parkland Hospital with her aging father." If I localize, it gives credibility and causes the audience to better picture the problem or the solution I am illustrating.

We should make every attempt to make socio-cultural identification with the audience in a way they can understand gender, race, religion, ethnicity, economic strata, education, and a thousand other criteria. If I am speaking at a Goth Convention, I am probably not going to use an illustration more suitable for an old woman's knitting social.

Environmental identification with an audience can also bleed over to connecting the **emotional factors** already discussed earlier in the book. A story can contain affective qualities appropriate to the audience, like joy, stress, worry, youthful insecurity, fears, elation, peace, stability, or things like that.

Emotional identification can exude negative or positive force. These forces can incline the listener to the sensitivities necessary to differentiate good and evil.

To illustrate this, consider this passage from Habakkuk 1:2: "O LORD, how long shall I cry for help, and you will not hear? Or cry to you "Violence!" and you will not save?" The verse already has emotional force. There is injustice and wrong within the experience of the prophet, yet it seems like God is not engaged in rectifying wrongs. How can this emotion be brought into an illustration?

If I shared with the audience about the Smith family in Uvalde, Texas who lost a child in the school shooting there in 2022, people who lived through that would immediately know what I am talking about. If I recounted a story of policemen looking at the children from the outside while the perpetrator was inside unchallenged, the ire would rise in the audience. Mind you, this may not be appropriate in some settings, but if the audience could bear the force of the illustration, it would clearly get the message across because most families have children in school. They worry on a regular basis of whether their child is safe. The emotional force of Habakkuk becomes even more real.

Temporality

The basic aspect of narrative is **time**. Time is the carpet on which the story walks. For example, "I did this, then this, then this." Or it can also move backward. "I did this, but before that I did this, and before that, you would not believe how this all started."

The storyteller's use of time is called a **disclosure sequence**. Sometimes that disclosure has a **rhythm** and sometimes not. The time-sequence can be in **equal lengths,** "The first day, the second day, the third day." It can be **unequal**, "Tuesday she took time to… and then the next week, she did these other things."

Time can be **retrospective** (past tense) or **anticipatory** (fictional future). In the case of the latter, a person can say, "Imagine, if you will, what your marriage might look like if you obey Paul's command to love your wife as Christ loved the church. You walk in at 5:30 p.m. next Friday after a hard week of work. Your wife Sue tells you this and that…."

There can also be **flashbacks** in a temporal sense. In this case, time sequence in a story is suspended while the speaker fills in the illustrative narrative with some backstory. This delay in meaning is very reflective of the way we think. We often dream about the future and immediately start thinking about a past incident that directly relates to our future vision of ourselves. The preacher should be encouraged to use this natural way of thinking.

Non-Temporal Progressions

Stories do not always have a controlling feature of time, even though they usually have an implicit temporal quality. The two most common ways that stories progress apart from time are through **change of venue/place** or **evolution of ideas**.

Jesus often told stories in which there were changes in venue—the Prodigal Son, the Parable of the Talents, etc. When stories advance by change in venue, it is very easy for the listener to follow clear indicators in the story. "When I was at work, it was one thing, but when I went home, it was quite another." Change in venue usually signals a change in idea or violates the expectation of the listener who *thinks* there should be a change of an idea. "You might think that my anger stopped when I left work and got on the tennis court, but it was even more of a trial than dealing with my boss."

When there is a shift in **idea**, the listener tracks with the speaker as well, very similarly to when there is a change of locale or of time. "My typical thought was to first wake up by drinking my coffee, but that morning, all I could think about was finishing the project. The setback came when I failed to do this step, and my mind became captive by depression."

Thought development is part of a larger idea of **tension** in a narrative, which we will discuss below. However, now it is important to understand that thought progression can be from **positive to negative or the reverse**. It can be from **ignorance to knowledge**, from **knowledge to doubt**, or a host of other changes. All indicate progression to the listener and should be emphasized by the preacher who wants to teach people how to think and live biblically.

Image Clips

The basic story-telling component is an image, something that is eventually connected through a string of movements and laid down over the top of a framework of time. A narrative is a set of orally imaged frames that create pictures in the mind of the listener. The speaker strings together one point after another, modifying the narrative picture as the message unrolls.

These images or short clips create episodes for the listener. It is what creates a story unit.

Sometimes those images represent a shared experience. Sometimes they do not. The speaker tries to create as many connect-points as possible with the audience. The delivered story challenges reality as it is known to the listener. Hopefully, the biblical illustration and glory of God displace the refuge of lies known to, and believed by, the listener (Isa. 28:15, 17).

Stories have a wide variety of components, and I will elaborate just a few below. A speaker should decide in advance the precise message s/he is trying to communicate, otherwise, the story can be an end in itself. The preacher is not an entertainer.

Tension

Stories have latent emotion, and the telling of stories creates a reaction in the mind of the listener. It can be relief, satisfaction, encouragement, wonder, or a host of other feelings. This tension-creation or tension-resolution is the central idea in stories but sometimes not in parables, especially if those parables are more imaged without much narrative.

Stories have a way of correcting us or meeting our needs in some way. Beside the inherent wonderment, there is a moral value in storying. Nevertheless, that moral quality is shrouded in a form that functions on tension.

Parental Advice

Listen to advice and accept instruction, that you may gain wisdom in the future.
Proverbs 19:20

You are 16 years old and hanging out with friends from school who are part of the 'popular group.' However, these friends are very influential in a bad way; they skip class and like to vape and pressure you into it. You are a young Christian who is already struggling with your faith, and right at this point, you just want to be popular and seen. You don't want to sound stupid to these friends, even though you know these things they are doing are wrong. Consequently, you find yourself hanging out with these people all the time, and you don't know how to get out of it. You also start to believe that maybe what you are doing is alright. Your parents find out about your vaping when they find a vape in your room. They begin to ask you questions, so you confess to them what is going on. They speak directly to you about how your friends are taking you down a destructive path. They encourage you and walk along with you on this journey of redemption and help you break free from these friends with their addictions. As a result, you change schools, where you are now able to make new friends that are real, loving, encouraging, and leading you down the right and godly path. Because you listened to counsel and received instruction, you become wise in the way you make friends now. These new friends influence you and shape you for your 'latter days.'

Aaron Moore

Storied tension is foundational to so much of what takes place in stories. The listener is in suspense about the resolution of the narrative.

Tension exists at multiple levels in any story. How is the main character like me but not like me? How will the narrative be resolved? What will happen next? Who else will we see in the story?

The types or levels of tensions in a story are endless because a human capacity for detail is almost incomprehensible. Tensions can involve almost anything, but there are some common ones. Some of the most frequent forms of **story tension are conflict, journey disclosure, safety, problem/solution, and challenge**.

Creating a story is not difficult, but when it comes to using narratives to support a biblical idea, the first thing that needs to be done is that the speaker must find and isolate the illustrative crux of a passage. This is somewhat different from the main idea of a biblical passage because the main idea needs to be converted from its biblical clothing that is steeped in cultural forms of prior centuries into a universal that can be applied in a contemporary context.

A speaker trying to relate how individuals can attempt to undermine your spiritual strength from Judges 14:16, when Samson's wife cried to get the answer to the riddle, might create a parallel story of a young married man whose wife wants to find out where her husband invests his money, since she does not know. She would like to get at it to invest it in a family venture with her relatives. In this scenario, the conflict exists in the non-disclosure of investment secrets.

The nature of tension should be evaluated and clarified with precision. Is there a journey involved? In that case, the story that is created must start somewhere and end somewhere, and the issue clarified in the story has to elucidate the main idea of the text.

Often there is a certain anticipation in the tension-resolution. The listener guesses how the problem will be resolved. If it is a journey, the listener asks how it will end. If it is a problem of security, the listener yearns for stability. Problems and challenges, like most tense situations, often have clear solutions.

Need-Fulfillment

Although emotional tension in stories cries out for an implicit solution, there is the overarching concept of **need**, something basic to all stories. This is different from tension that emerges from human desire. Tension is often imposed from the outside, while personal need is defined internally and demands satiation.

Need implies both lack and fulfillment. It is often accompanied by failure, and can be developed around physical, emotional, or spiritual yearning.

While most needs are emotional in nature, occasionally there is a cognitive or intellectual need. These are something entirely different but can often appear in the scriptures. For example, in Joshua 7, the leadership wanted to know the cause of the failure. The lack was knowledge. Who or what was responsible for the failure of Ai?

Story-Pivots

Stories pivot at certain points. As the plot develops in a story, the crisis or tension shifts toward resolution. In technical story language, this is called dénouement. The importance of the resolution is critical to understand. How is the tension resolved? There is a spiritual and communicative importance to this idea.

In a God-centered illustration technique, the solution-turn for the tension might be identified as divine or human, as contrived or supernatural, as from God or from men. The preacher must be God-centered ultimately. It is our job to exalt the Savior and the magnificent deliverance of God for His people. To do this, the preacher can create a story that illustrates the pivot-point of the text or its negation.

Pivots in stories can be toward resolution or toward deepening conflict. When one identifies what is at stake, and often there is a great deal at stake, the resolution becomes obvious. Is purity at stake? Is it safety? Is it health? Is it heaven? Is it hell?

When the principle that is at stake is clarified, the speaker designs how to resolve the suspense or tension. If spiritual welfare is the focus, the tension pivots on resolution of spiritual health or its opposite.

Story Paradigms

There are several story paradigms that are useful for stories in the Bible. The most basic idea behind all story paradigms after one considers the 'temporal' nature of narrative is the idea of **conflict**. Conflict creates tension, and tension holds the listener toward resolution.

This pattern of **conflict-to-resolution** is extremely important and does not always mean there is friction. Conflict is an idea of unresolved settlement in the heart of the listener. It is not necessarily battles between people.

Very similar to this is the idea of **problem-to-resolution**, something much more general. Tension is created when basic human needs are not met. When this is the problem, it may or may not involve conflict as we think about it.

Problems are infinite, and stories can be created around a myriad of tense dilemmas. In the Bible, Paul might be in jail. A man is born lame. A king makes an evil edict. A child might die. God could be absent. If the biblical story has a natural problem like the silence of God, I can create a story where the expectation is that the child wonders why her father is not speaking with her.

Within the broader categories of conflict or 'problem' dilemmas, there are standard story forms that are everywhere in life and in the media. Here are just a few of the more typically seen ones that make it easy for the teacher of biblical material to create corresponding stories. When a speaker is sharing from the scriptures on a story or set of verses that match these story models, it is very easy to create a parallel story from the modern context that causes resonance with the listener.

Journey stories are epic, from Homer's *Iliad* and *Odyssey* to modern day motion pictures. In a **journey story**, there is a basic model of **pilgrimage-to-goal** or **journey- and-return**. A story can also depict something **lost-to-found**. Some biblical examples of these types of stories might be Jacob's trip to Laban and back to Bethel (Gen. 25-49); Joseph and Mary to Egypt and back (Matt. 2:13-15); Paul and his return to the fledgling churches (Acts 15:36); Barnabas seeks Paul, who seemed to be lost to the early church (Acts 11:25); or the disciples being sent out and returning (Luke 10:17).

Parallel or invented journey stories do not simply have to be used to describe actual journey narratives from the scriptures. They work very well with many scriptures, describing a person who goes out from point A to point B. For example, were I preaching on Proverb 6:2 and the subject of promising too much, I could conceive of telling a story of someone who ensnared himself in some way by over-promising but later comes back after being humiliated or crushed by under-delivering.

One type of story involves **desire-to-satisfaction**. The desire could be a need. It could be eagerness for someone or something. The desire could involve almost anything. People are driven by their passion(s). Stories are easy to create when people want something dearly. That desire can be satiated, unmet, prolonged, intensified, or mixed with other factors. Ultimately, the preacher's goal would be to show the dangers of unholy desire or the positive quality of life with God when our desires are purified.

Similar story-patterns are the **struggle-to-success** narrative (Joseph) and the **struggle-to-justice** paradigm, as in the narrative of the widow in Luke 18. This story below addressing the sovereignty of God exemplifies a tension over justice, but it has no struggle. It is just a declared outcome, just as the text on which it is based implies.

Sovereignty in the Story

But who are you, O man, to answer back to God? Will what is molded say to its molder, "Why have you made me like this?" Has the potter no right over the clay, to make out of the same lump one vessel for honorable use and another for dishonorable use?
Romans 9:20-21

An orchard owner goes out to look at his 1000 trees. When he goes to his workers, he says, "500 trees should be used for harvesting fruit." He determines that the other 500 will be used for various other uses–land development, burn pile, etc. The trees and the workers do not have the right or ability to question their use because the owner is the one with all the knowledge and oversight.

Alina Lozovinsky

A frequent model that is used in movies, sometimes even in conjunction with other story forms is the **choice-to-outcome** scenario. In this type of story, a person makes a choice and processes through the outcomes. It is very easy to create for teaching. If I am teaching on a moral principle, I can create one person or even more, all who are faced with similar moral choices. Those choices have contingent consequences. The story reveals how each reaped a respective outcome.

In an **opposition-to-mediation** story, there is something to overcome. Often in the Bible, there is an obstacle that is foreboding. A person is faced with a conflictual power that demands intervention. A rather complicated example of this involves the imprisonment conflict of Simeon in Genesis 42:24 or Judah's mediation of famine relief in 43:8.

Because human nature desires freedom and not restriction, a frequently used story form is when there is **bondage-to-freedom**. This works well when preaching on sin, deliverance, spiritual warfare. The Bible teacher might herself ask what story do I know or what story might I invent where a protagonist is bound by a habit, a system, a falsehood, or a person that needs to be broken by the power of God? By probing into corresponding elements, the speaker can create a parallel story showing how God or scriptural principles bring freedom.

Some of the greatest components of redemption in the Bible involve bondage-to-freedom journeys. Mankind's eternal salvation, Israel's delivery from Egypt, and the death and resurrection of Jesus all follow this paradigm.

Refuge of Lies

"But I tell you that every careless word that people speak, they shall give an accounting for it in the day of judgment."
Matthew 12:36

You are going to your boss's office to get a review on your work. Your work performance is great, and you are nice to your co-workers. Consequently, you look forward to this meeting because you are doing a good job. At the meeting your boss goes over your portfolio and sees that your performance is solid. Then the meeting takes a shift. He says they are also reviewing the words you say at work. He pulls up emails and recordings from around the office of the words you have spoken. All of a sudden, the meeting gets awkward because you have said many careless things about your leadership and fellow employees, and now you are up for judgment. You realize that you are not as good of a worker as you thought you were, and you are in need of mercy.

Jacob Kuchmiy

There is a **lie-to-truth** model that is often found in the scriptures. It is similar to what is sometimes seen today in **fantasy-to-reality** models. Unfortunately, many characters in the Bible live a lie and are subject to the negative consequences of false foundations. It might be profitable at some point, for example, to create a story that resembles the biblical material very closely, showing how someone lives a lie and suffers the end of deception. Similarly, it is possible to bring someone out of his/her lie by obeying biblical mandates and principles.

Story Form and Delivery Method

There is some controversy about whether preachers should invent stories or even tell them, when teaching the scriptures. However, this question can only be answered by the prayerful speaker him/herself when considering the scriptural passage, the audience, and certain expectations that the audience holds.

If Jesus is any example for us in how to communicate, the gospels make a strong polemic in favor of figured and imaged delivery that is created. This, however, does not help speakers decide between various forms of correlative images and narrative. As stated above, it must be entered into prayerfully.

Stories can be realistic or imaginary. They can even be fabled. Stories that use personification are helpful in certain circumstances.

The speaker chooses a delivery method and a host of other oral characteristics such as voice, tone, volume, and speed, disclosure rhythm, volume, etc. This book is not a guide to speech delivery, however, but addresses the advisability of figured delivery in controlled ways. Story delivery is a complex process and involves plot resolution and dénouement. It can also involve shifts in point of view and other alternative delivery methods like drama, formally outside the purview of this book.

Delivery method is a topic in and of itself, and in many respects, involves vocal factors and story form, both of which are very complex subjects. If the student is particularly interested in oral performance and story form, there are many books on the subject.

I would just say a few things before moving on. Disclosure rhythm involves learning the fundamentals of delivery. Disclosure is built around expectation and expectation can be very dangerous as a guiding principle. If a preacher wants to avoid entertainment, it will be important to carefully design a correct delivery posture that is humble and not full of theatrics.

Audience Expectation and the Danger of Performance

There is a quality of speech that is helpful in being a good communicator. However, this road is a double-edged sword. Paul was clear when he wrote in 1 Corinthians 2 that wise words are not necessarily faith-building.

It is important to grasp so that a speaker is not enamored by performance orality. This is a dangerous precipice. Polished delivery can bring pats on the back but leave the heart of the listener unmoved. It is one thing for a listener to pay attention out of curiosity; it is quite another to have someone bend to God.

Yet every person listens with expectation. That is the nature of listening. We want to see storied conflict resolved, and in turn, want to see our own lives made more orderly.

We all listen with our cultural filters, so coming to a context with expectations is quite normal. We listen for familiarity and strangeness, for vividness or generalization, even if we do not know that we are doing it.

The speaker wants a captivated audience and wants to bring personal issues to resolution and positive outcomes through the power of the scriptures. There is nothing wrong with these things, if we have pure motives and are not doing it to be congratulated as we shake hands at the door.

A speaker needs to be minimally proficient with forward movement in story delivery and engineer time sequence and delivery rhythm to be effective. We don't need to be poor communicators to be effective, if that's even possible. Moses is a good example of one who spoke with authority without rhetorical skills.

Questions for Engagement

1. What is a narrative?
2. How is time related to movement in a story, and how is it not the same thing?
3. How can the illustrator avoid entertainment in story-use?
4. In what ways do stories address fundamental realities in a culture?
5. How is the force of a story multiplied when identification is evident?
6. What types of identification are there in a story?
7. What is a disclosure sequence?
8. What are some ways that stories 'progress' over time?
9. What is story-tension and how is it created?
10. How is the reality of need-fulfillment useful to the illustrator?
11. What is a story pivot?
12. What are some story paradigms that are often used in books and movies?
13. What are some performance dangers for a teacher of the Bible?

22 Illustrating with Parables

Jesus was the master preacher. It goes without saying that we should be more like Him in our speaking habits. However, we often complicate our exposition with complex outlines and discourse. Jesus was much more direct.

> **Matthew 15:14**
>
> **"Let them alone; they are blind guides. And if the blind lead the blind, both will fall into a pit."**

The Savior had a simple way of communicating profound truth using common objects and scenarios. A parable is a comparison, and our Lord preached by employing day-to-day happenings to strike at the heart of spiritual realities.

The above quote is an image parable. Many Bible readers do not realize that not all parables are stories or similitudes. They are often image clips.

In the same way that parables captivated the poor and drove people to the desert to hear this simple Teacher, they can yield similar results in ministry today.

Good teaching is filled with similar stories and images. Stories are a series of concrete images strung together by time, anticipation, and suspense, things we all live every day.

When a person tells a story, there is also a certain satisfaction. We are pleased when we can guess an outcome, feel, and move along with the cadence of the story, or identify with a character or situation that is common to us.

The Savior showed accommodating love for people in the way He talked with them. We should also. Unfortunately, the style that appears so simple is not so easy to reproduce without help. I have struggled for years to identify the essential ingredients of parabolic delivery. Ultimately, there are some simple ways that can help the preacher illustrate the textual idea and assist in grabbing hold of the wayward human will through the use of parabolic images and extended narratives.

Mark 4:34 tells us that Jesus "did not speak to them without a parable, but privately to his own disciples he explained everything." It appears that engagement with the crowd was with parables, but in-depth discipleship was through explanation in private. The text seems to imply that Jesus had two communication methods, imaged delivery for the crowd and exposition for His disciples.

Parables are not stories as we know them; they are proverbs or extended narrative with a wisdom-message. Let's examine this idea in detail.

The Jewish Context of Parables

Jesus was not the first person to use parables. The parables of Jesus were actually proverbs. This is the way the Jews of Jesus' day understood them. They were stories with contrast, with episodes, and with shock.

For background's sake, the reader needs to know that the prophetic role is sometimes tied to imaged delivery in the Old Testament. Moses states this in Numbers 12:6, for example. "And he said, 'Hear now my words: If there be a prophet among you, the LORD will make myself known unto him in a vision, [and] will speak unto him in a dream.'"

Among others, here are two examples of parabolic personification used in a prophetic manner. Jotham's Parable is recorded in Judges 9:8-15 and is a proverbial indictment on corrupt leadership. Jehoash's 'parable' to Amaziah is, in fact, a political provocation and is recorded in 2 Kings 14:9. These are not fables. The chief difference being that the application was immediate and has a sense of harsh realism that is not clear in its export like a fable has. Fables generally have more universal applications.

Additionally, there is often a sense of boldness and shock in proverbial instruction. Consider the brief historical snippet in Proverbs 24:40: "I went by the field of the slothful, and by the vineyard of the man void of understanding...." The author is using physical, agricultural life as Jesus did in order to instruct people in spiritual reality.

The parable is not a story in our sense of the term. It is a culturally different delivery system.

> **Hitting Home**
>
> As it is written in Isaiah the prophet, "Behold, I send my messenger before your face, who will prepare your way, the voice of one crying in the wilderness: 'Prepare the way of the Lord, make his paths straight.'"
> Mark 1:2-3
>
> Just like how we straighten and neaten up the house before we have guests over or our parents come over, we neaten and straighten our way before the Lord comes back.
>
> Olivia DeMacedo

As was stated earlier in this work, a parable is throwing one idea alongside another. It is teaching by comparison. Often a parable is defined in the sense of a noun from the Greek, as some 'thing' thrown alongside. However, I think it is better to understand, not the 'thingness' of a parable, but the action-aspect of the parable and how it is 'thrown.' A parable is a forceful communicative exchange, not just a narrative.

The directness of parable-use is accentuated by the fact that Jesus used common things in His parables to teach about truth. According to Horne, of the 61 stories that he considers parables: 34 deal with people (55.7%); 16 with things (26.2%); 7 with plants (11.5%); 4 with animals (6.6%).[9] The commonness of an idea, or better yet, the clothing in which that idea was dressed, made the reality that much more difficult for the listener to avoid.

Parables are not easy. They look like they are easy to understand on the surface, but once a reader gets into them, they are confrontational. Parables reveal or hide the truth and for this reason are sometimes viewed as dark. The easiest way to see this is to examine the Old Testament proverbs, which are antithetical in their parallelism (parables of negation). They have shock value (see Prov. 10:1-22:16).

The reader might ask, "What is 'dark' or hard about these sayings of Jesus?" Mark 4:11 tells us that parables hide spiritual truth. It does not get much harder than that. "To you has been given the secret of the kingdom of God, but for those outside everything is in parables."

The term 'parable' in the Greek language is used to translate the "dark sayings" in the Greek translation of the Old Testament (Ps. 49:4; 78:2; cf. Matt. 13:35). Also, the term παροιμία (proverb) is a synonym for *parabolé* in John 10:6 and John 15.

It is sometimes hard to wrap our minds around the idea that Jesus was interested in concealing truth, but that is pretty clear, even for His disciples. In John 10:6, John tells us this when they heard one of Jesus' parables: "This figure of speech Jesus used with them, but they did not understand what he was saying to them."

In Psalm 78:2-3, the Psalmist prophesies what kind of teacher Jesus would be. What does he say?

> I will open my mouth in a parable;
> I will utter dark sayings from of old,
> things that we have heard and known,
> that our fathers have told us.

Jesus was a mystery teacher, one who told shocking stories. People loved it. He filled their ears with wonder and anger at the same time. He was not there to entertain people. He met them where they were in their everyday lives and was effective at reaching people with the truth. We need to emulate Him.

Jesus' Methods of Preaching by Comparison

What forms do parables take? The reality is that Jesus often intentionally spoke in images and underdeveloped plotlines. Modern storytelling technique confuses our reading of Jesus.

Notice the parable illustration in the textbox. It has a complicated plotline. Jesus did this in the parable of the Prodigal Son, for example, but this was not typical of His method.

Jesus also did not preach narrative sermons as we know them. The basic parable form is neither a complex narrative nor an illustration. Parables have 'flat' characters that are not convoluted. The storyline of a parable lasts between five seconds and two minutes.

Parables do not usually have much suspense, although some cyclical parables might build into a brief climax.

We might be inclined to follow our culture and believe that a good story works similarly to parables. Oftentimes, a story does not force a moral choice. However, a parable was a proverbial tool, not an entertainment medium.

Story tension and suspense are also not usually part of delivering a parable. Parables have vastly different objectives and results. They concern moral confrontation and correct choices.

When a preacher uses a parable, she may be dissatisfied with the lack of storied force. The parable lands abruptly. However, that is the point. While resolution to modern day stories is rather satisfying, parables are often unresolved, even harsh.

If we are to ever bring people to a saving knowledge of Jesus, it is impending upon us that we show them the futility of competing alternatives. This is the power of the parable. Unveiling the heart is not a delicate process. It is often a harsh reality.

So, while the wicket gate appears significantly narrow, it is an infinitely better choice than the alternative. In reality, we do people a favor by clarifying and simplifying what the devil has fogged up. Jesus gave us the tools for proper illustration of His word. They are simple and clear. There is no need to complicate them.

Clarifying Narrative Delivery

Using parables in preaching is not narrative delivery. As stated previously, parables are wisdom literature.

By contrast, narrative preaching is something entirely different. There are many variations of narrative preaching. To oversimplify, narrative preaching is exposition in the form of storytelling. When the preacher relives the story, narrates the events, puts them in order, speaks or personifies a character, preaches in episodes, then the preacher moves into narrative delivery.

For example, if I say, "God said to Abraham, "Get out of your country." Abraham replied, "But God, I like Ur. Why do I have to leave?" Then I am in narrative delivery. When this is extended over the course of the sermon or for an elongated duration and the preacher is not explaining in a discursive way, then it is considered a narrative sermon.

The preacher sometimes speaks in first person, "I left Ur of the Chaldeans at the command of God. I did not know where I was going. We got to Haran and God appeared to me and told me to get out alone. I took Lot with me. This was a big mistake. I should have never done it." At that point, the person is into 1st person narrative delivery. Many students have never done this and really appreciate the experience and how it helps the audience grasp the text.

Most expositional preaching is not narrative delivery; however, people respond well to hearing the story told from different perspectives. Jesus often used narrative delivery in brief durations.

Narrative delivery should be one tool in the toolbox. We often persecute our people with what Jesus never did, that is, endless explanation. He told stories that contained the explanation and encouraged people to live the details. People learn through identification with concrete correspondence to their own lives.

By attempting to encapsulate the first-person experience in narrative, the student of the scriptures will grapple with details that were previously ignored. For example, if we read the scriptures and attempt to describe what it might have been like for Paul to visit the Philippian church and the city of his imprisonment 5 years later during his third missionary journey, there is a certain reliving of the prior persecution and evangelism. If the preacher attempts to be a prosecuting attorney in the courtroom of God as was the case with Micah, it will bring new insights about God's argumentation with God's people when all is not well. Were you to preach a first-person narrative of Peter going to the tomb and talking about the Resurrection, it demands a certain detail-management.

"Imagine, there I was. The women came back and announced that the tomb was empty. I did not believe them. I started running to see if it was true. John outran me. I am old and slow, you know. When I got to the tomb, there it was, the head piece, all wrapped up and folded...."

You get the idea. This is narration. It is intended to be illustrative and should be treated as such. It is an explanation of a text without telling people you are explaining something. If you are uncomfortable with embellishment, you tell the listeners that we all imagine what that must have been like, but the Bible is the ultimate authority about the facts.

From a theological perspective, narrative delivery follows the embodiment principle. The speaker uses bodily reinforcement and utterance to generate proximity between the 2000-year-old message and the modern listener. There are endless corollaries between ancient culture and contemporary life, and it is the speaker's responsibility to make those scriptural realities live for the people through some sort of narrative clothing.

Jesus Spoke. He Did Not Write.

What is the difference between Jesus and Paul, between the gospels and the epistles, between written advice and spoken communication? The difference is that Jesus spoke, and Paul wrote. Jesus wrote nothing. He was the Word. He lived the word.

Good teaching is living. It is concrete. It has movement, action, questions, dialog, stories, and most importantly, images. Jesus wasn't just a teacher; He was the Bread of Life, the Good Shepherd, and the Light of the World. These are the name-images that capture our attention and speak to us at a deeper level than simple descriptors.

To move one step beyond the image, we develop the idea that narrative is a sequence of images. Story is the servant to the image, which is master. If narrative is the house, image is the brick. Pictures, billboards, ads are images. Even commercials and songs are images, feelings, clips.

Every Christian communicator should be able to communicate by life's setting. It is the platform that God gave us when He created Adam in the Garden of Eden. God did not create us with print in our heads. Literacy is something man invented.

Polarization Parable of the Two Sisters

Whoever finds his life will lose it, and whoever loses his life for my sake will find it.
Matthew 10:39

There were once two sisters who had been seeking God for their next steps in life, since they were going to be graduating from college. One sister, Ella, was engaged to her to-be-husband and anticipated a wonderful internship, where she would make good money and buy a new car and home. She could fulfill her dreams for the future of being a mom and teacher. One day in a church service, she heard the voice of God clearly say to her heart, "I want you to become a missionary in the Middle East after you graduate from college. She had never felt God speak so clearly to her before, so she took a couple of days to fast and pray about it. Upon receiving further confirmation from God, she left it all behind her and booked a trip to the Middle East. She ended up spending the next 30 years ministering in places that had been unreached by the gospel, and the result of her ministry brought thousands to Christ. She remained single during that time, and her ex-fiancé ended up getting married to someone else. She lost her car, her internship opportunity, and money, having to be constantly on the run and living under persecution and in danger of losing her own life. Despite the pain that this caused her, she was able to give thousands of people the message of the gospel of Jesus Christ, people who had never even heard His name.

Five years later, the other sister received a call to be a foster mother, but she instead chose to continue to pursue money, fame, marriage and success. She soon ended up living a very sensuous life. No souls were won, and the children that could have been reached with the gospel were robbed of the opportunity to hear about Jesus Christ as their Lord and Savior and to have a stable family.

Soffia Liffey

Parable Construction Technique

The following parable-construction techniques assume that the speaker has already done exegesis and has isolated the homiletical idea and the illustrative crux of the text. These methods are not intended to be formulaic, but they will show the reader just how easy it is to construct parables.

In codifying the easiest ways to construct parables, the readers must take note that they are not delivered like stories. Often, they end abruptly and might shock the listener or leave him or her puzzled.

The ensuing four techniques represent the most essential ways to create parables to illustrate biblical ideas. In almost thirty years of international education, global travel, and overseas mission work, I have never heard a single church speaker, either in the United States or in a foreign country, preach a sermon that in any way remotely resembled the parabolic delivery style of Jesus. This breaks my heart. The obvious conclusion is that we have chosen not to do what Jesus did. We are also probably not seeing the evangelistic results that He saw. It does not have to be that way, however.

The Image Parable

There are quite a number of very curious verses in the gospels that show that not all parables are stories. In fact, the abundance of images in the New Testament where Jesus speaks is quite obvious. Salt, light, villages on a hill, houses on sand or rock, and a host of other image clips exist throughout the gospels. Parables are often single images or extremely brief narratives without plot.

Image parables are forceful and shock the listener with their simplicity. The kingdom of heaven is like leaven or like a mustard seed. If the blind lead the blind, both will fall into the pit (Matt. 15:14). The gospel writers use the term 'parable' to describe these simple pictures (Matt. 3:23-26; 13:31-32; 13:33; Luke. 6:39). There is no reason why we cannot follow Jesus' example by using verbal images that force listeners to examine their belief systems.

Original parabolic images are created using analogies from the context in which the audience lives. For example, while preaching on the tongue in James 3, the preacher might find similar images to those of James. Instead of using bits, fire, rudders, or animal tamers, the speaker can move to application by analogy and ask husbands if their tongue is like a tornado that touches down in town and rips through the neighborhood. Tongues might be like termites that destroy the beautiful home unnoticed or like a tsunami that comes ashore unannounced.

Cyclical Parables

Jesus often told parables using cycles. The term "cyclical" is a story formatting term.[10] Jesus uses this form of circling through phases, people, or options, and here are some examples (Matt. 7:24-27; 20:1-16; 24:45-51; Mark 4:2-9; Luke 10:30-35; 14:15-24; 16:1-8; 19:11-27).

These are like childhood stories most of us heard during our youth: The Three Bears, The Three Little Pigs, or Three Billy Goats Gruff. Each cycle brings the listener back to common language or themes (e.g. "I'll huff and I'll puff and blow your house down").

In cyclical parables, there are a series of vignettes that demonstrate several levels of obedience or types of individuals. For example, in the Parable of the Sower there are four types of soil, each yielding varying results. Multiple types of ground represent different types of people. Among other parables with clear cyclical plots are the parable of the minas and the parable of the laborers in the vineyard (Luke 19:11-27 and Matt. 25:14-30.). Jotham's parable in Judges 9:8-15 is also a very good example of a parable with cycles.

Parables that stratify individuals through varying levels of obedience are simple to create. Once the preacher locates what he wants to illustrate, he finds two to four other secondary or poor choices to contrast the ideal choice.

If a speaker needs to preach on Acts 6 and the selection of godly deacons, for example, it would be feasible to create a brief story with three or four fictitious deacon candidates that might all be flawed in some way. However, the deacon who God would want over the local church would certainly be the one man filled with the Holy Spirit and faith.

Morally Polarizing Parables

The parable is a tool that divides those that hear from those that don't hear (Matt. 13:10-17). When Jesus used it, it was not an entertainment device. It was certainly not narrative preaching as we know it today, although some would like to think so.

Jesus placed people in a moral dilemma. He gave them two choices: right or wrong, heaven or hell, good or bad. There was no middle ground.

He asked them if they were on the wide road or the narrow one, in light or darkness, among wheat or tares, like the Good Samaritan or the priestly hypocrites, like a self-righteous older brother or a repentant prodigal, guided by the divine master or mastered by money (Matt. 6:22-23; 6:24; 7:3-5; 7:9-11, 17-20; 12:28-31; 13:24-30; 25:31-46; Luke 7:41-43; 18:9-14).

Parables in preaching create a moral crisis. They divide the heart, leaving one's choices subject to the conviction of the Holy Spirit.

Anyone wanting to create a polarizing parable should identify the two opposite choices and then create a story intending to lead the listener to choose the lifestyle that God would approve of. The parable could begin with phraseology similar to Jesus' parable of the two men who went up to the temple to pray: "Once there were two church members…" or "In a town there lived two sisters…." The parable would then briefly sketch two behaviors. One, of course, is the godly choice.

The term "moral polarization" was used in medieval times to describe an illustration that demanded a choice.[39]   Anyone wanting to create a polarizing parable should identify the two opposite choices and then create a story intending to lead the listener to choose the lifestyle that God would sanction.

The Parable of the Two Preachers

Two preachers went up to the pulpit to preach. One took his complicated outline, full of subordinations. His manuscript was dotted with illustrations he had downloaded to his iPad. He said to his people, "Congregation, I have three points I would like to make today." His audience was duly impressed with his clarity.

The other preacher would not take his eyes off his people. He opened his mouth and said, "Dear folks, two congregants went to the church to pray...." The people listened with intensity. They sat in astonishment.

I tell you a truth. The preacher that spoke in parables had a full altar and went to his house justified rather than the other.

Daniel Sheard

Parabolic Illustration by Negation

Often Jesus used negative parables or shockingly bad examples (Matt. 7:3-5; 18:23-35; 23:25-26; 24:28; Mark 9:50; 12:1-11; Luke 6:39; 6:43-44; 12:16-31; 14:34-35). He did this by demonstrating truth or correct action by picturing the opposite. Unfortunately for those who listened to Him, they often found themselves just like the person or thing He described.

He talked of evil tenants and rich fools because they were so common (Mk 12:1-11; Luke 12:16-21). They were also not well liked. Who would want to be one of those people?

Jesus told us that if we see eagles, we might find a dead carcass (Matt. 24:28). Even animals know when there is food nearby. We will be able to see when His coming is near. We should not be surprised when Jesus comes back because, after all, the circling eagles gave away the future reality that was just around the corner. Eagles meant death, judgment, and by extension, the return of the Messiah. The export of Jesus' words were clear to His listeners.

When preachers are at a loss for a way to picture correct action or proper thought, it is often possible to come up with a myriad of poor alternatives. This is a valid pedagogical technique, often easier and more effective than pointing out true behaviors, which people often wrongly assume they already practice. Negative examples, however, can be woven into a sermon as contrastive elements that demonstrate by improper action what the scriptures are really trying to say.

How do we create illustrations by negation? Negation is a way of clarifying the identified subject. That is, any item, its movement, its cause, its effect, its moral implications, its feeling, or any number of other specifics can be made clearer to the listener when the speaker highlights its opposite.

The speaker is not restricted by form. Cyclical parables usually have many wrong choices–the man who buried his mina, the seed that fell on the wayside, the man who prayed arrogantly, thanking God he was not like the 'other guy.'

The negated allusion can be realistic or fictional, actual or invented. A person can create any type of story to show the futility or the consequences of an idea or decision simply by helping the audience visualize some alternatives that do not make sense or are not appropriate.

Negative images may or may not be put into narrative form and might not even have plots at all. Certainly, they do not have complex plots. When Jesus said that the blind lead the blind and both fall into the pit, He did not carefully construct an intricate scenario on which to deliver His material.

Medieval preachers were also fond of laying out options by degrees. Showing someone different levels, steps, grades, or phases is an easy way to differentiate several levels of obedience or love. Generalizing about something is far less effective than creating a cyclical parable that has multiple negative outcomes that are concrete and real.

Where Do We Go from Here?

If we are to approach the effectiveness of Jesus, there still is a lot of work to do with respect to parable-practice and research. Modern sermonic techniques do not reflect the comparative methods of Jesus or of Hebrew literature in general. We must aspire to a judicious management of figured communication.

In academic literature, homiletics has remained a subset of theology and is not in missions departments within the academy. This means that preaching is not typically subject to settings where lost people gather. Preaching, as was said earlier, has become defined as pulpit speech, when the Bible does not even remotely present this idea.

We must embrace the need and vision for original thinking with respect to doing exposition by means of figured communication as Jesus did. We should validate biblical sermonic methods and effective delivery styles, otherwise we succumb to the tendency to see preaching as information-transfer.

There are still unanswered questions related directly to the foregoing chapters. For example, what factors determine the durability of a figure in the mind of a listener? How does audience size affect engagement technique? How do different delivery contexts affect engagement? How do figures reinforce truthful aspects of the text and how do they deform the scriptures? There remain issues concerning the speed of student acquisition of certain imaging methods, differences in figure generation under different environmental conditions, reversion tendencies, and advantages or disadvantages of image complexity and simplicity.

Certain critical ramifications of impromptu creation of sermonic material are still yet to be analyzed. This is a whole field in and of itself. It must be examined. The reason for this is that impromptu speech is the soil on which most evangelistic witnessing takes place. Sharing Christ in an unexpected moment is the reality. We have to be ready, and we have to be ready with our story.

Beyond this, there are other related questions. Breaking down issues related to preaching in differing physical contexts, interacting with those elements, making sermonic content changes during that interaction, and how engagement is altered based on the myriad of audience factors are all questions that would be fruitful fields of research and add valuable new insights to the homiletical endeavor.

Methods for examining spiritually effective methods for preaching do not exist. Organizationally driven ways of creating and assessing the sermon are still the norm and go unquestioned.

Apprenticeship methodologies with sequenced progressions using the suggestions in this book would be helpful in turning the tide of teaching homiletics. A new outlook would be toward oral methods of delivery, rather than the informational management methods now in use in institutions around the world. Going one step further, if we could test those methods among those that do not know the Savior rather than within the confines of a church building, we would approximate a biblical definition of preaching.

Jesus' method was the way of wisdom, the way of the proverb and parable. This was a healthy, non-entertainment approach to human communication, one that brought great satisfaction and results among listeners. Because storied communication crosses all demographic lines and has a greater change effect on the listener than discursive discourse, we must shift our explanatory-type of delivery toward what Jesus showed us 2000 years ago, when He traveled around the countryside preaching by comparison.

Questions for Engagement

1. According to the Bible itself, why did Jesus use parables?
2. What are some realities of the Jewish context of Jesus' parables?
3. What are some differences between Jesus' use of parables and typical narrative delivery?
4. What are some of the qualities of Jesus' spoken word in comparison to Paul's written letters?
5. What are some qualities and characteristics of the 'image parable'?
6. What does it mean that some parables have cycles or a cyclical quality?
7. What does it mean that parables often have an implicit, moral polarization built into them?
8. What are some of the advantages of negative parables and what do they illustrate?

Appendix A: The New Testament Audience of Biblical 'Preaching'

'Preaching' Jesus to Those that Do Not Know Him

There is significant additional rationale for Bible application that has not been discussed in this book. When we examine the audience for biblical preaching, there is a very clear need for a dedicated practice of illustration.

Who were the listeners when Jesus, Paul, Peter, and the other apostles went about preaching? Very simply, the audiences were unbelievers.

This fact is critical because it changes the paradigm of the preaching model. Preaching is a passionate heralding of the good news of Jesus to people who don't know Him.

If what I am proposing is correct, and it is, it has vast implications. The structural and methodological implications are revolutionary and should change the whole nature of church life.

We need to ask, who is the preacher? It is the fisherman, not the trained clergyman. It is the average man or woman who follows Jesus.

For the sake of showing the implications of this idea, I offer the following excerpts from the New Testament. In the gospels and epistles, there are many words for preaching. All of them are used, almost universally, with the sense that the audience is composed of the uninitiated. Here are just a few examples, something that can be multiplied over 100 times from every corner of the Bible, even the Old Testament.

Lexical Clarity for Redefining Preaching

To bring back modern-day preaching and New Testament models of illustration, it is important to show just how far we have deviated in 2000 years. Essentially, there are about 10 different Greek words translated as 'preaching' in the English New Testament. Unfortunately, the essential qualities of their differences have been lost and deformed, especially the evangelistic nature of words and their cognates.

It is necessary to excerpt just a few samples from the overwhelming clarity of New Testament writings, demonstrating the fact that the audience of preaching was lost. If what I am proposing is the case, we will see just how far we have strayed from our calling.

The central word for preaching in the New Testament is the word *kērussō* (κηρύσσω with its cognate *prokērussō*, προκηρύσσω). It is used about 60 times. It is a term that means 'public heralding,' and addresses the open proclamation that was done by the early church. Examine these uses; the audiences are lost. 'Preaching' does not mean to herald to the already-convinced. It is the announcement of the message of the gospel.

The word is clearly about proclamation to people who have yet to believe in the Savior. A careful study of all the instances of this word in the New Testament reveals many interesting things about audiences. Suffice it to say, that preaching is what the early church did among outsiders. Here are a few examples: Matt. 24:14; Mark 1:38, 3:14, 16:15; Acts 8:5, 9:20, 28:31; 1 Cor. 1:21 & 23; 1 Tim. 3:16; 2 Tim. 4:17; 1 Pet. 3:19. From these, I want to point out some interesting *audience* considerations.

> And this gospel of the kingdom will be proclaimed throughout **the whole world** as a testimony to all nations, and then the end will come. (Matt. 24:14)

> For since, in the wisdom of God, **the world did not know God** through wisdom, it pleased God through the folly of what we preach to save those who believe. (1 Cor. 1:21)

> And he appointed twelve (whom he also named apostles) so that they might be with him and he might **send them out to preach.** (Mark 3:14)

> And he said to them, "Go into all the world and proclaim the gospel **to the whole creation.** (Mark 16:15)

> ...in which he went and proclaimed **to the spirits in prison**. (1 Pet. 3:19)

> And immediately he proclaimed Jesus **in the synagogues**, saying, "He is the Son of God." (Acts 9:20)

By multiplying examples, I am not being strategically selective. The word for 'preaching' or 'proclaiming' (*kērussō*) is used to describe what men did when they addressed lost individuals that did not know Jesus. The careful reader of the Bible will scarcely find a scenario that resembles what we would know as 'church preaching.' The audience is lost. The use of this word is rare in the New Testament in conjunction with exposition, something described more frequently by words linked to 'teaching' terminology.

Please don't think I am redundant, but we need a further examination of other words in the New Testament to paint a full picture of what the New Testament writers knew as *preaching*. In particular, the term *euaggelizō* (εὐαγγελίζω and its cognate *proeuaggelizomai,* προευαγγελίζομαι) is mutated almost beyond description into the verb 'preach' in the English language. Be that as it may, I want to focus again on the *audience* found in the following passages describing this word, which means to 'announce good news.'

By implication in these passages, the audience needs good news. They need something positive to be declared to them. They are lost. This is certainly *not* church-style delivery. To validate this idea, one might look up even a few of the following verses: Luke 7:22; Acts 8:2, 14:15, 16:10, 17:18; Rom. 10:14-15, 15:20; 1 Cor. 15:1; Gal. 1:16; Eph. 3:8; Heb. 4:2). I want to specifically highlight five instances where it is clear that the listeners are not initially believers. It is common in almost every use of the Greek word.

> But **when they believed** Philip as he preached good news about the kingdom of God and the name of Jesus Christ, they were baptized, both men and women. (Acts 8:12)

> And when Paul had seen the vision, immediately we sought to go on into **Macedonia**, concluding that God had called us to preach the gospel to them. (Acts 16:10)

> Some of the **Epicurean and Stoic philosophers** also conversed with him. And some said, "What does this babbler wish to say?" Others said, "He seems to be a preacher of foreign divinities"—because he was preaching Jesus and the resurrection. (Acts 17:18)

> ...and thus I make it my ambition to preach the gospel, **not where Christ has already been named**, lest I build on someone else's foundation. (Rom. 15:20)

There is a very particular passage that uses this word in the context of expository preaching. It is Acts 8:35. There we read that "Philip opened his mouth and began at the same scripture, and preached (from the verb *euaggelizō*) **unto him** Jesus." In this passage, the audience was 1 person, but he was lost. In other words, preaching was using the Bible to announce good news to lost people. The audience was not saved.

It is hard to find even just a few passages where the term preaching had anything to do with teaching established believers about Jesus. The term is universally 'teach' (didaskō, διδάσκω) when referring to what Jesus and others did in the context of the synagogue (e.g. Mark 6:2, John 6:59, 18:20). In Acts 13:05, they declared (*kataggellō*) the Word of God in the synagogues. Paul preached in the synagogues in Acts 9:20, but the audience was clearly lost. The issue was not the venue but the spiritual state of the audience. In Mark 1:39, Jesus did 'preach' (*kērussō*, κηρύσσω) in synagogues, but this use of the term is the exception, not the rule. Even at that, the audience was obviously not clear on the gospel and the identity or mission of Jesus Himself.

Often early church leaders reasoned (*dialegomai*, διαλέγομαι) in the synagogue, as in Acts 18:4, 18:19, and 19:8; however, they did not 'preach' there. This term is used in Acts 20:7 and 20:9 and seems to support a preaching model similar to what we see in modern churches, but to extrapolate this instance of 'reasoning' with Ephesian believers before Paul's departure about the implications of their faith as an example of a 'preaching' model would be seriously weak.

It's important to ask why Jesus, Paul, and other New Testament figures did not preach in synagogues. The venue was one of teaching and reasoning. *Preaching* was essentially what we know as *evangelism*. Unfortunately, most translations of the New Testament in English lose this distinctive.

The term *diaggellō*, which essentially means to declare more thoroughly through reasoning is joined by several other words that are similar in nature. These words are sometimes translated 'preach,' and usually refer to pointed talk of some kind, something akin to proclamation or declaration (*laleō,*). However, even there, the context is people who don't know the Savior. Look at these examples.

> And they went through the region of **Phrygia and Galatia**, having been forbidden by the Holy Spirit to speak the word in **Asia**. (Acts 16:6)

> But when the Jews from Thessalonica learned that the word of God was proclaimed by Paul at **Berea** also, they came there too, agitating and stirring up the crowds. (Acts 17:3)

> Him we proclaim, warning everyone and teaching **everyone** with all wisdom, that we may present **everyone** mature in Christ. (Col. 1:28)

> Let it be known to you therefore, brothers, that through this man forgiveness of sins is proclaimed to you, and by him **everyone who believes** is freed from everything from which you could not be freed by the law of Moses. (Acts 13:38)

Beyond these instances, the classical term for the content of preaching is the term *kērugma* (κήρυγμα). It is used 9 times in the New Testament and the audience is never composed of saved individuals.

This nominal form addresses the substance of the message, the preaching, and was something for those who had not heard the gospel before. Jonah heralds the *kērugma* (Matt. 12:41, Luke 11:32). Paul's gospel, that content, which was preached to lost Gentiles, was *kērugma* (Rom. 16:25, 1 Cor. 1:21, 1 Cor. 2:4, 1 Cor. 15:14, 2 Cor. 10:14, 2 Tim. 4:17, Tit. 1:3).

The cognate term for a preacher (*kērux*, κήρυξ), is used three times in the epistles and refers to Paul as a preacher and apostle as well as Noah, the preacher of righteousness in the middle of a very ungodly audience, none of which believed his message (1 Tim. 2:7; 2 Tim. 1:11; 2 Pet. 2:5).

Without exception, the Greek words for speaking to lost people in the New Testament are translated with the English word 'preaching' or 'proclaiming.' However, in contemporary evangelical usage, the term 'preach' is almost universally applied to what we do on Sunday morning within the confines of a building.

In speaking to believers, or mostly believers, within the context of a church gathering, we should not be using the term 'preaching.' Preaching is what we do when we share Jesus with people who don't know Him personally.

The ramifications of this idea are critical. First and foremost, the preacher is not a professional with a graduate degree. Preaching is what we all should be doing.

The idea of pulpit oratory cuts across the clear and central teaching that preaching is for the foolish and weak (1 Cor. 1:26). God loves using weak individuals because the message is more powerful in the hands of humble messengers.

What transpires in this logic is that evangelism is revitalized and gospel sharing is accessible. The scores of verses that address preaching in the New Testament now apply to the common person. Preaching is ours, not theirs. The preaching burns in us and not in the formally trained theologian.

A New Look at Old Biblical Models for Preaching

Once we identify what preaching is--crossing the culture between saved and lost by the simple, unschooled person—the Bible becomes quite a different book. Literally, the world becomes open to all of us. We no longer say, "Come hear our preacher this Sunday." That world is dead, and our calling is clear. We can no longer escape the reality that we Christians are the preachers, regardless of our past educational levels.

The picture we have of Jesus is one of a humble, unschooled carpenter. He enraptures listeners with stories, reminding them that the King has arrived. He communicates His death and draws them close.

Joseph is the imprisoned slave promoted to political power in a foreign country. He is bold to tell pharaoh that the true God Yahweh is the only revealer of secrets.

Abraham is the herdsman, raising a family 700 miles from his homeland. He brings worship of the Most High God with him in what will be a lifelong missionary endeavor with no turning back.

Jonah obviously was sent to Nineveh in Assyria. While he spoke a cognate language, somehow, he had to overcome communication difficulties when crossing the cultural divide.

Amos, a man counted among the most famous untrained preachers, was neither a prophet nor the son of a prophet. He was a herdsman and orchardman (Amos 7:4). God did not let him use his lack of heritage as an excuse for hiding from God's call. In calling Amos, God gave us an example of how He desires to remove some of the cultural distance that even existed almost 3000 years ago, separating the vocational speaker and the common person.

I could go on and on with examples, but notably we have to talk about Paul the lawyer. God purposely made him apostle to the Gentiles. He fell from prominence as a Jewish lawyer, but still began his preaching in Jewish synagogues. God took this Roman-born man from Cilicia and sent him to the ends of the earth, at least as far as what is now

Albania, Montenegro, Bosnia Herzegovina, and maybe even Croatia (Rom. 15:19).

When someone crosses cultures, no matter how seemingly insignificant, the cost is great. A person's weaknesses rise to the surface. Preaching takes place from a platform of human frailty, one in which the communicator relies upon the Spirit of the living God.

In this model, the communicator no longer leverages the superiority of his message because the message is foolishness in worldly terms. Oratory becomes useless.

By contrast, the speaker leverages God Himself. There is reliance upon the Creator of the model, not the medium. The medium is not the message. The medium is weak; the message is strong. Antibiotics are a powerful thing, but if I hand someone a bottle of them, I am not the healer. I am only the instrumental cause. The healing is done by the pills.

Imaged Communication for Change

There is a heaven and earth difference between illustrating for clarity and illustrating for change. In advocating for a more imaged homiletic, I am not saying that the preacher is there to entertain people. The speech figures are there to cut to the heart of the hearer and initiate change.

Jesus was an entertaining speaker. He drew large crowds. He did not do this with exposition; He did it with parables.

The power of comparison cannot be underestimated. Widows, trees, sheep, goats, and pearls are all hard to avoid. We know from experience what these items are like. When the speaker refers to the experience of the listener, the conclusions of stories are inevitable because the meaning is seated in the past of the hearer.

So, while the parable might be entertaining, and while the image may be striking, the real power is in the export, so to speak. The catchiness of the construction entraps the listener in the ethical implications. The ultimate rationale for the image is listener change.

While many speakers seek illustrations to keep the attention of the audience, this is an incorrect motivation for imaging preaching, especially considering the lostness of the preaching audience. We who speak, seek to implicate people in the life-call of God, to bring people near to the Savior.

If I look for illustrations that simply picture my biblical or textual idea, I have lost the intention of Jesus' methodology. He spoke to separate, convict, and convince people of His theological teachings, the chief one being to recognize who He was.

For the expositor, the illustration must clearly correspond to the text first, but then it must also bring the listener to an ethical crisis. The latter is the personal or contextual application.

For example, when Peter found himself in a trance in Acts 11, a sheet full of unclean animals was lowered from heaven. When God asked him to eat, he was squeezed between the Eternal God and Jewish tradition, not simply food laws but also Jewish/Gentile conduct codes. He did not know what to do. God revealed that He was opening His salvation to the Gentile world. It was a new direction.

God taught Peter through an illustration, a vision, and through verbal revelation. The illustration forced an ethical dilemma. The picture created a crisis. This is the purpose of illustration, not entertainment.

In Revelation, John's apocalyptic vision has a similar effect on the reader. Lamps, beasts, seals, trumpets, scrolls, blood, crowns, angels, sickles, grapes, wine presses, smoke, darkness, thieves, scarlet women, famine, smoke, horses, incense, locusts, people eating scrolls, swirling creatures, singing crowds, and white robes all evoke strong associations in the reader's or listener's mind.

The implications of the images force the reader to ask: Is this judgment about me? Am I going to be part of the crowd that is judged? Will I die from famine? Am I lukewarm? Am I alive but my works are dead? Am I following the Savior on a white horse or am I trampled? Is my blood splashing on the garment of King of Kings as He treads the winepress of God's wrath?

An image forces participation and interpretation. The sense of the text is not immediately evident, but there is an invitation into the deeper meaning.

This separation within listeners and audiences is not the purpose of most of the Pauline illustrations. Paul's language can be highly metaphoric without being parabolic. Often, he does not polarize with his illustrations. He speaks of: the armor of light (Rom. 13:12), leaven of wickedness (1 Cor. 5:8), members as weapons (Rom. 6:13), sin as service (Rom. 6:16), teaching as milk (1 Cor. 3:2), the body as a temple (1 Cor. 6:19), Christ's freedman (1 Cor. 7:22), knowledge as a mirror (1 Cor. 13:12), the body as a tabernacle (2 Cor. 5:1), sin as a murderer (Rom 7:11), life as a contest (1 Cor. 9:24-7), church as a body (1 Cor. 12:12), and the body as seed (1 Cor. 15:35).[11]

While Paul sometimes uses his illustrations to show separation, he does not do this in the same way that Jesus does. For example, in 2 Corinthians 2:16, Paul shows that incense creates differing realities for the captives than it does for the victors. The listener might find himself asking if he is among the chained or the free, but the Pauline allusion is not really a crisis-creating figure *in the same sense* that a parable that is preached by Jesus or Jotham, for example.

Appendix B: Parables as Contextual Engagement

Beyond the issue of crisis and moral polarization is the idea of contextualization. Contextualization is the local fabric into which a parable is clothed.

If I am walking through the shopping mall and I see an Arab in a *galabeya* (Egyptian outer garment) or a Saudi woman in a black *abaya*, I have a sense that they are out of place. They stand out, and for many, their clothing strikes strong feelings of anger or puzzlement.

For the preacher, an illustration needs to be a cultural bridge to the audience. If the audience is women, the speaker might use an illustration about NASCAR's Jimmie Johnson, but only if the speaker is in Daytona. However, if you are in Mumbai, India at a women's meeting, it might be better to talk about cooking or dress, for example.

On-the-spot relevance is a quality seen clearly in the parabolic teaching of Jesus. Parables are pictured truth applied to an immediate setting. Their general universality is not nearly as poignant as their contextual relevance.

Parables as Central to a Preaching Model

As was already discussed, the importance of the parable for developing a biblical model for circumstantially relevant preaching cannot be underestimated. The parable is a *contextual engagement* medium. Within this idea is encapsulated the issues of personalization and localization.

To begin with, Jesus' parables are verbally delivered to real people with real issues and questions. They employ culturally appropriate material from within the environment to explain divine truth. This idea is clearly seen in the parables of the Lost Sheep, the Lost Coin, and the Prodigal Son in Luke 15, when Jesus addressed the Pharisees' criticism that the Lord associated with sinners.

Abstract ideas, by contrast, are universal and far less contextual, and while abstraction is to some extent determined by language and physical setting, a story or an image is integrally tied to a situational framework. The parable or narrative is localized by detail and is impossible to understand apart from its concrete wrapper.

For example, I can talk about the abstract idea of witchcraft to most audiences. However, I cannot tell a story about a *kenbwazé* (sorcerer) just anywhere without adequate explanation about Creole magical practices.

Behind oral communication is the immediate situational dynamic, but New Testament scholars address this issue in many ways. They do not all agree on the *purpose* of parable discourse.

A Survey of Approaches

In William Barclay's treatment of New Testament parables, he identifies one of Jesus' chief reasons for using the parables as the desire for "the sudden awakening."[12] "He wanted to persuade men to pass a judgment on things with which they were well acquainted, and then to compel them to transfer that judgment to something to whose significance they had been blind."[13]

Barclay's focus is the urgent demand for a response. For him, Jesus' story was intended to raise consciousness and elicit a decision. Jones' identification of direct appeal in the parables through the means of using the question, "Who among you…?" is also a good example of an immediate response mechanism.[14]

Jesus' parables are considered by some to be ideological subversion/reconstruction.[15] Dodd considers various ones "parables of crisis"[16] because of their soliciting type content, while Jeremias refers to their call to "resolute action" as "the challenge of the hour."[17] Wright calls the ethically evocative quality of the parable "an invitation to refashion a whole out of the part they had been given" and "a moral challenge."[18]

Borsch's way of looking at this type of immediate involvement is through the arena of drama. He believes the story invites listeners to become "participants" in the "play" by means of identification with the "characters."[19] In his discussion of "extravagant stories," he says that the parables make "outrageous demands," offer "incomprehensible grace and new ways of belonging," and he goes on to say that "[t]hey indicate that now is the time for decisions of the greatest importance."[20]

Parables are stories that throw listeners into a crisis or that create spontaneous joy. They give clarity to moral dilemmas or hope to discouraged people. They are immediately applicable and relevant, and they bring form to a preaching idea that involves clothing the presence of God for people who have trouble seeing Him.

Historical ways of classifying synoptic figures do not adequately define their performative power. Parables can be defined clearly and precisely as *contextual engagements*. They *are* what they *do*. However, this is not the general descriptive trend in scholarship.

Parable studies can be divided into interpretive movements. Dodd and Jeremias viewed the parables according to the historical-eschatological currents of their day.[21] Linneman and Via followed the thoughts of Schleiermacher, Dilthey, Heidegger, Bultmann, and Fuchs in a historical-existential way,[22] although Via was principally concerned with parables as aesthetic objects.[23] Jones similarly defined the parables in terms of art,[24] and Bailey in terms of literary cultural concerns.[25] Wittig saw the possibility of viewing parables according to the principles of semiotics, which opened up a sort of "indeterminacy" of parable sign meaning based on the interpretive perspective of the reader.[26] Many of these, however, are definitional perspectives generated according to what a parable is and not what it does.

Jesus' figurative teachings have been described by numbers of technical and literary terms including allegory, simile, metaphor, synecdoche, example, symbol, similitude, and a host of other words used to describe figures of speech, both tropical and non-tropical. Unlike a traditional way of viewing the New Testament use of the term *parable* as a generic term to mean an extended figure of speech, I move away from an abstracted definition of a parable to an active one.

I prefer to focus on the engagement aspect of the parable rather than its thing-like qualities, even though it is grammatically a noun. A parable is *throwing alongside* not just some-*thing* thrown alongside. This is the nature of a story. It is a communicative exchange, not just a narrative.

Many of the historic differentiations and definitions of the biblical parable do not recognize this idea of engagement. Early Christian interpretations saw the parables in an allegoric fashion,[27] although their tendency was to avoid the label.[28] More recently, the parable is seen as metaphoric. This idea is developed in contemporary literary criticism, seen, for example, in the works of Bernard Brandon Scott who would view the symbolic representations of the parable texts as having "endlessly renewable meaning."[29] This idea has hermeneutical dangers, however.

Among similar figurative examples of broad hermeneutical structures for understanding the parables is Adolf Jülicher in *Die Gleichnisreden Jesus* who saw "the essential nature" of the parables as one of simile, stories with correspondences of "clear purpose," not veiled truth.[30] Wright has developed a theory of synecdochic meaning for the parables, where he believes "*Jesus focused the world in realistic stories of characters intended as exemplary*" [italics his].[31]

Wright identifies the element of meaning construction by stating that the responsibility falls on the listener to "complete" the synecdochic meaning implied in the example story.[32] In one way, this is the nature of all listening, as we search for understanding of what we read or hear. A cautionary note can be made, however, in that God's intentional purposes are not simply subject to human interpretation in a sort of reader-response fashion. We must always have exegetical precision as the basis for meaning construction.

Additionally, there are rules of figure invention that guide the speaker and present a predictable framework for meaning as people hear the message. Most preaching theorists don't talk about illustration rules unfortunately.

The engagement paradigm functions on the premise of parabolic use, where words are constructed with intention and precise analogous correspondence. Ideas are engineered by the speaker and decoded by the listener with some joy and experiential resonance.

In speech figures, meaning is thrown down to be picked up by the listener. The basic terms for parabolic speech forms are similitude, parable, allegory, and illustration.[33] As already stated, they are nouns. While the similitude generally speaks about "typical situations," parables are based on more "particular case[s];" illustrations are argumentative examples of real-life situations without corresponding analogies while allegories are stories with figures that mean something by extension.[34]

These distinctions have long histories with origins in classical Greek authors. Specific categorical subtleties have long been under analysis, particularly with respect to the terms parable, metaphor, simile/comparison, and allegory.[35]

Parables as Contextual Engagement

It is my contention that regardless of what meanings are applied to the word *parable* and its contingent terms, the *purpose* of the parable is engagement. The medium is the figure.

Defining the parable in terms of its functional interaction upon the listener, one can more clearly grasp the sense of the synoptic decree that Jesus never spoke except by parables.[36] He spoke to them to engage them, to reveal to them, to blind them to His kingdom purposes.

A sermon that is truly engaging at every level functions in a full-orbed orality, something that utilizes the vast concrete world and its pool of figures, something beyond a sequentially outlined delivery. Within that adjacent world are poetic and illustrative components that capture the imagination. They need to be used because that is what Jesus did.

Preachers who aspire to communicate well with diverse audiences seek engagement, that simultaneous and mystical resonance of their words, divine truth, and revelatory surprise in the understanding of the listener. When the preacher's message rings true with both the listener's experience and the voice of God, they vibrate together like a harmonic. That is engagement, a personal meeting in the *hEAR*-and-now.

This model clarifies the nature of preaching as a relational discipline and not an informational task. It involves a vibrant, personal call to encounter the living Christ along with the speaker as the details of the text are unfolded on a tapestry of human language and experience.[37] This communal idea of exchange draws attention to both the unavoidable obligation of the preacher to engineer an assembly of the hearer with her God as well as the potentially intimate interaction of speaker and audience.

The physical setting becomes central to this model of preaching, and consequently, the aspect of immediacy in delivery narrows the interchange aspect of preaching to one of "apocalyptic" engagement.[38] The importance of the circumstantial quality of the meeting comes to the forefront of the preacher's communicative task because the encounter is localized. It is not simply auditory and cognitive exchange but is also a physical and material meeting of people with their God in a hall, in a home, or under a tree.

That local engagement brings together the biblical text, the speaker, and the listener into a vibrant convergence of understanding. The carefully chosen language of the speaker illuminates the scriptures through shared threads of experience. The Holy Spirit uses the communication exchange to draw the listener to Himself as the speaker preaches by comparison.

Appendix C: Essential Questions for Creating Biblical Applications

1. What is your text, and what key word, phrase, or phrases do you want to illustrate?

2. What quality do you want to apply/illustrate: relationships, parallel emotion, movement, moral human behavior, desire, fixed object, or abstraction?

3. What is the sub-domain within that quality? For example, you might illustrate *discontinuance* within moral human behavior or perhaps *speed* of movement.

4. How might you probe down in detail, nuancing your subject as much as possible using the appropriate sub-methods?

5. How will you analogize the illustrative crux to a contemporary experience through a set of images that clarify the meaning of the text?

6. What audience demographic issues do you have and how might you make the application contextually appropriate to the listeners?

7. What are the circumstantial/immediacy factors present in your context that are important to consider for you to reach your listeners?

8. If you are creating a story, what is the controlling aspect: Ignorance-to-knowledge, knowledge-to-doubt, conflict, journey, safety, problem/solution, challenge, choice-to-outcome, bondage-to-freedom, lie-to-truth, fantasy-to-reality?

9. What type of parable construction technique might you use in order to create an appropriate parable (a series of images, similitude, cyclical method, moral polarization, negation, etc.)?

Appendix D: Bible Application Matrix

Relationship	Parallel Emotion	Movement
Relational Direction • Construction or Improvement • Faithful Maintenance • Disruption of Relationship **Behavior** • Adoption • Continuance • Discontinuance • Deterrence/Avoidance	**Positive Emotion** • Surprise, Excitement, Amusement, Admiration, Adoration **Negative Emotion** • Sadness, Shame, Anxiety, Horror, Pain, Confusion, Fear **Shock** • Surprise, Awe, Satisfaction, Relief, Entrancement, Appreciation of Beauty **Passion** • Elation, Craving, Boredom, Calmness, Empathy, Anger, Pride, Awkwardness	**Who is Moving?** **Power Under Which Someone Acts** **The Thing Acted Upon** **Effects of the Action** **The Function of the Action- 'Why?'** **The Position of the Action** **Directional Movement** **Speed, Timing, Rate Issues** **Sequence** **Triggers to the Senses**
Moral Human Behavior	**Desire**	**Fixed Objects**
Adoption **Continuance** **Discontinuance** **Deterrence/Avoidance**	**Motive** **Passion** **Need**	**Form** **Place in Space** **Symbolism** **Human Qualities**
Abstraction	**Analogous Story or Parable**	

Abstraction	Analogous Story or Parable

Nuancing the Abstraction
• By Definition
• By Quality
• By Magnitude
• By Distortion/Negation
• By Amplitude or Number
• By Privation and Lack
• By Excess
	Finding a Paradigmatic Character(s)
	Identifying Emotional Factors at Stake
	Deciding on Temporal Issues and Time-Chunks
	    • Disclosure Sequence–Retrospection, Flashback, Anticipatory Foreshadowing
	    • Rhythmed or Cycled Disclosure
	Creating the Relatable Environment/Setting/Venue
	Story Progression Sequence
	    • Change of Venue, Person, Time, etc.
	    • Idea Evolution or Change of Mind
	Tension–Journey, Conflict, Lost-to-Found, Safety-Seeking, Problem-to-Solution, Challenge-to-Victory, Choice-to-Outcome, Desire/Satisfaction, Opposition/Mediation, Lie-to-Truth, Fantasy-to-Reality, Struggle-to-Justice, etc.
	Pivotal Moment(s)/Denouement
	Parabolic Delivery through Image, Cycle, Polarization, Negation, Comparison

Endnotes

Forward

[1] "The greatest thing by far is to be a master of metaphor. This alone cannot be imparted by another; it is the mark of genius, for to make good metaphors implies an eye for resemblance," Aristotle, *Poetics* 1459 a 5-8.[1]

[2] The idea of 'symbolic extrication' is detailed in George Walley's, *Poetic Process* (London: Routledge & Kegan Paul Ltd., 1953). The fundamental components of creating main ideas are dependent upon the student's ability to create universals from language and life experience. "Analogy of intrinsic attribution" is a term to describe the notion that there are innate qualities of words that encourage or discourage imaging. It is explained in Stephen J. Brown, *The World of Imagery: Metaphor and Kindred Imagery* (New York: Haskell House, 1965), 229-30.

Capturing the Ordinary

[3] Whalley, *Poetic Process*, 63

[4] Brown, *The World of Imagery: Metaphor and Kindred Imagery*, 229-30.

'Preaching' is a Missionary Term

[5] Much of the material in this chapter was published earlier under the title, "Preaching in the *Hear* and Now: The Circumstantial Quality of the Preaching Engagement," *Journal of the Evangelical Homiletics Society* 4:2 (2004):10-22.

Illustrating through Parallel Emotion

[6] Most of the emotions listed are from: Alan Cowen, "How Many Different Kinds of Emotion are There?" "Frontiers for Young Minds," May 9, 2018. Accessed July 10, 2023. https://kids.frontiersin.org/articles/10.3389/frym.2018.00015. Doi: 10.3389/frym.2018.00015. However, some terms have been modified or eliminated, and the categories into which I have placed them are differentiations created by me for illustration purposes.

Illustrating by Analyzing Movement in a Text

[7] This table is constructed around the ways that thoughts are often associated according to Sir William Hamilton: successive in time; adjoining in space; dependent by cause/effect, effect/means, means/end, whole/part; contrast or similarity; operations of the same power; sign and signified; or same sound; see Stephen J. Brown, *The World of Imagery*, 62-63, in his discussion of *Lectures on Metaphysics*, 1865.

[8] See Harry Caplan, *Of Eloquence: Studies in Ancient and Mediaeval Rhetoric*, Anne King and Helen North, eds. (Ithaca: Cornell University Press, 1970), 61.

[9] Herman Horne, *Jesus the Teacher* (Grand Rapids: Kregel Publications, 1998), 79.

[10] Françoise Tsoungui's, *Clés pour le conte africain et créole* (Paris: Conseil International de la Langue Française, 1986), 10ff.

Appendix A: The New Testament Audience of Biblical 'Preaching'

[11] References are from Friedrich Hauck, "παραβολή," *Theological Dictionary of the New Testament*, ed. Gerhard Friedrich, (Grand Rapids: Wm. B. Eerdmans Publishing Company, 1967), 760.

Appendix B: Parables as Contextual Engagement

[12] William Barclay, *And Jesus Said* (Edinburgh: The Saint Andrew Press, 1970), 13.

[13] Ibid.

[14] Peter Rhea Jones, *Studying the Parables of Jesus* (Macon: Smyth & Helwys, 1999), 51.

[15] Craig L. Blomberg, *Interpreting the Parables* (Leicester: Apollos, 1990), 66. Blomberg uses the term "subversive" in an anti-rabbinical, anti-traditional sense.

[16] Dodd calls the parables that have to do with preparedness, "parables of crisis," namely, the Faithful and Unfaithful Servants, the Waiting Servants, the Thief at Night, and the Ten Virgins. See C. H. Dodd, *The Parables of the Kingdom* (London: Nisbet & Co. Ltd., 1935), 154.

[17] Joachim Jeremias, *The Parables of Jesus* (Bloomsbury: SCM Press, Ltd., 1963), 180.

[18] Stephen I. Wright, *The Voice of Jesus: Studies in the Interpretation of Six Gospel Parables* (Carlisle: Paternoster Press, 2000), 206.

[19] These are issues used by Borsch to open his community-slanted reading of the parables. Frederick Houk Borsch, *Many Things in Parables: Extravagant Stories of New Community* (Philadelphia: Fortress Press, 1988), 1.

[20] Ibid., 15.

[21] Kenneth E. Bailey, *Poet & Peasant* and *Through Peasant Eyes: A Literary-Cultural Approach to the Parables of Luke* (Grand Rapids: William B. Eerdmans Publishing Company, 1976), 16-17.

[22] Ibid., 19-23; E. Linnemann, *Parables of Jesus: Introduction and Exposition* (London: SPCK, 1966); Dan Otto Via, *The Parables: Their Literary and Existential Dimension* (Philadelphia: Fortress Press, 1967).

[23] Via, *The Parables*, ix.

[24] Bailey, *Poet & Peasant* and *Through Peasant Eyes*, 23; G. V. Jones, *The Art and Truth of the Parables* (London: SPCK, 1964).

[25] This is the major concern of Bailey's *Poet & Peasant* and *Through Peasant Eyes: A Literary-Cultural Approach to the Parables in Luke*.

[26] Mary Ann Tolbert, *Perspectives on the Parables: An Approach to Multiple Interpretations* (Philadelphia: Fortress Press, 1979), 35, 39.

[27] Wright, *The Voice of Jesus*, 62ff.

[28] Blomberg, *Interpreting the Parables*, 31.

[29] Wright, *The Voice of Jesus*, 155ff, 174.

[30] Ibid., 115-16.

[31] Ibid., 195.

[32] Ibid., 219 and 202.

[33] Linnemann, *Parables of Jesus*, 3-8.

[34] Ibid., 3. By contrast, Harold A. Bosley views the parable as "quiet, earnest conversation. It is a teacher explaining a point to a listener" (*He Spoke to Them in Parables* (New York: Harper & Row, 1963), vii).

[35] Hauck, "παραβολή," *Theological Dictionary of the New Testament*, 5:745-6.

[36] Matt. 13:34; for other uses of parables in the synoptics see: Matt. 10:18-20; 12:9-13; 22:15-21; 13:31-35.

[37] Col. 1:27-28; 2 Cor. 4:5; Gal. 1:16; Phil. 1:15-21; John 5:39-47.

[38] Brian K. Blount's "Preaching the Kingdom: Mark's Apocalyptic Call for Prophetic Engagement," *The Princeton Seminary Bulletin* 15 (1994): 33. Blount correctly identifies the eschatological sense of the preaching task by highlighting the *urgency* of kingdom proclamation.

www.ingramcontent.com/pod-product-compliance
Lightning Source LLC
Chambersburg PA
CBHW081147270326
41930CB00014B/3071